Responsive Pedagogy

Engaging Restoratively
with Challenging Behaviour

Responsive Pedagogy

Engaging Restoratively
with Challenging Behaviour

Valerie Margrain
& Angus H. Macfarlane (Eds.)

NZCER PRESS
Wellington 2011

NZCER Press
New Zealand Council for Educational Research
PO Box 3237
Wellington
New Zealand

ISBN 978-1-927151-15-0

Designed by Lynn Peck, Central Media

Cover illustration by Richard Matla

Printed by Printlink, Wellington

This title is also available as an e-book from
www.nzcer.org.nz/nzcerpress

Distributed by NZCER
PO Box 3237
Wellington
New Zealand
www.nzcer.org.nz

Ka whāngaia, ka tupu, ka pūāwai

That which is nurtured will blossom, then grow

Contents

PART III: ENABLING RESPONSIVE PEDAGOGY

Foreword

Education is a fundamental human right, as is a child's right to safety. Children and young people can only learn effectively if they feel safe and secure in their educational environments.

This book is timely. Perceptions of escalating rates of challenging behaviours in our schools and early childhood services have heightened the need to rethink how we deal with these incidents. Reasons for the perceived increase are complex. However, most children have a need for social connectedness and this book examines a number of different theoretical frameworks, all of which underscore the importance of relationship-based and culturally responsive approaches. Clearly, responsive pedagogy can make a difference by preventing, teaching and responding to behavioural issues and individual needs in ways that are respectful of both children and their educators.

There will always be times when teachers have to respond to incidents that they could not have prevented but by adopting restorative approaches teachers will be able to understand children and young people's views of their experiences and actions to ensure they deal with their challenging behaviours in meaningful ways. In contrast, punitive and exclusionary responses to discipline typically result in a passive experience, with little or no participation by the offending child, who often feels resentful and alienated from the school/early childhood community as a result. Punishment does not help those children to take responsibility for their own learning and behaviour, or for treating people with respect. On the other hand, a restorative approach to behaviour management puts the responsibility back on the child or young person and teaches accountability to those affected by the misdeeds as well as teaching him or her to handle situations differently next time.

The authors offer a set of practical and restorative responses to challenging behaviour that cross all types of educational settings, from early childhood through to secondary school. Locating the principles of responsive pedagogy within a Māori worldview gives the book particular relevance to New Zealand researchers and practitioners. Whatever the context, a practitioner lens is applied to the theoretical influences underpinning the philosophy of responsive pedagogy so that readers can easily relate the relevant principles and strategies to their own practice.

Responsive engagement with challenging behaviour through the modelling and supporting of positive and pro-social behaviours is always an important way for teachers to increase children's participation in learning. However, these authors effectively use case studies to illustrate other alternative responses that involve engaging restoratively to rebuild respectful relationships. These practices (for example, restorative conversations and for more serious infringements, restorative conferences) focus on restoring a healthy, respectful relationship between the aggrieved parties and the offending children, by actively involving them in directly repairing, or restoring, the damage their actions have caused.

Rather than attributing blame and exacting retribution, there is a consistent evidence-based message across all chapters that restorative approaches shift the emphasis from viewing challenging behaviour as confronting the authority of the school or early childhood service to viewing it as damaging to the relationships within. Embedding restorative processes into the school or early childhood setting therefore fosters a safe environment for working through conflict. Not only will this help those involved to reach agreement on how to repair the damaged relationships; the processes of forgiveness and reconciliation also facilitate reintegration back into their centre/school communities.

This book highlights the need for a complete paradigm shift so that restorative practices are not implemented as a stand-alone process. Rather, they are integrated within a whole school or early childhood management system where appropriate behaviour, school culture, and restorative processes are taught within the curriculum so that the principles of restorative justice have relevance and practical application in everyday interactions.

As the proverb says:

> Mā te huruhuru ka rere te manu
> With feathers the bird will fly

Dr Janis Carroll-Lind, Principal Advisor (Education)
Office of the Children's Commissioner

Preface

The writers of this book care deeply about students, children and teachers. We are a diverse group of researchers and educators who are connected by a belief that teachers can make a difference and that school and early childhood education settings can be places where behaviour is addressed with courage and conviction. We know that the media is quick to report negative instances of bullying and misdemeanour. Statistics also tell us that suspensions and expulsions are not remedies. We hope that the philosophy, discussions of practice support, and authentic case studies provided in this book support constructive and responsive pedagogical decisions.

The words in the book title have been carefully chosen. *Responsive Pedagogy* captured our belief that at the heart of effective teaching is relationship-based practice that takes account of content and context, and of culture. Equally, the work of teachers is professional, evidence-based and reflective. The subtitle begins with the word *Engaging*; we make no apology for insisting that teachers, management and places of learning must work with students and children to acknowledge the reality of challenging behaviour, but in ways that are respectful, constructive and restorative.

During the process of developing this book Christchurch was rocked repeatedly with major earthquakes. The book cover is graced with an image of a charcoal drawing by Richard Matla, one of the contributing authors from Christchurch. This art work, of nikau palms from the South Island of New Zealand, honours our Canterbury colleagues, family and friends. The flax palms also reflect our desire to weave concepts and values, including: research and practice; culture and care; assertiveness and warmth; curriculum and relationships; responsibility and restoration.

Throughout the book we include consideration of both school and early childhood education contexts. At times our discourse refers to "schools", but the broader education context is relevant because challenging behaviour begins with the very youngest in society.

Equally, young learners can learn to accept responsibility and be supported to "put things right". Universal applicability of restorative practice and responsive pedagogy is an example of one of the seven imperatives we have woven throughout the book, based on the concept of TAPUWAE (footsteps): effective teaching, well-considered aims, partnership, universality, wisdom, accountability and evidence-based practice.

Part I: Foundations for responsive pedagogy begins in Chapter 1 with historical and philosophical influences on teachers' responses to challenging behaviour. This is developed in Chapter 2 with examination and definition of our understanding of what challenging behaviour is. Culturally appropriate and responsive pedagogies are presented in Chapter 3, followed by connections to curriculum in Chapter 4, in which both school and early childhood curricula are acknowledged.

Restorative practice in education settings is a strong feature of the book. Working restoratively includes acknowledgement of harm, relationship-based accountabilities, and practices that seek to restore harmony. Within the book a range of approaches are considered, including informal chats and formally arranged hui (meetings). *Part II: Restorative practices* focuses on the imperatives that guide and direct this kind of approach, connecting theory and practice to support teachers to engage with challenging behaviour restoratively. Examples of restorative practice in action are supported in Chapter 5 by describing review tools which teachers and management can use. Restorative conversations are explained in further detail within Chapter 6, as selected aspects of practice at the heart of pedagogical relationships are explored. Case studies in Chapters 7 and 8 report on indigenous contexts and individual responses respectively.

Part III: Enabling responsive pedagogy focuses on approaches that will support systems-level engagement and responsiveness to challenging behaviour. Chapter 9 highlights the importance of educational leadership for restorative practice to be successful and sustained. Chapter 10 addresses the important issue of adults modelling restorative practices in their own staff interactions and relationships. We then return to challenging behaviour in Chapter 11, with consideration of the most challenging of situations. Chapter 12 concludes the book with consideration of footsteps to guide the future. This is achieved by returning to the seven concepts of TAPUWAE. An important consideration to keep in mind is that what constitutes effective restorative practice in one classroom or school setting may not do so in another. The reasons for this include differences in students' backgrounds, prior knowledge, parental support and school climate.

The world has experienced tremendous change over the past two decades, and an authentically commensurate approach for the delivery of educational practice is needed—one that moves in harmony with the new social direction. Summoning our individual strengths and areas of interest, the authors endeavoured to collectively generate new ways of thinking and doing in the craft and art of managing challenging behaviours. One of our important contentions was to move people's ideas and philosophies in an articulate and fair manner. We considered that a preferred way of doing this was to approach the research tasks inclusively, in the true sense of the word, emphasising progress toward a better understanding of the challenges that we encounter daily in a multidimensional and multicultural society. More compellingly, we were adamant that the majority of teachers and principals working in schools and early childhood settings today, like their counterparts of yesterday, are critical consumers of knowledge and are adept at applying this knowledge in the most effective of ways. These leaders respect the heritage and dignity of local and global understandings and they consciously respect the authoritative positions they hold within the profession. Because they are genuinely concerned about tomorrow, their footsteps can guide us forward. The whakatauki surely is a fitting one: *He tapuwae o mua — Footprints from the past; Mō muri — To guide the future.*

Angus H. Macfarlane & Valerie Margrain

Ka whāngaia, ka tupu, ka pūāwai.
That which is nurtured will blossom, then grow.

He tapuwae o mua mō muri.
Footsteps from the past to guide the future.

Me āta tirohia ki te take.
The problem is the problem;
the person is not the problem.

He aha te mea nui o te ao?
He tangata! He tangata! He tangata!
What is the most important thing in the world?
It is people! It is people! It is people!

PART I:

Foundations for Responsive Pedagogy

RESPONSIVE PEDAGOGY

1.

He Tapuwae o Mua:
Footsteps Towards Responsive Engagement
with Challenging Behaviour

Angus H. Macfarlane & Valerie Margrain

Introduction

How to respond appropriately to the diverse range of challenging behaviours in society has been a topic of ongoing theorising and debate for more than a century, but it has received renewed attention in recent years (Macfarlane, 2007; Thorsborne & Vinegrad, 2006). This increased attention stems from a growing awareness that many of the current educational processes and practices are not working for a large and growing percentage of the student body—indeed, they may inadvertently be serving to perpetuate alienation and under-achievement for many students.

Traditional policies and practices may no longer manage to address many challenges arising in today's classrooms and playgrounds.

Dilemmas abound in schools and early childhood services about how to respond to challenging behaviour, pitting individuals or ideals against one another. The community's response is often to demand swift decisions and astute results, but swift decisions in educational settings may not be based on evidence, or may not reflect social justice, fairness or an ethos of care. Many knee-jerk approaches (such as "zero tolerance") may actually work against achieving a potentially positive outcome for students and teachers (Lewis, 2009; Ministry of Social Development, 2007).

In this context it is worth exploring relationship-based and culturally responsive approaches such as restorative practices. Usually offered as a progressive alternative to the conventional model of exclusionary measures to control youngsters and dispense discipline, this approach is a more constructive form of conflict resolution. It may take more time, and can be supported through the use of specific protocols, but with crafted facilitation the knowledge base on restorative practices can be translated into actions that will work towards better outcomes and strengthened relationships.

Learning contexts (schools and early childhood education settings) are fundamentally *relational* enterprises. Authentic, caring relationships between teachers and students are fundamental to learning, as are relationships between and among students (Prochnow & Macfarlane, 2008). Add to this the reality that close, positive relationships with teachers have tangible benefits for student skill development, motivation, behaviour and learning, and the actuality becomes stark and compelling (Prochnow & Macfarlane, 2011): teaching and learning require a disposition of caring and social responsibility by teachers towards all students. This disposition must be predicated on an understanding of others. Inclusive and caring classrooms and early education settings engage learners and teachers with each other and also reach out to the community. In these settings, the values of responsibility and accountability are reinforced, and young people are supported to contribute constructively to society.

We argue that learning is socially constructed: based on social values and developed through social interactions. In a social relationship-based approach to learning, schools and early childhood services necessarily engage with challenging behaviours in responsive ways. The use of restorative practices exemplifies having a positive belief about students, applies the constructive teaching of relationship skills and provides a positive resolution to situations that are causing conflict or harm. Relationships reign and productive partnerships between people are central: they are at the core of how people interact, build trust, support each other and behave. The more that parties work together, the greater the opportunity they have to get to know one another and to build relationships. Relationships affect everyone, and everyone can affect a relationship. However, with relationships come two key collective responsibilities: maintaining *productive* social interconnections and *repairing any harm* or damage that has affected these connections, whether caused intentionally or inadvertently.

In this chapter we set the philosophical scene for the other chapters in the book by discussing key approaches, a model for evidence-based practice and the principles of restorative justice. The remaining chapters in Part I continue to provide a rationale for responsive pedagogy when engaging with challenging behaviour, including concepts of behaviour, pedagogical care and curriculum. Part II focuses on restorative practice as a specific responsive approach that teachers use to engage with challenging behaviour. The final part of the book considers the kind of systems-level support in educational settings that enables effective teacher engagement with challenging behaviour, including leadership, staff relationships and integrated responses to the most challenging behaviours.

Footsteps from the past

It is rare that any supposedly "new" concept is truly unique. Responsive pedagogical engagement with challenging behaviour has been historically evident in many cultures and contexts (Macfarlane, Hendy, & Macfarlane, 2010). In this section we examine the historical influences on restorative practice and tie these to a range of contemporary philosophical approaches—sociocultural, ecological and inclusive, along with circumspection and cultural responsivity—in order to illustrate the pedagogical connectedness of any response. The following whakataukī illustrates the importance of not overlooking the uniqueness and richness of past experiences and practices:

He tapuwae o mua mō muri.
Pathways from the past to guide the future.

Historical influences

Any New Zealand historical review of educational development through the decades should acknowledge the indigenous people of Aotearoa (New Zealand). Bowen (2008) points to the constructive use of responsive engagement with challenging behaviour in traditional Māori society, stating that "prior to European contact, Māori had a well-developed system of custom and process that ensured the protection of individuals, the stability of social life and the integrity of the group" (p. 7). The indigenous nature of restorative practice initiatives and the extent of commitment to this approach in New Zealand should not be underestimated. Speaking through an international e-forum, Wachtel (2007) argued that these aspects of New Zealand's journey are significant:

While it would be an exaggeration to say that restorative justice (RJ) has completely overtaken conventional forms of justice in New Zealand, RJ has made as much headway on the island nation as it has anywhere in the world. RJ processes—mainly conferencing, based on practices adopted from the Māori people of New Zealand, in which offenders, victims and their supporters meet face to face to repair the harm caused by crimes—are being implemented in the country of 4.1 million throughout the criminal justice system. (p. 1)

An example of a community-developed indigenous restorative practice model is Te Ara Āwhina. This model has been working constructively since 1970 and continues today (Bowen, 2008). In 2007 the Ministry of Justice launched Te Whānau Āwhina, based on the model of Te Ara Āwhina. Another example of a restorative approach to effect positive change is the introduction of family group conferences to resolve complex situations.

An increase in crime rates during the latter third of the 20th century led to ongoing questioning of the effectiveness of retributive models of justice. It was becoming increasingly clear that the traditional "lock up and throw away the key" approach was not an effective or sustainable deterrent, particularly for the increasing number of disaffected male Māori youth. At the New Zealand Police Conference (Ngakia Kia Pūāwai) in 2005, Judge Becroft reported on the offending and recidivist offending rates of male Māori youth, stating that these were disproportionately high—indeed the punitive approach, he declared, appeared to be a counter-productive process (Becroft, 2005). By the 1990s, prominent Judges Brown, McElrea and Curruthers publicly articulated their concerns about the existing justice system and led the call for restorative approaches to be recognised as legitimate judicial options (Bowen, 2008; Drewery & Winslade, 2003). Formal trialling of conferencing referrals occurred within the Ministry of Justice between 2001 and 2004, followed by a thorough evaluation of conferencing concepts and procedures. The findings indicated sufficient positive outcomes for both the victims and the perpetrators of wrongdoings, resulting in restorative practice becoming recognised as a constructive judicial process.

A more recent example of wider social engagement with restorative practice is the publication of resources that link Catholic values and restorative practice. One example, *A Justice that Reconciles* (Caritas Aotearoa New Zealand, 2009), promotes the benefits of forgiveness. In Scotland, research has confirmed the importance of school-wide commitment to restorative practice across a range of educational settings (Kane et al., 2007). These examples illustrate that although restorative practice is new as a key concept in education, it is not entirely new in the wider society.

The first funded project to trial restorative practices in education (the University of Waikato pilot project) was undertaken in 1999/2000. The initiative was driven by the Ministry of Education's acknowledgement that suspensions and expulsions from school were unsatisfactorily high—an acknowledgement that ultimately initiated the Suspension Reduction Initiative (SRI). The Waikato pilot initially focused on conferencing, but later the more comprehensive te hui whakatika approach was developed (see Chapter 7). Key researchers and leaders of restorative practice in education at that time included Wendy Drewery, John Winslade, Angus Macfarlane and Ted Glynn and their associates. Mere Berryman and colleagues from the Poutama Pounamu Education Research Centre, as well as Tom Cavanagh (in New Zealand on a Fulbright Fellowship), were able to complement the work of the Waikato researchers and continue to publish and advocate for restorative practices.

Throughout the 2000s, Margaret Thorsborne has responded to calls from the teaching sector in both Australia and New Zealand for effective professional development on restorative practice interventions, such as conferencing and workplace conferencing (see Chapter 10 of this book). Most recently, Greg Jansen and Richard Matla established the educational practice-oriented website *Restorative Schools*, along with a restorative practice newsletter, *Restore*. Their contribution continues to provide New Zealand leadership and creative delivery of professional development (see Chapters 5 and 6, and http://restorativeschools.org.nz). This book both acknowledges and includes these contemporary contributors to restorative practice in education.

The Ministry of Education's *Positive Behaviour for Learning Action Plan* (2010) promotes a range of programmes and initiatives for parents, teachers and schools across the country to "turn around problem behaviour in children" ("Addressing disruptive behaviour in students", 2011, p. 4). One of the range of programmes and initiatives is The Incredible Years, introduced to New Zealand from the United States in 2002 (Hamilton & Litterick-Biggs, 2008). Over 400 early childhood and primary school teachers participated in an Incredible Years programme during 2010. The programme "provides teachers with approaches to help turn disruptive classroom behaviour around and create a more positive learning environment for their students", including "more consciously developing relationships with challenging students and providing incentives and praise for positive behaviour"

("Addressing disruptive behaviour in students", 2011, p. 4). This one example within the overall government strategy indicates an expectation that teachers will ensure the learning environment is supportive, responsive, accountable and safe. But one learning environment is never the same as another. According to a New Zealand authority on restorative practice, Wendy Drewery, "Every school that I have seen implement restorative practices has done it differently, and that is appropriate ... Every school has different strengths and growing edges—and different parent communities with a wide range of expectations" ("Restore and Research", 2011, p. 2). Students arrive in class with complex histories that include the dynamics that relate to physical, social, emotional and cultural forces. While we cannot expect to understand the full complexity of these forces, we can come to understand some of the fundamental influences if we consider some of the recognised philosophical approaches that attempt to help us better understand the mix of attitudes, beliefs and actions that are ever-prevailing. It is to some of these philosophical approaches that we now turn.

Philosophical approaches

Pedagogical decisions are not made in isolation, and teaching philosophies draw on a range of models and concepts. The approaches we refer to in this section draw from the past but continue to have a strong influence on how teachers engage with challenging behaviour in contemporary settings.

Sociocultural

Current conceptualisations of sociocultural theory draw heavily on the work of Vygotsky (1978), as well as later theoreticians (see, for example, Bruner, 1996). A key feature of Vygotsky's theory is that learning is constructed within the contexts of social interaction. Rather than looking solely at individuals, we need to consider social environments and community influences on learning. The early childhood curriculum, *Te Whāriki* (Ministry of Education, 1996), and the revised *New Zealand Curriculum* for schools (Ministry of

Education, 2007), are sociocultural documents with a vision of learners who contribute to society. Children and young people construct an understanding of what it is "right" to do in their social settings, and also learn the consequences when the rules are broken. Restorative practices of acknowledging harm and seeking to "put things right" are inherently sociocultural.

Ecological

The ecological model highlights the interaction between critical contexts, such as that between home and school, or home and the early childhood setting (Bronfenbrenner, 1979). These critical environments in a child's world include family, teachers and peers. Relationship-based and responsive pedagogical approaches acknowledge that we need to consult with families and learn about the strengths and experiences students bring from home and other contexts. It is critical that families are helped to feel valued, respected and able to contribute to restorative decision making.

Inclusion

Inclusion is a philosophical position that advocates the right of all students to access effective educational provision and support. The central contention of inclusion is that all students are equally entitled to be educated, and that their education should be available in regular educational settings within the community. Working within an inclusive philosophy means we should expect students with behavioural challenges to be acknowledged and accounted for within regular education settings. Inclusion demands that schools and early childhood education services are safe and positive places for all, and restorative practice supports this aim. Restorative approaches support us to accept a wrongdoing and work with those who have done wrong to set things right for everyone.

Circumspection

Circumspection is about being judicious, careful, well planned and thoughtful. It acknowledges that the increasing frequency and severity of bullying has led to specific deliberation and greater vigilance in more recent years about the importance of student safety and wellbeing (Macfarlane, 2007). Bullying behaviour needs to be effectively addressed. A fundamental aspect of restorative practice is an acknowledgment of the rights of victims to be safe and to be heard. It is important to understand that restorative practice is not a "soft" approach that avoids issues; restoration demands that those who do wrong face up to their victims and acknowledge their transgression(s), and also take responsibility for putting things right.

Culturally responsive

Culturally responsive teachers will use differentiated instruction to tailor teaching to the different needs and backgrounds of their students (Foorman, 2003; Tunmer, Chapman, & Prochnow, 2003) without resorting to cultural stereotyping or adopting a one-size-fits-all teaching approach. Culturally responsive teachers will develop a personal cultural awareness and understanding of their own biases so that they can develop the awareness and understanding of their learners in order to promote positive classroom relationships. Essentially, culturally responsive teaching is premised on building, maintaining and restoring productive and positive relationships. Restorative teachers working in culturally responsive classrooms focus on constructive experiences and resolution as opposed to resorting to punitive, reductive procedures (see reviews by Macfarlane, 2007; Meyer & Evans, 2006).

Evidence-based practice

Teachers are increasingly required to illustrate that pedagogy is informed by evidence. However, there have been conflicting interpretations of what "evidence-based practice" means. Traditional positivist or scientific notions of evidence are dominated by quantitative approaches. Such approaches can readily measure specific instances of behaviour but are less successful at understanding individuals, or at acknowledging contexts or the depth of relationships.

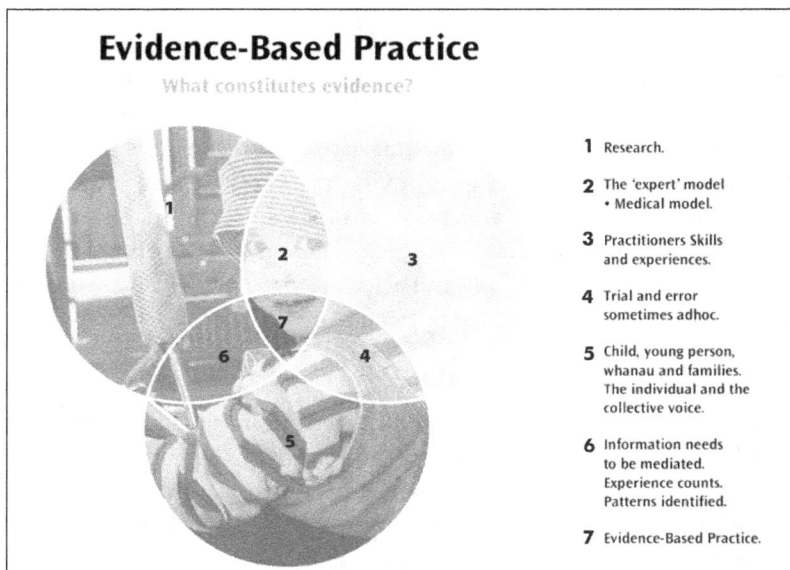

FIGURE 1.1 EVIDENCE-BASED PRACTICE: WHAT CONSTITUTES EVIDENCE?
Source: Bourke et al. (2005). Image reproduced with the permission of the authors.

A model for what constitutes evidence-based practice has been developed by Bourke, Holden, and Curzon (2005) (see Figure 1.1). This model clearly challenges practitioners to consider the ranges and relevance of the evidences from which they draw. Three types or *lenses* of evidence are acknowledged by these authors: the research lens; the practitioner lens; and the individual/family/community lens. Bourke et al. argue that evidence-based practice is only achieved when all three lenses inform understanding, and further declare that the process of defining "what constitutes evidence" will be fraught with difficulty should individual/family/community experiences and knowledge be overlooked or marginalised. If any one of the three lenses is missing in an analysis, the evidence will have limited validity, as follows:

- Use of the research lens and the practitioner skill and experience lens without the individual/family/community lens will result in an "expert" or "medical" model. Such a model is more likely to be deficient in its view of learner behaviour, and will fail to acknowledge family, cultural and community experiences or values.

- Use of the research lens along with perspectives from the individual/family/community, but without the practitioner lens, will be limited by the absence of practitioner skills, experience and mediation.
- Use of perspectives from the practitioner lens along with the individual/family/community, but without research evidence, will result in ad hoc, trial-and-error approaches that can result in unnecessary effort and energy.

Use of all three lenses is important to ensure effective and relevant evidence-based practice.

The model of Bourke et al. (2005) is valuable for supporting teachers in their pedagogical reflection when engaging with challenging behaviour. Teachers use the *research* lens when they read journals and books about ways to manage behaviour or use restorative practice. Documenting particular individual behaviours, antecedents and consequences is an example of teachers using research methods to collect relevant data. Teachers apply their own *practitioner skills and experience* in their everyday classroom management of individuals and groups. They also draw on the practitioner circle through professional staff/collegial discussions of challenging situations, whether in the staffroom or when working alongside specialist behaviour support staff. Practitioner skills are enhanced through professional learning and development (PL&D) opportunities.

The *individual and community* lens includes input from learners, parents/whānau and community members. Teachers become informed when they meet with parents at formal parent–teacher interviews, and at informal events such as family fish 'n chip nights or hāngi (earth oven used to cook food). Wider participation in communities also enables teachers to meet students and families in settings with different values, including church, cultural and sports events. In many of these settings, student behaviour and motivation can be markedly different from that observed in classroom contexts.

Restorative principles for pedagogical responsivity

In this section we briefly consider the definition and core principles of restorative justice, and consider how these inform restorative practices in education. Part II of this book explores restorative practice in greater depth. Restorative approaches can perhaps best be defined as being in fundamental contrast to retributive approaches— they are about "putting things right" (the notion of accountability) rather than punishment.

Philosophy and principles

Restorative practice has its roots in restorative justice, a judicial approach that focuses on repairing the harm done to people and relationships rather than on punishing offenders. McCold and Wachtel (2003) describe how it originated in the 1970s as a mediation approach between victims and offenders, then broadened its scope in the 1990s to include communities of care, with victims' and offenders' families and friends participating in collaborative processes. At the forefront of our ideas in this book is a vision that schools and early childhood education services can use this approach to create and enhance positive learning contexts for children and young people.

Zehr (2002) describes restorative justice as "a process to involve, to the extent possible, those who have a stake in a specific offence and to collectively identify and address harms, needs and obligations, in order to heal and put things as right as possible" (p. 37). Three principles are key:

- misconduct violates people and relationships
- violations create obligations and liabilities
- restorative practice seeks to heal, put things right and restore harmony (Zehr, 2002).

This philosophy is not new, but clearly it is in opposition to the retributive philosophy. Thorsborne and Vinegrad (2004) suggest that restorative problem solving is a process that was evident in Anglo-Saxon and Roman law, and remind us that healing, compassion, forgiveness and mercy are human values that transcend many cultures

TABLE 1.1 COMPARING and CONTRASTING RESTORATIVE and RETRIBUTIVE PHILOSOPHIES and PRACTICES

Aspect	Principles/practices	
	Restorative	Retributive
Model	Fairness and accountability	"Just desserts"
Focus	Harm done in an incident	The "wrongdoer"
Misbehaviour	Harm done to people, property and relationships	Violation of school rules, against policy
	Creates obligations and liabilities that are acknowledged and shared	Requires guilt and blame to be apportioned
Justice	People's needs are addressed	Penalties/sanctions are applied
	Consequences are decided by those affected and by those responsible	Consequences are decided by school officials
	Harm requires healing, and relationships need repairing	Harm is not often addressed when punishment is delivered
Accountability	A shared concern	Directed at the wrongdoer and sometimes at the victim
Conversations and dialogue	About the past, present and future	About the past
	Two-way, relevant and concrete; facilitated by teachers and/or skilled students	One-way, abstract and managed by designated officials
The wrongdoer	Seen as a good person who has behaved badly	Labelled as a bully and as a bad person because of what he/she did
	Offered forgiveness and support from the community	May have to plead for forgiveness and might not be offered understanding and support
	Managed within their school or early childhood education community	Removed from their school or early childhood education community and "dealt with"
	Asked to fix things and supported to make amends for their behaviour	Told what is to happen to them and what needs to be said or done to others
Feelings and emotions	Acknowledged and managed with dignity and respect	Controlled and limited by school policy and protocol
	Shame is managed and discharged	Shame is induced and used to disgrace the wrongdoer
Victims	Asked what needs to happen to repair the harm and ensure future safeguards	Have little control over the process and outcomes
Support groups and families	Significant in rejecting the bullying behaviour while supporting the wrongdoer	Often viewed as part of the problem

Source: Adapted from Thorsborne and Vinegrad (2006)

and communities. Restorative practices and philosophies have been important and fundamental elements of many relationship-oriented indigenous cultural groups, including Māori.

Table 1.1 (adapted from Thorsborne & Vinegrad, 2006) compares and contrasts restorative problem-solving philosophy with the traditional retributive and punitive approach. The table clearly shows that restorative approaches cannot be implemented at a practical level without a commitment to restorative philosophy and a rejection of retributive philosophy. Restorative justice is thus both a process and a set of values (Morrison, 2007). Chapter 5 looks in more detail at punitive versus restorative practices, along with constructive examples of restorative practice strategies and methods.

So far we have been discussing restorative justice in very general terms. Claassen (1996), at the National Conference on Peacemaking and Conflict Resolution (NCPCR), identified 10 principles of restorative justice that provide more precision to the concept:

1. Crime is primarily an offence against human relationships.
2. Restorative justice recognises that crime is wrong and should not occur.
3. Restorative justice is a process to make things as right as possible.
4. The primary victim(s) of a crime is/are the one(s) most impacted by the offence.
5. The situation is an opportunity for teaching and learning.
6. Restorative justice responds at the earliest possible time with the greatest amount of co-operation.
7. A co-operative and community structure is used.
8. Not all offenders will choose to be co-operative.
9. The impact of the crime on victims should be emphasised.
10. Follow-up and accountability are important.

These principles apply across cultures and settings to diverse learners and communities. They can be applied to communities, within schools or in early childhood education services, in families and across societies.

Restorative practice is an approach based on respect, empowerment, collaboration and healing. These aspects are constructive and affirming, ensuring positive outcomes for all involved, and are in opposition to retributive approaches. In fact, the rejection of retributive approaches is perhaps the key aspect of understanding restorative practice. Restorative practice in schools and early childhood education services might be defined as much by what it is *not*. Table 1.2 clarifies elements of what restorative justice is and is not. Teachers might use this table to reflect on the philosophy they wish to foster and represent in their work with learners.

TABLE 1.2 RESTORATIVE PRACTICE IS, and IS NOT

Restorative practice is...	Restorative practice is not...
• about maximising a learning opportunity	• about attacking a person for mistakes and failures
• a healing process	
• a purpose-driven response	• punishment
• victim centred	• reactive
• a focus on working to make things right	• offender centred
• a creation and fostering of relationships	• a focus on the offence
• empowering	• alienating or isolating
• individualised	• humiliating
• collaborative	• one-size-fits-all
	• lecturing

Source: Adapted from Ashworth et al. (2008)

Social discipline

The restorative matrix, or social discipline window, devised by Wachtel and McCold (2000), further explains the restorative approach (see Figure 1.2). Four quadrants are formed through the intersection of two axes: the vertical axis defines structure and limits, and the horizontal axis defines support and care. Approaches to challenging behaviour can be located in one of the four quadrants, as follows:

- The top-left quadrant is high on structure and limits but low on support, resulting in a punitive and authoritarian approach. This approach results in actions being done *to* others.

- The bottom-right quadrant is high on support and care but low on structure and limits, resulting in approaches that appear permissive, rescuing, or *for* others.
- The bottom-left quadrant, being low on both structure and support, is neglectful and does *not* resolve.
- The top-right quadrant is high on both structure and support. This approach results in respectful problem solving, collaboration and restoration *with* others.

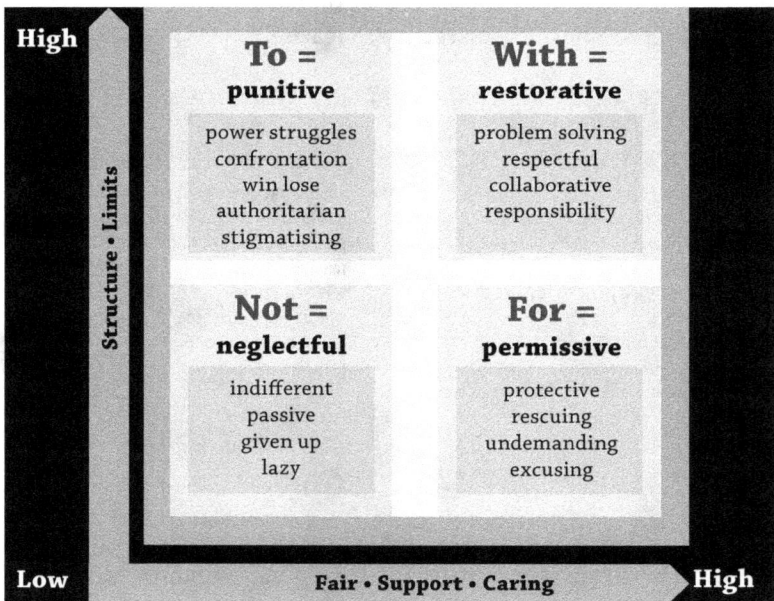

FIGURE 1.2 THE SOCIAL DISCIPLINE WINDOW
Source: Adapted from Wachtel & McCold, (2000) © restorative schools.org.nz

Wachtel (2005) draws from this matrix by challenging us to find ways of responding to behaviour that ensure we operate within the top-right quadrant, working responsively *with* others. This book provides authentic case studies and practice suggestions from teachers engaging responsively with challenging behaviour.

Conclusion

There is continuing national and international frustration over how to respond more appropriately to the increasing incidence of challenging behaviours in schools and early childhood education settings. Both the education sector and wider society are increasingly considering culturally responsive and relationship-based principles and practices as a methodology to use for sound professional intervention. Principles of restorative justice, applied most noticeably in the legal setting, can be translated to the field of education as restorative practice, highlighting their universality. That said, restorative practice is no miracle intervention. The ways in which teachers, students and whānau (families) can engage constructively with students who behave in challenging ways is contingent on a range of factors. Different situations require different responses, and knowing when and how to respond requires knowledge and reason.

When we are confronted with behavioural challenges we often wonder "why?" We want to know what causes that behaviour and how best to respond. Sometimes, despite our best intentions, relationships between students and teachers are tested, and matters that have gone wrong have to be put right. Engagement with challenging behaviour is most effective when informed by sound and systematic understanding, grounded in theory. The next chapter considers a number of theoretical models that provide empirically based frameworks to guide practice.

This chapter has contributed to the discussion of the historical and philosophical influences on the ways in which teachers choose to engage with challenging behaviour. It has aimed to raise consciousness by encouraging reflection about personal values, and to encourage ways of working towards constructive, relationship-based and culturally responsive practices. We argue that in order to engage effectively with challenging behaviour, seven imperatives need to be taken into account. Premised on the concept of TAPUWAE (footsteps) these seven imperatives include: effective teaching, well-considered aims, partnership, universality, wisdom, accountability and evidence-based practice, and will be revisited in many of the chapters that follow.

References

Addressing disruptive behaviour in students. (2011, February 14). *Tukutuku Kōrero: New Zealand Education Gazette*, 90(2), 4–5.

Ashworth, J., Van Bockern, S., Ailts, J., Donnelly, J., Erickson, K., & Woltermann, J. (2008). The restorative justice center: An alternative to school detention. *Reclaiming Children and Youth Journal*, 17(3), 22–26.

Becroft, A. J. (2005, November). *Māori youth offending*. Paper presented at the Ngakia Kia Puawai New Zealand Police conference, Nelson.

Bourke, R., Holden, B., & Curzon, J. (2005). *Using evidence to challenge practice: A discussion paper*. Wellington: Ministry of Education.

Bowen, H. (2008). *Restorative and healing justice in Aotearoa: A way forward for schools*. Paper presented at the New Zealand Edmund Rice conference, Oamaru. Retrieved 26 April 2010, from http://www.restorativejustice. org/10fulltext/bowen-helen.-2008.-restorative-and-healing-justice-in-aotearoa-a-way-forward-for-schools/view

Bronfenbrenner, U. (1979). *The ecology of human development: Experiments by nature and design*. Boston: Harvard University Press.

Bruner, J. (1996). *The culture of education*. Cambridge, MA: Harvard University Press.

Caritas Aotearoa New Zealand. (2009). A justice that reconciles. In *Caritas Social Justice Series, 14*. Wellington: Author.

Church, R. J. (2003). *The definition, diagnosis and treatment of children and youth with severe behaviour difficulties: A review of research*. Report prepared for the Ministry of Education.

Claassen, R. (1996). *Restorative justice: Fundamental principles*. London: Home Office, Information and Publications Group.

Drewery, W., & Winslade, J. (2003). *Developing restorative practices in schools: Flavour of the month or saviour of the system?* Paper presented at the AARE/ NZARE conference, Auckland.

Foorman, B. (2003). *Preventing and remediating reading difficulties: Bringing science to scale*. Baltimore: York Press.

Hamilton, M., & Litterick-Biggs, A. (2008). The Incredible Years parent training programme in Tauranga. *Kairaranga*, 9(1), 44–49.

Kane, J., Lloyd, G., McCluskey, G., Riddell, S., Stead, J., & Weedon, E. (2007). *Restorative practices in three Scottish councils: Final report of the evaluation of pilot projects 2004–2006*. Scottish Executive. Retrieved 8 August 2009, from http://www.scotland.gov.uk/Publications/2007/08/24093135/20

Lewis, S. (2009). *Improving school climate: Findings from schools implementing restorative practices*. A report from the International Institute for Restorative Practices GraduateSchool. Retrieved 21 August 2009, from http://www.iirp.org

Macfarlane, A. (2007). *Discipline, democracy and diversity: Working with students with behaviour difficulties*. Wellington: NZCER Press.

Macfarlane, A. H., Hendy, V., & Macfarlane, S. (2010). Young people experiencing behavioural difficulties: Discourses through the decades. *Kairaranga, 11*(2), 5–15.

McCold, P., & Wachtel, T. (2003). *In pursuit of paradigm: A theory of restorative justice*. Paper presented at the XIII World Congress of Criminology, Rio de Janeiro. Retrieved 28 October 2009, from http://www.realjustice.org/library/paradigm.html

Meyer, L. H., & Evans, I. M. (2006). *Draft final report: Literature review on intervention with challenging behaviour in children and youth with developmental disabilities*. Wellington: Ministry of Education.

Ministry of Education. (1996). *Te Whāriki: He whāriki mātauranga mō ngā mokopuna o Aotearoa: Early childhood curriculum*. Wellington: Learning Media.

Ministry of Education. (2007). *The New Zealand curriculum*. Wellington: Learning Media.

Ministry of Social Development. (2007). *Inter-agency plan for conduct disorder/severe antisocial behaviour 2007–2012*. Wellington: Author.

Morrison, B. (2007). *Restoring safe school communities: A whole school approach to bullying, violence and alienation*. Sydney: The Federation Press.

Positive behaviour for learning: Addressing disruptive behaviour in students. (2011). *New Zealand Education Gazette*. Retrieved 22 February 2011, from http://www.edgazette.govt.nz/Articles/Article.aspx?ArticleId=8275

Prochnow, J., & Macfarlane, A. (2008). *Managing classroom behaviour: Assertiveness and warmth*. Paper presented at the first Educational Psychology forum, Faculty of Education, University of Auckland, Auckland.

Prochnow, J., and Macfarlane, A. (2011). Managing classroom behaviour. In C. Rubie-Davies (Ed.). *Educational Psychology: Concepts, research and challenges* (pp 150-166). London: Routledge.

Restore and research. (2011, May 23). *Tukutuku Kōrero: New Zealand Education Gazette, 90*(2), 2–3.

Thorsborne, M., & Vinegrad, D. (2004). *Restorative practices in classrooms: Rethinking behaviour management*. Queenscliff, VIC: Inyahead Press.

Thorsborne, M., & Vinegrad, D. (2006). *Restorative practices and bullying: Rethinking behaviour management*. Queenscliff, VIC: Inyahead Press.

Tunmer, W. E., Chapman, J. W., & Prochnow, J. E. (2003). Preventing negative Matthew effects in at-risk readers: A retrospective study. In B. Foorman (Ed.), *Preventing and remediating reading difficulties: Bringing science to scale* (pp. 121–162). Timonium, MD: York Press.

Vygotsky, L. (1978). *Mind and society*. Cambridge, MA: Harvard University Press.

Wachtel, J. (2007). *RJ in the land of the long white cloud: New Zealand embraces restorative justice for adult offenders*. Paper presented at the Restorative Practices e-forum, Bethlehem, PA. Retrieved 26 April 2010, from http://www.restorativejustice.org/articlesdb/articles/7975

Wachtel, T. (2005). *The next step: Developing restorative communities*. Paper presented at The Next Step: Developing Restorative Communities, IIRP seventh international conference on Conferencing, Circles and Other Restorative Practices, Manchester, UK. Retrieved 28 October 2009, from http://www.realjustice.org/library/man05_wachtel.html

Wachtel, T., & McCold, P. (2000). *Restorative justice in everyday life*. In J. Braithwaite & H. Strang (Eds.), *Restorative justice in civil society* (pp. 117–125). New York: Cambridge University Press.

Zehr, H. (2002). *The little book of restorative justice*. Intercourse, PA: Good Books.

2.

Student Behaviour:
Towards a Theoretical Understanding

Angus H. Macfarlane & Jane E. Prochnow

Introduction

This chapter considers the definition and dimensions of challenging behaviours, while bearing in mind the different theoretical lenses through which we see and understand challenging and disordered behaviours. Challenging behaviours have continued to elude being defined concretely for many reasons including children's developmental stage and behaviours as perceived by others. However, any teacher can identify students they consider to be exhibiting disordered behaviour and recount examples of challenging behaviours. Some researchers have suggested (perhaps cynically) that the definition of severely challenging behaviour depends on the level of funding available to provide services for those students identified by the definition (Kauffman & Landrum, 2009). The potentially transient nature of challenging behaviour—including the idea that challenging behaviour will be outgrown—and the effect of labelling children as having a behaviour disorder cause us to pause and be circumspect when considering a definition of challenging behaviours. These behaviours are difficult to define because they are affected by the environment, background and tolerances of the person identifying a problem behaviour (most often the classroom teacher). This chapter therefore focuses on clarifying what we mean by behaviour problems and misconduct, in order to facilitate our understanding of pedagogy that is responsive to them.

Five broad types of behaviour are discussed in this chapter: aggression; immorality; defiance; disruption; and goofing off (Charles, 2008). These behaviours are illustrated in terms of their prevalence and severity along a continuum. Students who present challenging behaviours often have difficulties relating effectively with peers, teachers and/or parents. They also often have difficulty accomplishing academic tasks, which further compromises their access to core areas of the curriculum for their education. It is therefore important that educators have a sound understanding of the various influences that help to explain the causes of the problems, the types of behaviours and why definitions of challenging behaviours and behaviour difficulties are necessary.

In addition to presenting challenging behaviours as a continuum, the chapter discusses the theoretical background of contemporary models and approaches for understanding these behaviours. The theoretical models focus on environmental aspects and personal characteristics, including a person's physical/medical condition and cognition. The perspectives of the theoretical models further complicate the process of defining challenging behaviours, although they do present various strategies for engaging positively with each behaviour.

The different theoretical perspectives introduced in this chapter also contribute two imperatives: to outline the complexities involved in defining challenging behaviours, and to present various strategies for positively dealing with them while taking into account the context in which such behaviours are manifested. Implicit in the theories and strategies outlined here are philosophies, skills and interventions that are congruent with responsive pedagogy in addressing challenging behaviours. These approaches refer to the shift from retributive intervention, to building and nurturing relationships in order to prevent harm occurring in the first place, or introducing skills to engage in repair processes after the harm has occurred. Overall, the focus of this chapter is on clarifying what we mean by challenging behaviours in order to better understand responsive pedagogical engagement.

Definition and continuum of challenging behaviours

Defining challenging behaviour

An acceptable definition of challenging behaviour is an important prerequisite for accurate identification, appropriate assessment and programme placement. Varying definitions and a range of terminology are used in the field of human behaviour. These have emerged from differing theoretical views presented in the literature over recent decades. Although arriving at a definition is difficult, establishing one that is suitable for a particular context can be helpful in terms of assessment, programme planning and the placement of students with challenging behaviours.

The difficulty reaching an acceptable definition of challenging behaviour has been frequently described. Kauffman and Landrum (2009) argue that reaching an agreed definition has been made more difficult by:

- the different conceptual models used in the field—psycho-dynamic, biophysical, behavioural, ecological, sociocultural and (the most recent) restorative
- the variety of aims involved in reaching a definition (e.g., educational, legal, psychological, health related)
- the fact that any definition is developed within a social context and is embedded in cultural rules.

Although no single definition is acceptable to all theorists and practitioners, Bower's (1981) description of severe behaviour disorders has been widely recognised in the field of education. Bower includes:

- an inability to learn, which cannot be explained by intellectual, sensory or health factors
- an inability to build or maintain satisfactory interpersonal relationships with peers and teachers
- inappropriate types of behaviour or feelings under normal conditions
- a general pervasive mood of unhappiness or depression
- a tendency to develop physical symptoms, pains or fears associated with personal or school problems (pp. 115–116).

Bower proposes that an individual should be considered to be "behaviourally disordered" if his or her condition exhibits one or more of these five characteristics over a long period of time to a marked degree, and to the extent that it affects educational performance.

Conway (2008) presents a different but related set of defining characteristics of a behavioural disorder:

- more than a temporary, unexpected response to stressful events in the environment
- consistently exhibited in two different settings, at least one of which is school related
- persisting despite individualised interventions within the educational programme (unless the student's history indicates that such interventions would not be effective) (p. 179).

Although other definitions vary considerably, Hallahan, Kauffman, and Pullen (2011) note that there are some features common to many of them, including:

- behaviour that goes to an extreme (i.e., behaviour that is not just slightly different from that which is perceived as the norm)
- a problem that is chronic—one that does not quickly disappear
- behaviour that is unacceptable because of social and cultural expectations.

STUDENT BEHAVIOUR: TOWARDS A THEORETICAL UNDERSTANDING

The behaviour continuum

A number of studies (Conway, 2008; Porter, 2000; Wheldall & Merrett, 1989) have qualitatively described these behaviours along a continuum, ranging from mild to severe. These studies lend support to the way Charles (2008) categorises different types of challenging behaviours, along with their severity and level of prevalence. In descending order of seriousness, as judged by social scientists, the five types of misbehaviour are:

1. aggression—physical and verbal attacks on the teacher or other students
2. immorality—acts such as cheating, lying and stealing
3. defiance of authority—refusal, sometimes hostile, to do as the teacher requests
4. class disruptions—talking loudly, calling out, walking about the room, clowning and tossing objects
5. goofing off—such as fooling around, out of seat, not doing assigned tasks, dawdling and daydreaming (Charles, 2008, p. 2).

According to Charles, there is general agreement among researchers and teachers that the most dreaded behaviours teachers face at school are aggression, immorality and defiance. However, he also points out that teachers seldom encounter these types of behaviours. It is the less serious behaviours, such as goofing off and paying insufficient attention, that are far more prevalent. These apparently innocuous, repetitive behaviours not only stress teachers to the point where their responses may often be counter-productive, but they are also the behaviours that waste instructional time and interfere with learning (Macfarlane, 2007; Prochnow, 2006; Wearmouth, Glynn, & Berryman, 2005).

That said, the notion that teachers seldom have to deal with the more serious behaviours is now being challenged. The *Inter-agency Plan for Conduct Disorder/Severe Antisocial Behaviour 2007–2012* (Ministry of Social Development, 2007) estimated that "approximately 5% of children and young people [have] conduct disorder/severe antisocial behaviour" (p. 22). Similarly, the Ministry of Education (2008) indicated that "around five per cent of children in New Zealand demonstrate the more severe forms of disruptive and challenging behaviour ... this would equate to around 37,500 school-aged children" (p. 5). The Ministry of Education also notes that "studies suggest that up to 20 per cent of children at some time demonstrate these sorts of more serious behaviours" (p. 5).

Meyer and Evans (2006) argue that the presence of such challenging behaviours is a growing problem internationally. They cite an escalating number of media reports and television programmes that present case studies of children with severe behavioural problems. While the number of media reports cannot be considered evidence that the number or intensity of challenging behaviours exhibited is growing, it is an indication that the behaviours are attracting attention nationally as well as internationally. According to Moore, Anderson, and Sharma (2005), internationally, schools are reported to be resorting increasingly to suspension and expulsion as a way of dealing with the growing issue of severe misbehaviour.

Despite the difficulty of gaining a general consensus on a definition of challenging behaviours, it is possible to identify a number of behaviour clusters with recognisable features. These clusters can be represented along a continuum that ranges from mild to serious (see Table 2.1). The location of students on this kind of behavioural continuum has a significant bearing on who introduces the intervention strategy and what form the strategy is likely to take. That said, responsive pedagogy is applicable to students across the whole continuum. Behaviours on the continuum are represented as a range rather than distinctly separate categories. The ranges are more reflective of the different levels of behaviour problems that students may display at any given time.

TABLE 2.1 MACFARLANE and PROCHNOW'S
CONTINUUM of PROBLEM BEHAVIOUR

Level 1 Mild to moderate	Level 2 Moderate to severe	Level 3 Severe to serious
Displays rather innocuous behaviours; seen as more to do with adjustment difficulties because of slowness to respond to the usual range of management strategies.	Displays more salient behaviours; consequently judged by more than one authoritative adult to be excessive, deficient or inappropriate within given social situations.	Displays more damaging behaviours; often seen as defiant or uncouth, which consequently interfere seriously with either their own or other people's wellbeing, learning and teaching. Often continues at an unacceptable level after the intervention, even when this has been implemented thoroughly and with fidelity.
Irritating, frustrating and distracting behaviours.	Disruptive and challenging behaviours.	Defiant, aggressive and intense behaviours.
• Affects quality instructional time in the classroom • Low-end need; inexpensive resourcing required per student or programme	• Affects the quality management time of school leaders • Moderate need; medium resourcing required per student or programme	• Affects the quality time of teachers, school leaders, whānau, caregivers, as well as professional and voluntary services • High-end need; costly resourcing required per student or programme

Level 1 (mild to moderate) behaviours are those that interfere with the orderly environment of the classroom. Responses to these more common behaviours are usually implemented by the teacher and/ or the resource or support teacher of learning and behaviour. They should be developmentally appropriate, instructive and positive. Level 2 (moderate to severe) behaviours are those that interfere with the orderly environment of the school and are potentially dangerous to the wellbeing of the student and staff. The teacher, senior staff member(s), school counsellor and specialist assessor are likely to be involved in implementing responses to these behaviours. Level 3 (severe to serious) behaviours are the most serious violations and represent a direct threat to the orderly operation of the classroom or school. More specialised personnel from a psychological service or community agency are likely to be involved in implementing responses to these behaviours. It may be necessary to exclude the student for a period of time that is commensurate with the seriousness of the behaviour.

Theoretical models

Theoretical background

For nearly 50 years educators have actively sought ways to promote acceptable student behaviour by employing means other than intimidation and punishment. In the last 30 years, discipline has risen to the top of the list of teacher concerns (Charles, 2008). Pioneers in the field of student behaviour include Redl and Wattenburg (1951), who focused on group behaviour and explored how individual behaviour within groups could more easily be understood and managed. Redl and Wattenburg's research contributed significantly to our understanding of the way in which group expectations strongly influence group and individual behaviour. In the 1960s Skinner's work on the consequences of behaviour focused on shaping desired student behaviour using the principles of reinforcement (Skinner, 1953, 1974). Skinner's research added to a general understanding of the contingencies that shape and control many human behaviours. Notable research and publications continued, including Kounin's (1977) landmark studies on behaviour management through classroom management practices oriented toward teaching and learning, and Jones's (1987) focus on positive discipline.

Theoretical models: A platform for understanding behaviour

What makes us behave as we do towards ourselves, others and the environment? How can we change our behaviour and the behaviour of others from inappropriate to appropriate, and from unacceptable to acceptable? As Walker and Shea (2006) point out, theories can help us respond to these questions. These theories can provide a useful guide for teaching practice, as well as for the type of assessment and intervention required to address specific challenging behaviours. This is because theories help to reveal and rationalise a structured set of ideas and practices; and the more organised one's ideas, the more effective one can be in responding to challenging behaviour. More generally, theories can provide what Porter (2000) refers to as "an orderly set of beliefs, concepts and models that is used to describe, explain and predict behaviour" (p. 7).

Figure 2.1 illustrates our adaptation of work by Walker and Shea (2006). In it we present six models that influence contemporary practice: psychodynamic; biophysical; behavioural; ecological; sociocultural; and restorative. As Figure 2.1 illustrates, theoretical models influence the principles for practice, and in turn the methods and strategies for action. Teachers need to think about whether particular models support relevant interventions for the behaviours they regularly encounter, and how the models fit their own context and influence.

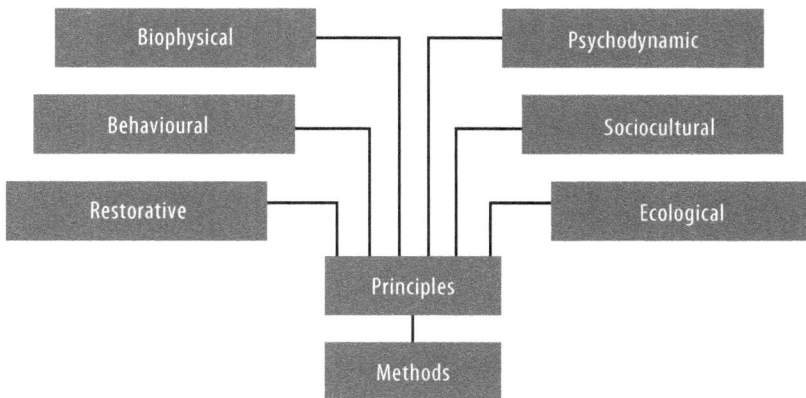

FIGURE 2.1 THEORETICAL MODELS OF DISCIPLINE

It is worth noting that there is a vast range of explanatory models of human behaviour, and the list given here is by no means exhaustive. The intention is to offer an overview of how behaviour is understood from different theoretical perspectives rather than provide the kind of comprehensive review provided by Kauffman and Landrum (2009), Charles (2008) and Walker and Shea (2006). The selected models also provide a framework from which to consider the connections between theoretical models and the practice of professional responses to a behaviour.

The psychodynamic model

Psychodynamic theorists perceive the causes of human behaviour as residing within the individual. The many forms of psychodynamic theories suggest that undesirable behaviour is the result of some form of inner turmoil or tension among the dynamic parts of one's personality. Brigham and Brigham (2005) contend that acceptable behaviour is impossible until these tensions are resolved through a psychotherapy-oriented approach. They argue that the implication for educators working within a psychodynamic model is to provide a permissive and accepting classroom environment so that the student is able to work through his or her emotional conflicts.

Counselling and other forms of talking interventions are often associated with this model for understanding behaviour. There is an association here with the restorative intervention theory in terms of the interactions between victim and offender, because both involve personal reconciliation, atonement and potential forgiveness. A criticism of this approach might well be its overemphasis on the individual nature of restorative thinking and practice. Such criticism is often refuted on the basis that with this model the emphasis in the classroom is placed on developing a psychologically healthy atmosphere, accepting the young person and the pathological condition without reservation and encouraging and assisting the student to learn. In order to promote and enhance the student's learning, the teacher pitches learning activities at a certain level and in ways that enable the student to experience success.

The biophysical model

The biophysical model emphasises the organic origins of human behaviour. It postulates a relationship between physical defects, malfunctions and illnesses, and the individual's behaviour (Walker & Shea, 2006). Two primary subgroups of this model are the deficit and the developmental theories (Walker & Shea, 2006). Deficit theory sees the causes of behavioural disorders as related to genetics, temperament, nutrition and neurological dysfunction. Development theory sees the causes as including identifiable conditions such as neurological organisation, perceptual motor learning, psychological readiness, sensory integration and development.

Not surprisingly, intricate intervention processes are often indicated for the behaviours explained in the biophysical model. Brigham and Brigham (2005) assert that educators need to be aware of biophysical explanations because they will see a number of students whose behaviour is related to a genetic or chemical condition. Although it is not the dominant theory of causation in the education of young people, the biophysical model does have its proponents among restorative professionals and parents of children with profound emotional and behavioural disorders. For example, schizophrenia, autism, depression, hyperactivity and selective mutism can all be associated with organic origins. Some forms of behavioural disorders, such as those just mentioned, respond better to medical treatment than to other forms of intervention (Brigham & Cole, 1998). Brigham and Brigham (2005) point out, however, that educators are not trained in a biophysical discipline and should therefore be cautious about offering a biophysical explanation for a given behaviour without conference with or feedback from a medical doctor, psychologist or psychiatrist.

The behavioural model

The behavioural model, which includes behaviour modification techniques and other applications, has its roots in the writings of Bandura (1977) and Skinner (1953, 1974), among others. Walker and Shea (2006) argue that although the traditional debates have lingered in terms of the various constructs and interventions within this model, practitioners have successfully applied its principles to a variety of human situations.

The behavioural explanation suggests that all behaviour is learnt as a function of events within the environment. Brigham and Brigham (2005) expand on this explanation:

> When maladaptive behaviours are observed, they should be considered to be the outcomes of inappropriate learning. Similarly, adaptive behaviours are the result of learning appropriate responses to various prompts in the environment. Behavioural practitioners support or change behaviour by arranging antecedent events and consequences. A great deal of effort goes into making precise definitions of the behaviour in question and collecting objective reliable data regarding frequency, duration, setting, antecedent events, and the consequences surrounding the behaviour. (p. 2)

Applied behaviour analysis refers to the overall process of changing student behaviour through antecedents and consequences, but particularly by reinforcing those behaviours that are appropriate. According to Wearmouth et al. (2005), the field of applied behaviour analysis employs strategies based on an examination of behavioural principles in the environment for antecedents to and consequences of behaviours, as well as the reinforcements and punishing circumstances that can maintain or reduce behaviours.

The ecological model

The ecological or integrative model stresses that understanding human development and behaviour requires an examination of the contexts of a person's interactions in several settings (Bronfen-brenner, 1979). The home and the school are the critical environments in a child's world, which usually include the family, classroom and peer group. Proponents of this approach insist that rather than focusing exclusively, or primarily, on the behaviour of the student, ecological practitioners need to assess environment–behaviour inter-actions, as well as the ecological contexts in which student behaviours occur. This ecological approach has the benefit of being less intrusive, because it employs naturally occurring supports that already exist in the environment (Brigham & Brigham, 2005). Development of the teachers' skills to understand the wider environment is also essential in the ecological model.

In order to be effective, teachers and parents should focus their primary efforts on the microsystem of the school and home. According to Ysseldyke and Christensen (1998), the child's instructional needs within the classroom, as well as the home as a source of support for classroom learning, should be of primary concern when designing restorative interventions. This is because educators have more direct control over the influences that occur at the microsystem level. At the classroom level, the prominent factors include lesson organisation, presentation and momentum, student engagement and accountability, as well as the mixture of joy and challenge. Those at school and home need to listen to and respect the integrity and status of each other.

The sociocultural model

Current concepts of sociocultural theory draw heavily on the work of Vygotsky (1978), as well as later theoreticians (see, for example, Bruner, 1996). A key feature of this emergent model of human development is that higher order functions develop out of social interaction. Vygotsky argues that a child's development cannot be understood simply by studying the individual. We must also examine the social world in which that person has developed. Vygotsky claimed that children could learn and develop best within their zone of proximal development. Within this zone, a child can learn and develop in interaction with peers, teachers and family further and more easily than the same child can progress alone. The zone of proximal development, for example, is an area of activities that individuals can navigate with the help of more capable peers or adults. This zone can include not only individuals with different levels of knowledge and experiences, but also artefacts such as books, computers and other information technology materials. This approach also promotes the notion that students working in groups can master learning better than students working alone (see Slavin, 1995).

The sociocultural model supports the idea of a culturally responsive teacher (Villegas & Lucas, 2002) engaging in responsive practice. Assuming that a child's thinking is shaped by the cultural context in which he or she is reared, and which provides the tools for organising meaning and shaping behaviour, then the sociocultural model has profound implications for teaching and schooling. As an example of this approach, Māori scholar, Makareti (also known as Maggie Papakura), presents a depiction of the social world for a Māori child. She describes the child as being absorbed into and mentored by the whānau, just as the whānau is absorbed into the hapū, and the hapū into the iwi (see Penniman, 1986).

Barbara Rogoff (2003) begins her text on the cultural nature of human development by stating that as a biological species humans are defined in terms of their cultural participation. This is compatible with Phinney and Rotheram's (1987) contention that there are ethically linked ways of thinking, feeling and acting that are acquired through socialisation—meaning the way that young people are raised, along with the cultural tools that are both inherited and transformed by successive generations.

The restorative model

Restorative practices based on this model are constructive, solution-oriented responses to behaviour derived from the principles of restorative justice. The restorative justice philosophy is distinct from approaches involving retribution and punishment. Key elements of restorative justice include an acknowledgement that misconduct violates people and relationships, violations create obligations and restorative practice seeks to heal, put things right and restore harmony (Thorsborne & Vinegrad, 2006; Zehr, 2002). These aspects are forward looking, constructive and support positive outcomes for all.

In broad terms, restorative approaches to discipline constitute an innovative perspective on both offending and challenging behaviour. They put repairing harm done to relationships and people over and above the need for assigning blame and dispensing punishment (Thorsborne & Vinegrad, 2006). Wisdom and a wide understanding of interventions are essential because the offenders are also recognised as having been affected and therefore should be part of the problem-solving pathway. The restorative model sees problems and problem solving as bidirectional. This approach to discipline challenges many notions embedded in Western society (at least) and dispensed in many homes, schools and institutions. We contend here that restorative discipline must include a pervasive set of skills that complements the ethos of the seminal theoretical models of behaviour that have influenced literature and professional development constructs for many decades. This skill set includes remaining open minded and aware of the factors that contribute to the behaviour, whoever and whatever these may be. These skills include: active and empathic listening; development of rapport; offering empowerment to others to come up with solutions rather than imposing or suggesting ideas; use of creative conversations; and maintenance of warmth and compassion.

Theory into practice

Classroom management is the careful orchestration of classroom life so that students are able to maximise their opportunities to learn. This is no easy task. The classroom is a unique, multidimensional physical and human space, populated (generally) by a sole adult and many students, with a host of different activities taking place at the same time. The teacher is regularly required to implement a variety of tasks simultaneously with little time to pause or reflect. The classroom is also an unpredictable place, where a combination of human mannerisms (e.g., noncompliance) and natural elements (e.g., weather conditions) can determine the dominant mood within its walls. In addition, the classroom is a place to which each student and teacher brings their previous histories and experiences (see Doyle, 1986).

Teachers therefore have to draw on a range of particular qualities required of their profession, including attitudes, skills, knowledge and experience. According to Jensen (1995), a further quality, *acumen*, describes the high professional standards that good teachers set for themselves. Acumen includes learning about the various cultures represented in the classroom; discovering what has been done by other teachers in the past; looking through local archives; and asking colleagues and community members about the local traditions, rituals and legends. Having acumen is in line with Blumberg's (1989) notion of "developing a nose for things—having a sense of process", so that the management of the classroom can be carried out efficiently (p. 56).

In early childhood education, teachers aim to provide positive guidance rather than "management" of behaviour (Ministry of Education, 1998). Redirection and resolution are considered both age-appropriate and philosophically relevant. Several of the school-based classroom management and disciplinary strategies that have emerged from early scholarship continue to be vehicles for establishing a positive classroom climate in which students feel valued and motivated. From previous research (Ginott, 1971; Good & Brophy, 2008), for example, we are aware that effective communication is both fundamental to student motivation and based on positive and reciprocal teacher–student relationships. These in turn are integral to effective classroom organisation and management because the particular strategies a teacher employs in a classroom are more likely to be successful in a climate of mutual respect (Macfarlane, 2007). Effective communication and mutual respect begin with positive support of behaviour and a culturally responsive classroom.

An important aspect of responsive pedagogy is collaborative and bidirectional problem solving. Restorative practices exemplify responsive engagement with a challenging behaviour by providing an opportunity for those who have been most affected by an incident or a behaviour to come together to share their feelings, describe how they were affected and develop a plan to repair the harm done or prevent a recurrence. The restorative approach confronts and disapproves of wrongdoing while accepting the intrinsic worth of the individual wrongdoer. The restorative approach is also reiterative, allowing the offender to make amends and shed the offender label, while allowing the offended to retain or reclaim his or her integrity.

Conclusion

This chapter has provided a range of definitions for challenging behaviours and behavioural difficulties, along with a continuum of these behaviours. We have considered key historical perspectives of behaviour, including an analysis of methods and strategies for behaviour management and how they can better be understood in the context of their origins. Inherent in the different models and perspectives are ideas and beliefs that can guide educators' actions with young people to support students' learning and behaviour. Theoretical models provide a framework to support teachers in their understanding of the factors that cause behavioural difficulties that exist in schools and society. The theoretical models also provide us with the background for examining our own beliefs about children's behaviour and the malleability of behaviours. What we believe about the behaviour of students affects how we respond and act towards them.

Kauffman and Landrum (2009) stress that there are many theories for understanding children's behaviour. However, they contend that not all ways of understanding are equal. Rather, they argue that some ways of knowing and understanding are better than others depending on the behaviours and the purpose for explaining the behaviours. Contemporary approaches to responding to behaviour acknowledge context and culture, and use constructive, restorative methods. It makes sense that if we want a constructive solution, we should use constructive, responsive methods in our response to behaviour.

References

Bandura, A. (1977). *Social learning theory*. Englewood Cliffs, NJ: Prentice Hall.

Blumberg, A. (1989). *School administration as a craft: Foundations of practice*. Boston, MA: Allyn and Bacon.

Bower, E. M. (1981). *Early identification of emotionally handicapped children in school* (3rd ed.) Springfield, IL: Thomas.

Brigham, F. J., & Brigham, M. (2005). *An introduction to understanding behavior*. Charlottesville, VA: University of Virginia.

Brigham, F. J., & Cole, J. E. (1998). Selective mutism: Developments in definition, etiology, assessment and treatment. In T. E. Scruggs & M. A. Mastropieri (Eds.), *Advances in learning and behavioral disabilities* (pp. 183–216). Greenwich, CT: JAI Press.

Bronfenbrenner, U. (1979). *The ecology of human development: Experiments by nature and design*. Cambridge, MA: Harvard University Press.

Bruner, J. (1996). *The culture of education*. Cambridge, MA: Harvard University Press.

Charles, C. (2008). *Building classroom discipline* (7th ed.). New York: AddisonWesley Longman.

Conway, R. (2008). Behaviour support and management. In A. F. Ashman & J. Elkins (Eds.), *Education for inclusion and diversity* (3rd ed., pp. 177–208). Frenchs Forest, NSW: Pearson Education Australia.

Doyle. W. (1986). Classroom organization and management. In M. C. Wittrock (Ed.), *Handbook of research on teaching* (3rd ed., pp. 341–392). New York: Macmillan.

Ginott, H., (1971). *Teacher and child*. New York: Macmillan.

Good, T., & Brophy, J. (2008). *Looking in classrooms* (10th ed.). Boston, MA: Pearson/Allyn and Bacon.

Hallahan, D. P., Kauffman, J. M., & Pullen, P. C. (2011). *Exceptional children: Introduction to special education* (12th ed.). Englewood Cliffs, NJ: Prentice-Hall.

Jensen, E. (1995). *Super teaching*. San Diego: The Brain Store.

Jones, F. H. (1987). *Positive classroom discipline*. New York: McGraw Hill.

Kauffman, J. M., & Landrum, T. J. (2009). *Characteristics of emotional and behavioral disorders of children and youth* (9th ed.). Upper Saddle River, NJ: Pearson Education.

Kounin, J. (1977). *Discipline and group management in classrooms* (Rev. ed.). New York: Holt, Rinehart & Winston.

Macfarlane, A. H. (2007). *Discipline, democracy, and diversity: Working with students with behaviour difficulties*. Wellington: NZCER Press.

Meyer, L. H., & Evans, I. M. (2006). *Literature review on intervention with challenging behaviour in children and youth with developmental disabilities* (Final report commissioned by the New Zealand Ministry of Education). Wellington: College of Education, Victoria University of Wellington.

Ministry of Education. (1998). *Providing positive guidance*. Wellington: Learning Media.

Ministry of Education. (2008). *Setting boundaries: Plan of action for addressing behaviour issues in schools and early childhood centres: Actions to 30 June 2009*. Wellington: Author.

Ministry of Social Development. (2007). *Inter-agency plan for conduct disorder/ severe antisocial behaviour 2007–2012*. Wellington: Author.

Moore, D., Anderson, A. & Sharma, U (2005) *Reducing challenging behaviour initiative: The effectiveness of off-site centres/ centers of extra support as an intervention for children and young people with severe challenging behaviour,* Ministry of Education, New Zealand

Penniman, T. (Ed.). (1986). *Makereti: The old-time Māori.* Auckland: New Women's Press.

Phinney, J., & Rotheram, M. (1987). *Children's ethnic socialization: Pluralism and development.* Newbury Park, CA: Sage.

Porter, L. (2000). *Student behaviour: Theory and practice for teachers* (2nd ed.). St Leonards, NSW: Allen & Unwin.

Prochnow, J. E. (2006). Barriers toward including students with difficult behaviour in regular classrooms. *New Zealand Journal of Educational Studies, 41*(2), 329–347.

Redl, F., & Wattenburg, W. (1951). *Mental hygiene in teaching.* New York: Harcourt, Brace & World.

Rogoff, B. (2003). *The cultural nature of human development.* New York: Oxford University Press.

Skinner, B. F. (1953), *Science and human behavior.* New York: Macmillan.

Skinner, B. F. (1974). *About behaviorism.* London: Cape.

Slavin, R. (1995). *Cooperative learning: Theory, research and practice* (2nd ed.). Boston: Allyn & Bacon.

Thorsborne, M., & Vinegrad, D. (2006). *Restorative practices and bullying: Rethinking behaviour management* (2nd ed.). Queenscliff, VIC: Inyahead Press.

Villegas, A., & Lucas, T. (2002). *Educating culturally responsive teachers: A coherent approach.* Albany, NY: State University of New York Press.

Vygotsky, L. (1978). *Mind and society.* Cambridge, MA: Harvard University Press.

Walker, J., & Shea, T. (2006). *Behaviour management: A practical approach for educators* (9th ed.). Upper Saddle River, NJ: Prentice-Hall.

Wearmouth, J., Glynn, T., & Berryman, M. (2005). *Perspectives on student behaviour in schools: Exploring theory and developing practice.* London: Routledge.

Wheldall, K., & Merrett, F. (1989). Managing troublesome behaviour in primary and secondary classrooms. *The best of set: Discipline,* item 12. Wellington: New Zealand Council for Educational Research; Melbourne, VIC: Australian Council for Educational Research.

Ysseldyke, J., & Christensen, S. (1998). *TIES II: The instructional environmental system: II* (4th ed.). Longmot, CO: Sopris West.

Zehr, H. (2002). *The little book of restorative justice.* Intercourse, PA: Good Books.

3.

Listening to Culture

Ted Glynn, Tom Cavanagh,
Angus H. Macfarlane, & Sonja Macfarlane

Introduction

In this chapter we suggest that classrooms and schools should be safe places for learning that embody a *culture of care*. A culture of care is strongly supportive of improving both learning and behaviour outcomes for students. Within a culture of care, students and teachers are free to express themselves and their own cultural identities. They are free to develop reciprocal and supportive relationships as learners, and to construct the kind of classroom culture in which they all feel they can safely belong. They are also free to strive for learning outcomes that are both achievable and desirable.

Within a culture of care a blending of boundaries between teachers and learners can emerge. Teachers are comfortable as learners and learners are comfortable as teachers. There is a fusion of instructional and caring roles. Boundaries between teachers' professional identities and their personal identities are fluid. Trusting and respectful relationships establish and sustain both the instructional and the caring roles. Responding to each other's learning needs is as much about teachers and students caring for each other as it is about teaching and learning. Caring for each other extends beyond the time spent at school and extends into the families and wider communities beyond school, as evidenced in Glynn, Berryman, Loader, and Cavanagh's (2005) case study of a successful school and community literacy partnership in a rural Māori-immersion school.

We also discuss how establishing and maintaining a culture of care in classrooms and schools can be informed and guided by two different but complementary theoretical approaches: culturally responsive pedagogies and communities of practice. It is argued that a safe and caring classroom and school can be established as communities of practice that incorporate responsive pedagogies known variously as "culturally relevant", "culturally responsive" and "culturally inclusive".

Rationale for responsivity

The process of creating classrooms in which students and teachers can learn in safety within a culture of care involves resourcing and professional development that is targeted at supporting teachers to develop expertise in implementing culturally responsive, relation-ship-based pedagogies. This surely does more to facilitate culturally inclusive environments than endorsing the use of behaviour management strategies that embrace "crime and punishment" and "zero tolerance" approaches. One such approach—the resourcing and implementation of successful relationships-based restorative practices—was adopted by Brady Area School (a pseudonym) in New Zealand. In reporting on this activity, Cavanagh (2008) noted that "care before censure" was a key understanding of both teachers and students.

In order to move forward with responsivity, we need to reflect briefly on where we are currently in terms of classrooms and behaviour. In

New Zealand, and indeed in other countries, concern continues to be expressed at the levels of severe and challenging behaviour displayed in many classrooms and schools. The frequency and intensity of both verbal and physical aggression that occur in some classrooms by students and teachers alike is an ongoing issue. We propose that positive responsivity by teachers will minimise negativity, reinforce positive interactions between teachers and students and enhance the quality of opportunities for teachers to teach and for students to learn.

It is easy to understand how having to live and cope with the interpersonal harm that results from incidents of verbal and physical abuse can lead to students and teachers experiencing classrooms and schools as environments that are unsafe. It is also understandable how infrequent but extreme incidents, such as the disastrous school shootings in the United States, can lead to schools and teachers adopting "zero tolerance" approaches in response to such incidents in order to ensure that students and teachers are safe (in the sense of being free from harm). However, Cavanagh (2009) argues that zero tolerance policies as a response to severe and challenging behaviours in schools appear to oppose the fundamental purposes of public education. Excluding bullying students from school also removes opportunities for them, and for their victims, to learn safer and more respectful ways of living and learning together—to restore calm and to rebuild relationships.

Being free from extreme harm does not necessarily ensure that classrooms and schools will be safe. Students from a marginalised cultural minority background frequently find themselves in classroom and school environments that feel unsafe, uncaring and destructive of their cultural identities and their capacity to learn. Where students find their culture is not reflected in the curriculum and pedagogy of the school and that the knowledge they do have is never called upon in the classroom, school for them can become an alien, uncaring and unsafe place, where they feel they do not belong (Wearmouth, Glynn, & Berryman, 2005). This can often provoke increased challenging and disruptive behaviour or truancy.

There are clearly alternative ways to view safety in classrooms based on an understanding of a culture of care (Cavanagh, 2003, 2005a, 2005b; Macfarlane, 2007; Macfarlane, Glynn, Cavanagh, & Bateman, 2007; Noddings, 1992, 2002).

Exclusionary behaviour management strategies do little to respond to the diverse cultural learning and experiences that students bring with them to the classroom. Such approaches reinforce attitudes of intolerance and minimise opportunities for students and teachers to develop equitable, caring and respectful working relationships. Conversely, restorative practice strategies focus on repairing the harm and the hurt done to individuals, as well as to their families and communities, and on restoring harmony. We endorse such strategies because they allow teachers, students and their cultural communities to create communities of practice within their classrooms, which operate within a culture of care. Such communities of practice incorporate pedagogies that affirm and respond to students' diverse cultural identities and learning backgrounds. They ensure that our classrooms and schools are safe places for students and teachers.

Although there has been a wide range of professional development initiatives providing teachers with a variety of positivist, or scientific, approaches to managing student behaviour (Canter & Canter, 2001; Rogers, 2003; Watkins & Wagner, 2000), student stand-down and suspension continue to be the most frequently applied responses to challenging behaviour in New Zealand schools. Furthermore, for many years these responses have been applied disproportionately to Māori students, who experience stand-downs and suspensions at three times the rate of non-Māori students (Ministry of Education, 2005).

There is a pressing need for professional development that supports New Zealand teachers to build positive, equitable and reciprocal learning relationships with students, particularly students from different cultural backgrounds from their own, and especially with their Māori students. Not surprisingly, it can be challenging for many teachers to develop responsive and positive relationships with students whose language and culture they do not understand. Nevertheless, building such relationships is a central component of culturally responsive pedagogies (Bishop, Berryman, Cavanagh, & Teddy, 2007; Bishop & Glynn, 1999; Gay, 2000; Glynn, Wearmouth, & Berryman, 2005; Ladson-Billings, 1995; Macfarlane, 2004, 2007; Macfarlane, Glynn, Cavanagh, & Bateman, 2005). Knowing and understanding more about the language and cultural beliefs, values and practices of Māori students is a powerful way to ensure that their voices and their mana (ascribed power, prestige and authority), dignity and autonomy as Māori people are fully represented in the curriculum and pedagogical practices within the classroom.

By learning to "listen to culture" (Macfarlane, 2004), teachers can create classrooms that are safe communities of practice where "culture counts" (Bishop & Glynn, 1999) and where "culture speaks" (Bishop & Berryman, 2006). In these classrooms, Māori students (as well as students from other minority cultural groups) can experience a sense of belonging, and can participate and contribute on the basis of their own cultural identities. Success for these students will not have to come at the cost of leaving their family and community culture at the school gate, or, as one successful Māori student at Brady Area School put it, "turning the lights out" (Cavanagh, 2005b).

Culturally appropriate and responsive pedagogies

There have been numerous descriptions and profiles of pedagogical approaches that are labelled "culturally appropriate", "culturally relevant" or "culturally responsive". The work of Ladson-Billings (1995) provides us with one informative, foundational example, which aligns with the principles and characteristics of restorative practices and beliefs. In discussing the outcomes of her two-year intensive research study with eight highly effective teachers of urban African-American students, Ladson-Billings concluded that all eight teachers—both African-American and white American—displayed three important sets of characteristics.

The first set of characteristics concerned the teachers' perceptions of themselves in relation to others: they believed that all students were capable of success. These eight teachers saw their teaching as a work in progress, and they saw themselves as members of a community of practice with a commitment to give back to the community. The second set of characteristics concerned the way in which these teachers constructed their social relationships. Their relationships with students remained fluid, equitable and reciprocal. They established and maintained connectedness with their students and operated their classes as communities of learners. They also encouraged students to work collaboratively and to take responsibility for each other.

The third set of characteristics concerned the teachers' perception of knowledge. They believed that knowledge was not static but constructed, and that it must be viewed critically. There was also a strong social justice element to their curriculum focus and the learning tasks they devised. They believed that teachers need to be passionate and to facilitate learning through building bridges (e.g., to students' existing personal and community knowledge and life experiences). They believed that assessment needs to be multifaceted, recognising and incorporating multiple forms of excellence. In addition, while these teachers clearly had a deeply caring and nurturing role towards their students, they nevertheless all communicated high expectations that their students would achieve academic success.

The work of Ladson-Billings is a major contribution to our understanding of culturally responsive pedagogy in action within the classroom. Similarly, the work of Russell Bishop and colleagues in the *Te Kotahitanga* professional development project (Bishop, Berryman, Cavanagh, & Teddy, 2007, 2009) and the *Educultural Wheel* (Macfarlane, 2004) provide contemporary New Zealand examples of culturally responsive, relationship-based pedagogies that are firmly grounded in theorising and practices that reflect Māori world view perspectives. Te Kotahitanga has particular strengths in terms of providing in-school professional development for mainstream teachers, beginning with providing access to the powerful narratives of the school experiences of Year 9 and Year 10 Māori students in the students' own voices.

This approach has challenged teachers to change their discursive positioning in relation to their Māori students by adopting *unknowing* as well as *knowing* positions. It thereby positions students *and* teachers as *experts* as well as *novices* within behaviour and learning conversations. Through this change in discursive positioning, teachers and students learn to interact in ways that create mutually positive, affirming and respectful relationships. This in turn facilitates reciprocal learning and teaching, and is fundamentally restorative in focus.

Ongoing research by the Te Kotahitanga team has shown that the engagement and learning of Year 9 and Year 10 Māori students has improved significantly, as has their rate of retention at school, since Phase 2 of the project was implemented in schools during and since 2002. The findings from Te Kotahitanga provide strong support for culturally responsive, relationship-based pedagogy as an essential component of a culture of care within classrooms and schools. The Educultural Wheel offers strategies that are guided by the values considered to be core to te ao Māori (the Māori world).

Based on a wide range of research studies and their findings, we have identified four pedagogical principles that underpin teaching and learning strategies that contribute to culturally safe and caring classrooms and schools for minoritised or marginalised students (Cavanagh, 2003, 2005a, 2005b; Glynn, 1985; Glynn et al., 2005; Glynn, Berryman, O'Brien, & Bishop, 2001; Glynn, Berryman, Vanstone, & Weiss, 2009; Glynn et al., 1998; Macfarlane et al., 2007; Prochnow & Macfarlane, 2011). These principles are: routines; relationships; responsibilities; and respect. We look at each of these below.

Routines

Routines provide safe and familiar structures that focus and channel classroom behaviour. They ensure that everyone knows what sorts of behaviour are expected, and these are affirmed in different classroom learning contexts. Routines support the implementation of the protocols and processes that are fundamental to a particular context. They are therefore critical to providing pathways for appropriate behaviour and for establishing expectations for students.

However, establishing and maintaining routines is a collaborative process, requiring input from students and teachers alike, and especially from students who are marginalised or minoritised. It is important that classroom routines are negotiated mutually, and their rationale is clearly understood by students and teachers. It is also important that all class members can *initiate* changes, either to existing routines or to the way the routines are maintained. They are not expected to simply *respond* to changes imposed by others, however well intended. When all class members have taken part in the design and implementation of classroom routines, and are able to suggest changes in safety, a strong sense of ownership and affirmation of appropriate behaviour is a likely outcome.

All students benefit from having clearly understood routines for beginning and ending lesson activities, for moving from one activity to the next, for gaining peer assistance, for accessing and sharing classroom resource materials and for working together in safety on different learning tasks. Māori students benefit from the structure of classroom routines, especially when these routines incorporate processes and activities that affirm their cultural knowledge and identity. These include beginning with a karakia (traditional chant or prayer) or with an appropriate whakataukī (metaphorical saying) and ending with a waiata (song); engaging in tuakana–teina relationships (peer tutoring roles where there is a specific cultural expectation for the older or more skilled student to assist younger or less skilled students); engaging in mihimihi (greetings and introductions); or sharing the findings of a small working group with younger students, perhaps from a more junior class.

However, even classroom routines that do not arise from within a Māori worldview will have positive benefits for all students. Being greeted personally and warmly by the teacher at the beginning of each lesson, without emotional or other undertones and without challenging or threatening questions or observations, can help build positive and trusting relationships; for example, "Nice to see you back today, Tama" or "Good news about making the netball team, Hiria!" rather than "Still wearing the wrong T-shirt, Tama?" or "Late again, Hiria!" So, too, can a few moments of stillness at the end of a lesson, in which the teacher thanks students for their participation and contribution and lets them know that he or she has enjoyed being with them and working with them: "That was a great lesson today guys. I really enjoyed hearing all your stories about looking after animals."

All students in a class can benefit from helping to establish routines that structure ways they can safely address issues threatening the wellbeing of the group (e.g., calming down a group member who is angry or aggrieved), as well as addressing task performance and completion. Established and agreed routines support greater interpersonal safety than leaving these incidents to chance initiations and spur-of-the moment reactions by different individuals. Safe routines become embedded in the classroom's unique tikanga (classroom culture, including its values, beliefs and practices). Establishing and maintaining these routines help to define students' cultural identities, and their identities as members of a community of practice in a particular classroom.

Relationships

Equitable and reciprocal teacher–student and student–student relationships, where learning and teaching roles are freely interchanged, are fundamental to effective student engagement and learning. Establishing and maintaining such relationships characterises much of our work on exploring responsive social contexts for learning (Glynn, 1985; Glynn, Wearmouth, & Berryman 2005; Wearmouth et al., 2005) and culturally responsive pedagogies (Berryman, Glynn, Woller, & Reweti, 2010; Bishop & Glynn, 1999; Bishop et al., 2009; Cavanagh, 2003, 2009; Glynn, 1985). All the members of a safe and caring classroom can benefit from regular interchanges of teacher and learner roles. This is especially true for students who are minoritised or marginalised.

When teachers take up an *unknowing* position in the classroom, students are empowered to find their voice and to participate and contribute to classroom learning on the basis of their existing knowledge and expertise—at times, and in some domains, beyond that of the teacher. For example, in an inquiry learning study of Māori students learning science in a mainstream English-medium classroom, their teacher invited them to identify sources of information about their topic of local land forms (Glynn, Cowie, & Otrel-Cass, 2008). One student answered, "We could ask a kaumātua (tribal elder) or go on the net" (p. 8). This student thus identified an appropriate source of indigenous tribal knowledge and experiences, as well as an appropriate source of Western/European science knowledge. There then began a 20-week learning journey for the teacher and her students, which resulted in their gaining detailed knowledge about the volcanic land forms of mountains in the region surrounding the school, as well as oral narratives of the tribal histories and cultural significance of those mountains. In this way, new knowledge was jointly constructed and owned by the students and their teacher. The process of working and learning together also greatly enhanced the quality of their relationships with each other. The notions of power sharing, collaborative decision making and reciprocity that have been highlighted here are also key components of a restorative classroom ethos.

Responsibilities

Effective teachers encourage and support students to take respon-sibility for their own learning and behaviour, and for assisting other students to improve their learning and behaviour. This pedagogical value is entirely consistent with the Māori cultural value of whanaungatanga (exercising collective responsibility through engaging in family-like relationships). If a member of a group working on a task is experiencing anxiety, stress, frustration or sadness, which is interfering with the achievement of the task, then the group's energy is focused on restoring the wellbeing of that individual. With the collective wellbeing restored, the group can refocus its energy on addressing the task at hand. Such a restorative ethos espouses the sharing of responsibilities and collective problem-solving approaches. Sadly, however, when practised in many mainstream educational contexts, the value of whanaungatanga can conflict with the values of individual achievement and competition, which are prevalent in contemporary Western societies and educational systems.

The curriculum framework along with effective teaching practice should provide students with a choice of learning tasks and options for task completion and presentation (written, oral, visual, individual or group). As a result, they have opportunities to *exercise* responsibility in the classroom. When students learn to make responsible choices and to contribute from their own knowledge and expertise, teachers have increased opportunities to vary their own position with respect to their students. Teachers are no longer restricted to positioning themselves only as authoritative experts and behaviour managers. They can also be guides, collaborators and facilitators. These last three roles are also likely to support closer, deeper and more equitable relationships within the classroom.

Respect

Respect is a powerful human quality. It can bind the three collaborative processes of devising effective routines, building or enhancing relationships and accepting responsibilities within a culture of care. Respect is a quality that is freely given and humbly received. It cannot be required or demanded, but it can be offered to others and others can offer it in return. Both the giving and the receiving of respect are essential elements in creating a culture of care, and they are also fundamental to processes and practices that are restorative in their focus.

Within a Māori world view, respect can be understood as a response to the mana of another person. Rangatira (chiefs and leaders of the people) are not only persons of outstanding achievement, but they also earn the respect of their people by serving them and providing for their wellbeing. Chiefs and leaders are distinguished by their manaakitanga (commitment to care for people). Teachers who show respect for their students, who care about what is happening in their students' lives outside the classroom and who respect the knowledge, experience and expertise students bring into the classroom, will be respected in turn by their students. Although the reciprocal exchange of teacher and learner roles is an important element of culturally responsive pedagogy, the values of whanaungatanga and manaakitanga together define the respectful and caring teacher–student and student–student relationships that are essential characteristics of a culture of care. Within a culture of care these relationships are established as an ongoing covenant or commitment, rather than as a simple behavioural contract. These are relationships that are founded on trust and respect.

Classrooms as inclusive communities of practice

Our thinking about classrooms as communities of practice, and the discussion that follows, are based on the concept of communities of practice developed by Lave and Wenger (1991) and Wenger (1998), and more recently on the work of Wearmouth, Berryman, and Glynn (2009). They have all explored inclusion in educational settings in terms of participating in a community of practice. Furthermore, Hooper, Winslade, Drewery, Monk, and Macfarlane (1999) promote restorative practice as a means of enhancing schools and classrooms as inclusive communities of practice.

The concept of a community of practice involves a community of practitioners, a domain of knowledge, a body of shared practices and the negotiation and construction of identities. Within a safe and caring classroom context, students and teachers constitute a community of practitioners (learners) who are engaged within a domain of knowledge (a specific curriculum area), who participate in activities on the basis of shared values (e.g., an understanding of knowledge creation and of their relationships and connectedness with each other) and shared practices (e.g., engaging in routines and accepting responsibilities).

Participating

Learning within a community of practice means engaging in and contributing to the practices of that community. Continuing participation and engagement in the classroom community lead to learners becoming more competent. Learning within a community of practice is therefore a fundamentally *social* phenomenon, which occurs in the context of our experience of participation in the classroom community of practice.

Competent participation in a community of practice involves engaging with other members to establish relationships in which mutuality (e.g., freely exchanging expert and novice positions, and accepting collective responsibility for learning) forms the basis for an identity of participation. Participating and building safe and caring relationships with others in a community of practice engender a sense of belonging. Our identity as a member of a community of practice is constructed by negotiating the meanings and personal experiences of being a member of that community. In this way, identity and practice mirror each other: "We know who we are by what is familiar, understandable, usable, and negotiable; we know who we are not by what is foreign, opaque, unwieldy, and unproductive" (Wenger, 1998, p. 153).

Most importantly, competent participation involves being able to participate in changing the practices of a community. This supports a sense of agency among all the members of a community in terms of being able to initiate and negotiate changes in routines, relationships and responsibilities, as well as contributing to restoring harmony and balance if there is any turbulence. Given this understanding of participation within a community of practice, the successful inclusion of students from marginalised cultural backgrounds within a classroom community of practice clearly requires much more than just placement and engagement in classroom activities. Inclusion involves both the cognitive and the affective domains:

> Inclusion in a classroom implies active participation in learning, acquiring knowledge, developing a sense of self as able to contribute to its practice (to a degree that is viewed as legitimate), and having a sense of belonging. (Wearmouth et al., 2009, p. 63)

If Māori students are to be fully included in classroom communities of practice, if they are to feel that they belong and that they can initiate change or restore balance within the classroom community of practice, teachers need to make substantial changes to their pedagogical approaches. Teachers need to find out more about the cultural values, experiences and aspirations of their Māori students and whānau (family and/or extended family) to ensure these will be affirmed and incorporated within classroom practice.

The policy document *Ka Hikitia* (Ministry of Education, 2008) makes it abundantly clear that Māori aspire for their children to participate and succeed in education *as Māori*, and to be successful participants in the modern world. Māori want their children to be secure in their identity as successful participants in local, regional and national communities of practice that are culturally Māori; for example, kapa haka (cultural performing arts groups) and manu kōrero (language and oratory competitions). However, Māori also want their children to be successful participants in classroom and school communities of practice in all areas of the New Zealand national curriculum so as to become effective citizens of the world (Durie, 2003). Success for Māori students in general school subject areas should not have to be at the cost of further loss of opportunities to access their language and culture within their own country's public education system. They should not have to put their Māori language and identity to one side in order to participate fully in a classroom community of practice.

Crossing boundaries

Students are required to participate in multiple communities of practice before they enter the classroom. These communities of practice may include family activities, sports teams, service groups, church groups, music groups, arts and craft groups and community-based cultural groups. However, when different communities of practice define themselves in opposition to each other, crossing boundaries can be challenging and hard work. Learning can be either enhanced or impaired when individuals are expected to cross boundaries. Membership in one community of practice can mean marginalisation or nonparticipation in another. The understanding and practices (routines, responsibilities, relationships and activities) that are required for successful participation in one community may be inappropriate, or even offensive, within the practices of another (Wearmouth et al., 2009). The values, beliefs, relationships and practices of the home and cultural communities of minoritised or marginalised students, as well as their cultural identities, may be judged to be irrelevant or unacceptable in classroom communities. This engenders in marginalised students a feeling of alienation and of not belonging. It is a reality for many Māori students in New Zealand schools.

However, the boundaries that exist within the classrrom context need not be impervious to Māori students. Boundary crossing can be initiated and negotiated within the safety of classrooms that embody a culture of care. Within a culture of care, for example, Māori students can be invited to take on an expert teaching role in safety by sharing their cultural knowledge, experience and expertise with students and teachers. This is an example of a culturally responsive pedagogical approach that affirms their identities as Māori *and* their identities as participants in the classroom community of practice (Cavanagh, Macfarlane, Glynn, & Macfarlane, 2010). It also enhances their feelings of ownership and belonging, as well as their sense of being fully included in their restorative community of practice—the classroom.

Conclusion

If we are serious about improving the learning and behavioural outcomes for students in our classroom and early childhood education settings, then it is incumbent upon teachers and management to ensure that educational settings operate as inclusive and caring communities within which students feel safe, supported and valued. Establishing a culture of care requires educators to be aware of the four key principles of responsive pedagogy: routines; relationships; responsibilities; and respect. Adhering to these principles enables and promotes the notion of *participation*, whereby teachers and students collaboratively construct the content and context that support positive and ongoing classroom interactions.

Responsive pedagogy comprises two distinct yet philosophically congruent elements: preventive and reactive strategies. The preventive dimension determines the ethos or culture that is foundational and that is promoted. This includes the tone, expectations, boundaries, values and processes. The reactive dimension determines how challenges are responded to and managed if they arise. Clearly, the latter will need to be premised on the same four principles. Reactive classroom management practices need to be chosen wisely so that balance, restoration and harmony can be achieved and maintained in educational settings at all times.

Restorative practice is an approach that can be incorporated across and throughout the preventive and reactive elements of responsive pedagogy in order to support classroom management and maintain a culture of care. This particular approach will be unpacked and described in terms of its journey in Aotearoa New Zealand in Part II of this book.

References

Berryman, M., Glynn, T., Woller, P., & Reweti, M. (2010). Māori language policy and practice in New Zealand schools: Community challenges and community solutions. In K. Menken & O. Garcia (Eds.), *Negotiating language policies in classrooms: Educators as policy makers* (pp. 145–161). New York: Routledge/ Taylor & Francis.

Bishop, R., & Berryman, M. (2006). *Culture speaks: Cultural relationships and classroom learning.* Wellington: Huia.

Bishop, R., Berryman, M., Cavanagh, T., & Teddy, L. (2007). *Te Kotahitanga phase 3: Whanaungatanga: Establishing a culturally responsive pedagogy of relations in mainstream secondary school classrooms.* Wellington: Ministry of Education.

Bishop, R., Berryman, M., Cavanagh, T., & Teddy, L. (2009). Te Kotahitanga: Addressing educational disparities facing Māori students in New Zealand. *Teaching and Teacher Education: An International Journal of Research and Studies,* 25(5), 734–742.

Bishop, R., & Glynn, T. (1999). *Culture counts: Changing power relations in education.* Palmerston North: Dunmore Press.

Canter, L., & Canter, M. (2001). *Assertive discipline: Positive behavior management for today's classroom.* Bloomington, IN: Solution Tree.

Cavanagh, T. (2003). Schooling for peace: Caring for our children in school. *Experiments in Education,* 31(8), 139–143.

Cavanagh, T. (2005a). Constructing ethnographic relationships: Reflections on key issues and struggles in the field. *Waikato Journal of Education,* 11(1), 27–42.

Cavanagh, T. (2005b). *Creating safe schools using restorative practices in a culture of care: An ethnographic study conducted at Raglan Area School, Te Kura a Rohe o Whaingaroa.* Wellington: Fulbright New Zealand.

Cavanagh, T. (2008). *Schooling for peaceful relationships: Advancing the theory of a culture of care.* Paper presented at the Peace Education Special Interest Group (SIG), Education for the Promising Practices in Peace Education: Global Perspectives session, at the American Educational Research Association Annual Meeting, New York.

Cavanagh, T. (2009). Restorative practices in schools: Breaking the cycle of student involvement in child welfare and legal systems. *Protecting Children, 24*(4), 53–60.

Cavanagh, T., Macfarlane, A, Glynn, T. & Macfarlane, S. (2010, April). *Creating peaceful and effective schools through continuity of relationships.* A paper presented at the Expanding the Vision, Theory, and Practice of Peace Education in Diverse Contexts session, sponsored by the Peace Education Special Interest Group (SIG), at the American Education Research Association (AERA) Annual Meeting, Denver, Colorado.

Durie, M. (2003). *Nga kahui pou.* Wellington: Huia.

Gay, G. (2000). *Culturally responsive teaching: Theory, research, and practice.* New York: Teachers College Press.

Glynn, T. (1985). Contexts for independent learning. *Educational Psychology, 5*(1), 5–15.

Glynn, T., Berryman, M., Atvars, K., Harawira, W., Walker, R., & Kaiwai, H. (1998). Bicultural research and support programmes for Māori students, teachers and communities. In I. Livingstone (Ed.), *New Zealand Annual Review of Education* (Vol. 8, pp. 43–64). Wellington: School of Education, Victoria University.

Glynn, T., Berryman, M., Loader, K., & Cavanagh, T. (2005). From literacy in Māori to biliteracy in Māori and English: A community and school transition programme. *Journal of Bilingual Education and Bilingualism, 8*(5), 433–454.

Glynn, T., Berryman, M., O'Brien, K., & Bishop, R. (2001). Responsive written feedback on students' writing in a Māori language revitalisation context. In R. Harlow & R. Barnard (Eds.), *Proceedings of the conference, Bilingualism at the Ends of the Earth* (pp. 47–61). Hamilton: Department of General and Applied Linguistics, University of Waikato.

Glynn, T., Berryman, M., Vanstone, B., & Weiss, S. (2009). Responsive written feedback to improve the writing of minoritised students. *Journal of Australian Indigenous Issues, 12*(1–4), 12–21.

Glynn, T., Cowie, B., & Otrel-Cass, K. (2008). *Quality teaching research and development science hub (Waikato): Connecting New Zealand teachers of science with their Māori students.* Research report to the Ministry of Education. Hamilton: Wilf Malcolm Institute of Educational Research, University of Waikato.

Glynn, T., Wearmouth, J., & Berryman, M. (2005). *Supporting students with literacy difficulties: A responsive approach.* London: McGraw-Hill.

Hooper, S., Winslade, J., Drewery, W., Monk, G., & Macfarlane, A. (1999). *School and family group conferences: Te hui whakatika (a time for making amends).* Paper presented at Keeping Young People in School Summit Conference on Truancy, Suspensions and Effective Alternatives, Auckland.

Ladson-Billings, G. (1995). Toward a theory of culturally relevant pedagogy. *American Education Research Journal, 32*(3), 465–491.

Lave. J., & Wenger, E. (1991). *Situated learning: Legitimate peripheral participation.* Cambridge: Cambridge University Press.

Macfarlane, A. (2004). *Kia hiwa ra! Listen to culture: Māori students' plea to educators.* Wellington: NZCER Press.

Macfarlane, A. (2007). *Discipline, democracy, and diversity: Working with students with behaviour difficulties.* Wellington: NZCER Press.

Macfarlane, A., Glynn, T., Cavanagh, T., & Bateman, S. (2005). *Creating culturally safe schools: Culturally appropriate approaches to supporting Māori students.* Paper presented at the seventh World Peoples Indigenous Conference on Education (WIPCE), University of Waikato, Hamilton.

Macfarlane, A., Glynn, T., Cavanagh, T., & Bateman, S. (2007). Creating culturally safe schools for Māori students. *Australian Journal of Indigenous Education, 36,* 65–76.

Ministry of Education. (2005). *Report on stand-downs, exclusions and expulsions for 2004.* Wellington: Author. Retrieved from http://www.minedu.govt.nz

Ministry of Education. (2008). *Ka hikitia: Managing for success: Māori education strategy.* Wellington: Ministry of Education, Group Māori .

Noddings, N. (1992). *The challenge to care in schools: An alternative approach to education.* New York: Teachers College Press.

Noddings, N. (2002). *Educating moral people: A caring alternative to character education.* New York: Teachers College Press.

Prochnow, J., & Macfarlane, A. (2011). Managing classroom behaviour. In C. Rubie-Davies (Ed.), *Educational psychology: Concepts, research and challenges.* London: Routledge.

Rogers, B. (2003). *Behaviour management, classroom discipline and colleague support.* Melbourne: Paul Chapman Educational.

Watkins, C., & Wagner, P. (2000). *Improving school behaviour.* London: Paul Chapman.

Wearmouth, J., Berryman, M., & Glynn, T. (2009). *Inclusion through participation in communities of practice in schools.* Wellington: Dunmore Press.

Wearmouth, J., Glynn, T., & Berryman, M. (2005). *Perspectives on student behaviour in schools: Exploring theory and developing practice.* New York: Routledge Falmer.

Wenger, E. (1998). *Communities of practice: Learning, meaning and identity.* Cambridge: Cambridge University Press.

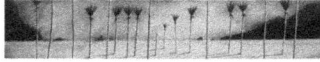

4.

Connecting Curriculum

Valerie Margrain & Vijaya Dharan

Introduction

Curriculum development is "fundamentally a political act" (Nuttall, 2003, p. 9) that documents social aspirations. As Bernstein (1971) states, "curriculum defines what counts as valid knowledge, pedagogy defines what counts as valid transmission of knowledge" (p. 85). Negotiating what is valid and valued demands that there is negotiation and articulation of the vision and hopes of parents, children, teachers, academics and society as a whole (Brostróm, 2003). The vision articulated in our current curricula is for young people to become confident learners, able to learn with others and to contribute positively to society (Ministry of Education, 1996, 2007). This vision is more significant than the detail within individual learning areas. Curriculum, therefore, supports relationship-based pedagogy, which includes those with challenging behaviours.

This chapter argues that responsive pedagogy is not just about curriculum delivery: it is at the heart of curriculum. There are four main sections in this chapter. Following the introduction, the New Zealand early childhood curriculum is discussed. It has a strong sociocultural and holistic approach, which has informed the more recent New Zealand school curriculum. Examples of principles and strands that particularly exemplify responsive pedagogy are identified. The next section provides two case studies that illustrate responsive and restorative practice with young children. The discussion highlights curriculum connections that can be made to these case studies. Dispositions for learning are then introduced as a means of linking children's actions, inclinations and behaviour to the curriculum. The final section discusses the links between the early childhood and school curricula. It argues that the use of dispositions for learning and key competencies illustrates a shared social commitment to learning, as defined by socially constructed aims and outcomes. Restorative practices are an illustration of a responsive curriculum in action.

Background

This section provides an overview of curricula in New Zealand and summarises core concepts for responsive pedagogy and restorative practice. Such a background is important for framing the discussion of the connections between curricula and restorative practice.

Overview of curricula in New Zealand

In New Zealand there are three curriculum documents:

- *The New Zealand Curriculum* (Ministry of Education, 2007) for Years 1–13, English-medium schools
- *Te Marautanga o Aotearoa* (Ministry of Education, 2008), which sets the direction for teaching and learning in Years 1–13 for both kura kaupapa Māori (Māori-medium schools) and Māori-medium classes in regular schools
- *Te Whāriki: He Whāriki Matauranga mō ngā Mokopuna o Aotearoa: Early Childhood Curriculum* (Ministry of Education, 1996), a bicultural document for all early childhood education services.

In this chapter we discuss *The New Zealand Curriculum* and *Te Whāriki*. The term "curriculum" is used in *Te Whāriki* "to describe the sum total of the experiences, activities and events, whether direct or indirect, which occur within an environment designed to foster children's learning and development" (Ministry of Education, 1996, p. 10). This interpretation of curriculum acknowledges a far broader view of learning than merely focusing on traditional learning areas such as mathematics and science. Curriculum includes aspects of a learning environment such as relationships, community, reflection and contribution.

Restorative concepts

Restorative practice provides an explicit example of responsive pedagogy. Restoration implies the notion of *wanting* to return to an acceptable previously existing condition. At the heart of restorative practices are human tendencies such as willingness, acceptance and, more importantly, the ability to forgive—qualities and dispositions that we believe children naturally possess. Yet for some children and young people, their teachers and whānau (family and/or extended family), these very qualities are often clouded when they are being viewed negatively. Often deficit discourse is taken from the pages of a medical dictionary and used rather loosely (Stanley, 2006a, 2006b). Common responses from teachers when describing certain students often include medically framed deficit discourse such as "she is oppositional", "he must be ADD", "never seen a child like him before" or "she is wild". Such comments provide flashing neon signs signalling "naughty kids", who then proceed to live up to their ascribed role, with some children appearing to relish the associated attention. Once on a downward spiral, these children seem to get caught in a vortex, often stopped only when the educational setting is changed.

For children whose initial problems include actions such as hurting other children to the point where their safety is compromised, or damaging property, punitive solutions may achieve little. One reason for this is that the focus is on ways to "fix" the child. Exhaustive observation, documentation and "testing" tend to problematise and label (Stanley, 2006a, 2006b). This does not mean that such children and young people are not given lifelines and support. However, the provision of education support workers, for example, who at times take on the role of minders, can further alienate children from their peers. This is where restorative practices, including conferencing and investigating influences and causes, are important. Such practices can be connected to curriculum principles and vision. Because the intent is to restore balance and harmony rather than to assign blame, restorative principles and practices can reduce the alienation of children by contributing positive narratives and new ways of thinking (Drewery & Winslade, 2005).

Curriculum in early childhood

The early childhood curriculum *Te Whāriki* (Ministry of Education, 1996) was developed over several years with extensive sector collaboration and through a bicultural partnership (Reedy, 2003; Te One, 2003). *Te Whāriki* is modelled on a metaphor of a woven mat (whāriki). Reedy's (2003) description of the whāriki clearly connects to the restorative practice principles of respect and relationships:

> *Te Whāriki* has a theoretical framework that is appropriate for all; common yet individual; for everyone, yet only for one; a whāriki woven by loving hands that can cross cultures with respect, that can weave people and nations together. *Te Whāriki* teaches us to respect ourselves and ultimately to respect others. (p. 74)

The following discussion explains the four curriculum *principles* (empowerment, holistic learning, family and community, and relation-ships), which are interwoven with five curriculum *strands* (wellbeing, belonging, exploration, communication and contribution), and indicates how these connect to responsive pedagogy.

Principles

The four principles in the early childhood curriculum *Te Whāriki* are: empowerment; holistic learning; family and community; and relationships. Responsive pedagogy is at the heart of these principles, as shown in Table 4.1 below. For example, the principle of holistic learning includes acknowledgement that "Children's learning and development are fostered if the well-being of their family and community are respected" (Ministry of Education, 1996, p. 41). Respect is both a curriculum principle and a broader principle supporting a relationship-based culture of care (see Chapter 2 of this book).

TABLE 4.1 *TE WHĀRIKI* PRINCIPLES and INDICATORS
of RESTORATIVE PRACTICE

Curriculum principle	Comment	Te Whāriki quotes (emphasis added)
Empowerment *Whakamana*	*Empowers* the child to learn and grow.	"... take increasing *responsibility* for their own learning and care ... Empowerment is also a guide for practice ... To learn and to develop their potential, children must be *respected* and *valued* as individuals. Their *rights* to personal *dignity*, to *equitable* opportunities for participation, to *protection* from physical, mental, or emotional abuse and injury, and to opportunities for rest and leisure must be safeguarded" (p. 40).
Holistic development *Whakamana*	Reflects the holistic way children learn and grow.	Learning and development should be integrated through *"consistent, warm relationships* that connect everything together"* (p. 41).
Family and community *Whānau tangata*	The wider world of family and community is an integral part of the early childhood curriculum. The wellbeing of children is interdependent with the wellbeing and culture of adults in the early childhood education setting, whānau and families, and local communities and neighbourhoods.	"Children's learning and development are fostered if the well-being of their family and community are *respected*; and if there is a strong connection and consistency among all the aspects of the child's world. The curriculum builds on what children bring to it and makes links with the everyday activities and special events of *families, whānau*, local *communities* and *cultures*" (p. 42).
Relationships *Ngā hononga*	Children make sense of the world around them by interacting with adults and other children. Adults provide the context that extends their thinking and creative learning.	"There are opportunities for social interaction with adults and other children ... Adults provide encouragement, warmth, and acceptance" (p. 43).

(Derived from Ministry of Education, 1996)

Strands

The curriculum strands in *Te Whāriki* are: wellbeing; belonging; contribution; communication; and exploration. Although these strands focus on opportunities for children, the curriculum demands responsive pedagogy through sociocultural values. Within each of the strands there are links to restorative principles and practices, as shown in Table 4.2. For example, within the strand of belonging is recognition that educational settings should be fair places for all. This is a fundamental tenet of restorative practice and an indicator of responsive pedagogy.

The elements of curriculum principles and strands identified in this discussion strongly illustrate the inclusion of relationships, accountability, responsibility and respect. Curriculum is presented as a socially constructed, dynamic construct that serves and supports society. The richness of social interaction provides value for children's spontaneity and ability to work co-operatively with other children and adults. Curriculum teaching and learning are therefore fundamentally sociocultural events (Dockett & Fleer, 1999).

Case studies

This section features two case studies of responsive pedagogical engagement with challenging behaviour. They have been disguised to ensure anonymity by the standard technique of "altering specific characteristics, limiting description of specific characteristics and obfuscating case detail by adding extraneous material" (American Psychological Association, 2010, p. 17). The first case study applies restorative practices in the strict sense of the term: child to child. In the other case study, responsive pedagogy and restorative principles were used to depersonalise "problems" and give a fresh start to what would have otherwise been an untenable situation for the child and his whānau. Neither of these case studies was articulated as being a restorative practice conference at the time, but their processes can retrospectively be identified as restorative in principle. Both case studies illustrate that curriculum in action is about more than content knowledge. They also show that early intervention can be framed within a constructive approach, using positive discourse.

TABLE 4.2 *TE WHĀRIKI* STRANDS and INDICATORS of RESTORATIVE PRACTICE

Wellbeing Mana atua	Belonging Mana whenua	Contribution Mana tangata	Communication Mana reo	Exploration Mana aotūroa
The early childhood curriculum (Ministry of Education, 1996) proposes that "Children moving from early childhood settings to the early years of school are likely to ... be increasingly in control of their emotional responses" (p. 47). Wellbeing Goal 3 states that children develop: • a sense of responsibility for their own wellbeing and that of others • an increasing sense of responsibility for protecting others from injury, and from physical and emotional abuse • respect for rules about harming others and the environment, and an understanding of the reasons for such rules (p. 53).	The strand of belonging endorses the importance of interdependence and interactions with community and the wider world. *Te Whāriki* states: "Children moving from early childhood settings to the early years of school are likely to ... understand basic concepts about rules, rights, and fairness" (Ministry of Education, 1996, p. 55). Belonging Goal 4 states that children develop: • the capacity to discuss and negotiate rules, rights and fairness • an understanding of the rules of the early childhood education setting, of the reasons for them, and of which rules will be different in other settings • an understanding that the early childhood education setting is fair for all • an understanding of the consequences of stepping beyond the limits of acceptable behaviour • an increasing ability to take responsibility for their own actions • the ability to disagree and state a conflicting opinion assertively and appropriately (p. 62).	The curriculum strand of contribution acknowledges that learning is bidirectional. Contribution Goal 1 states that children develop "an understanding of their own rights and those of others" and "some early concepts of the value of appreciating diversity and fairness" (Ministry of Education, 1996, p. 66). Contribution Goal 3 states that children develop: • strategies and skills for initiating, maintaining and enjoying a relationship with other children— including taking turns, problem solving, negotiating, taking another's point of view, supporting others, and understanding other people's attitudes and feelings in a variety of contexts • a range of strategies for solving conflicts in peaceful ways, and a perception that peaceful ways are best • an increasing ability to take another point of view and to empathise with others • a sense of responsibility and respect for the needs and wellbeing of the group, including taking responsibility for group decisions (p. 70).	Communication Goal 1 affirms the importance of children developing "language skills for increasingly complex purposes, such as stating and asking others about intention; expressing feelings and attitudes", negotiating, and affirming the importance of "the inclination and ability to listen attentively and respond appropriately to speakers" (p. 76).	Problem solving and negotiation are important elements of Exploration Goal 3, which states that children develop "confidence in using a variety of strategies for exploring and making sense of the world, such as in setting and solving problems ... asking questions, explaining to others, listening to others, participating in reflective discussion" (p. 88).

(Derived from Ministry of Education, 1996)

Case study: Lockie

Lockie lived in foster care, along with his younger sister. The foster family had grown-up children of their own. When he started at an early childhood education centre he had been with the new family for about three weeks. It is not known if Lockie had oral language difficulties earlier or if it was a recent development following a spate of traumatising incidents in his life. His personal hygiene was poor, and after an initial week of placidity he soon became the boy who "spoke" with his fists. Initially his behaviours were dealt with by staff at the centre using management techniques such as de-escalation, time out and loss of outdoor time (which he most preferred). But they seemed to have minimal effect on Lockie. Soon he began to target a rather fragile boy, Sam, who was no physical match for him.

The teachers were concerned about keeping Sam and other children safe from Lockie's outbursts, so they sought the help of specialist staff to assist them in managing Lockie's aggressive behaviours. As a necessary first step it was decided to involve the family in a meeting to share information and establish some goals for Lockie. This was part of an intervention meeting set up by staff at the centre. What was different from the normal individual planning meeting at this hui (a meeting held with Māori protocols) was the inclusion of both Lockie and Sam at the meeting. Although the term "restorative" was not explicitly articulated, the proceedings of the meeting and the outcome were truly restorative. Important elements of this meeting included: the "victim's" voice was given prominence; the problem was named; the effects of the problem on the victim were explained; and what would be required to stop a recurrence of the problem was determined (Drewery & Winslade, 2005). The "victim" child (Sam), with a lot of coaxing and assurances against a backlash, described how he felt. His mother spoke about his nightmares. At that point there was a poignant remark by the "offender" (Lockie) that he did not react in the same way when subjected to similar treatment.

This utterance by Lockie enabled the adults in the hui to see why the "problem" was external to him. They began to realise that Lockie may have been traumatised and victimised in some ways too. While it is doubtful that the "victim" and the "offender" fully comprehended the significance of this utterance given their young age, it changed the perceptions of the adults, especially Sam's mother. Rather than documenting a behaviour management plan to focus on the physically aggressive behaviours, a much wider plan of providing a safe and trustworthy environment both at home and in the early childhood education setting was discussed. A teacher was assigned to build a relationship of trust with Lockie, and agencies were approached to support his caregivers with positive parenting strategies.

What began as a hui to problematise Lockie ended up being a profound learning experience for all involved. It allowed for a total change in the way everyone in the early childhood setting perceived Lockie. Rather than continuing to focus on his negative behaviours, preventive strategies were put in place, such as modelling and frequent role plays, in order to understand and respect the feelings of all the children in the centre. In line with the curriculum, the staff helped Lockie to increase his sense of belonging and wellbeing. Communication was at the heart of the effective changes for Lockie, which opened the way for him to be able to participate more positively within the early childhood setting. The fundamental principles of *Te Whāriki* underpinned responsive pedagogy, including building a sense of belonging in Lockie that allowed him to interact more positively with other children and adults.

Proponents of restorative practice argue that the response to "crime" must begin where the problem begins—within relationships (Drewery & Winslade, 2005, p. 19). The case study of Alice highlights the extent to which problems and behaviour are socially and contextually constructed: the same child can be rejected in one setting but valued in another.

Case study: Alice

"Crime" is a harsh word when referring to children in early childhood, but in this case study the behaviours of Alice had escalated to the point where her "crimes" were punished by her being expelled as a four-year-old. Visual images of her unacceptable behaviours were caught on camera and displayed to parents and specialists. Having their child positioned as a "problem" created further strain in the relationship between the parents, and between Alice and her mother, with whom she lived.

Following Alice's expulsion from her early childhood service, a total change occurred in her next early childhood setting. Staff at the new early childhood service, along with two specialist support personnel, instigated a restorative process to respond to the problem rather than the child—to restore the child back from being the problem. In order to do so, they had gathered information that redefined what was important and that allowed them to move to a new space, which they wanted to share with the family. A hui was organised a few weeks after Alice was enrolled at the centre.

The hui was attended by all the early childhood staff, the two external specialists, both parents (although separated they were keen to support their "problem child") and Alice. Having been through a few such meetings, the parents braced themselves for an onslaught of complaints from the staff, and their body language was a testimony to this. The well-educated, employed and articulate parents sat in silence waiting for the tirade against their daughter to begin. Instead, the hui began with Alice showing all the work that she had been doing so far in the centre. There was stunned silence and a sense of disbelief in the parents, who felt that this was a kind of curtain raiser to precede something more ominous. Alice was asked to talk about her friends and the things that she liked, or about her time in the early childhood education setting. The crux of the discussions in the hui therefore focused on Alice's strengths and interests rather than the "problems". How was this possible? This was the question the parents wanted an answer to as the animosity of blaming each other turned into a more guarded smile between them. They were still anticipating some kind of backlash from the specialist support staff and the early childhood staff.

Each of the early childhood teachers said that they had decided to set aside the "problems" that Alice brought with her, basically because they had found the information they had been given on her so overwhelming that they didn't know where to start! Instead, each teacher decided to gather new evidence from a strengths-based perspective, each observing at least one positive aspect, and within a day they had a list of them. The common factor discussed by all teachers was Alice's cognitive ability, which made the team think that her "problems" could be the result of boredom. Working on this hypothesis, they had started to challenge and extend her thinking. What followed was an unexpected turn towards an increased participation in learning. Alice responded with keenness and interest and was always ready for more challenges. She began to thrive on the extension opportunities and the leadership-by-example role she was given. The teachers had identified her niche and there was no looking back. The "problem child" was never to be seen again.

For Alice—who had been branded as oppositionally defiant and who had a prognosis of exclusion even before entering school—and her parents, this conference was a turning point. It went beyond meeting the educational needs of their daughter. It was about restoring connections (Drewery & Winslade, 2005); in this case, restoring relationships between the parents, between the parents and their daughter and between the parents and the early childhood education staff. Most importantly, it restored the connection between Alice and her learning.

The hui was held within the *Te Whāriki* framework, with a clear focus on supporting Alice's wellbeing and sense of belonging, while providing opportunities for her to contribute in new ways. Teachers in this setting enacted the aspirations of the curriculum through their focus on Alice's competence. This is a responsive pedagogical approach that can be used by all teachers.

Dispositions for learning

Dispositions for learning are a means of linking children's actions, inclinations and behaviour to the curriculum. They contribute to students' intellectual thinking and academic development, as well as to their social responsibilities and participation. Dispositions have been referred to in various ways in the literature: as "good thinking" and "good habits of mind" (Perkins, Jay, & Tishman, 1993), as "habits of mind" (Katz, 1999a), as "habitus" (Bourdieu, 1993) and as "spirit" (Koenig, George, & Siegler, 1988). Perkins et al. (1993) describe three aspects of dispositions: inclination; sensitivity; and ability. Carr (2001) uses the terminology of being "ready, willing and able" to learn. Katz (2003) also reminds us of children's "inborn disposition" (p. 16) and "inborn quest" (p. 15) to learn. She also reinforces the need to support "basic intellectual dispositions" (Katz, 1999b).

Te Whāriki includes the statement "Dispositions provide a framework for developing working theories and expertise" (Ministry of Education, 1996, p. 45). Alongside the publication of *Te Whāriki*, the Ministry of Education funded research to develop and trial approaches that would link the strands and goals of the curriculum to the needs of practitioners. The Project for Assessing Children's Experiences (PACE) was funded to holistically consider ways that teachers could be supported to assess children's experiences, using an "empowering, holistic, transactional, and ecological" approach (Carr, 1998a). The project identified five domains of learning dispositions that could be linked to *Te Whāriki*: courage and curiosity; trust and playfulness; perseverance; confidence; and responsibility (Carr, 1998b). These five dispositions were re-explained as children's learning "decisions" (Carr, 1998b, p. 22), and teachers' "criteria for observing" (p. 29). Table 4.3 illustrates these connections.

TABLE 4.3 *TE WHĀRIKI* STRANDS, DISPOSITIONS and LEARNING DECISIONS

Curriculum strand	Disposition	Learning "decision" and teacher "criteria for observing" (Carr, 1998b)
Wellbeing Mana atua	Courage and curiosity	Taking an interest
Belonging Mana whenua	Trust and playfulness	Being involved
Exploration Mana tangata	Perseverance	Persisting with a difficulty, challenge or uncertainty
Communication Mana reo	Confidence	Communicating with others (or expressing a point of view or feeling)
Contribution Mana aotūroa	Responsibility	Taking responsibility (or taking another point of view)

In the case studies discussed earlier we can see Lockie acknowledging the experience of his peer and sharing his own experience. These actions link to the dispositions of courage, curiosity and confidence, which in turn link to the curriculum strands of wellbeing and communication. In the second case study, teachers supported Alice to be involved and to take responsibility. These dispositions of trust and playfulness as well as responsibility link to the curriculum strands of belonging and contribution. The examples show pedagogical responsivity through the teachers being alert to a child's dispositions for learning, and connecting these to curriculum planning and action.

Dispositions have become widely used by early childhood teachers, with one assessment tool linking observation to the curriculum via dispositions known as "learning stories" (Carr, 1998b, 1998c, 2001). The dispositions also became linked to "teaching stories" through research into teacher evaluation in early childhood (May & Podmore, 2000; Podmore & May, with Mara, 1998). These projects on teaching and learning dispositions have provided consistent messages about the importance of responsive pedagogy within the curriculum (Carr, May, & Podmore, 1998; Carr et al., 2000). The importance of dispositions continues to feature in New Zealand (Carr, 2004, 2010), including through the publication of early childhood exemplars that showcase learning story narratives (Ministry of Education, 2004/07/09). The assessment approach promoted in the exemplars is one that prioritises dispositions rather than focusing on skills and knowledge. Inherent in this approach are responsive pedagogical principles and practices that aim to focus on relationships, on belonging to social settings and on strengths, interests and competencies.

Connecting curricula

The 2007 revision of the school curriculum provided greater alignment with the early childhood curriculum, and both documents now provide a strong foundation for "lifelong learning". The five key competencies within *The New Zealand Curriculum* (thinking; using language, symbols and texts; managing self; relating to others; participating and contributing) have been aligned with the five strands of *Te Whāriki* (exploration, communication, wellbeing, contribution and belonging), and also with the aims of the tertiary sector (see Ministry of Education, 2001, p. 42).

Key competencies

The New Zealand Curriculum describes the key competencies as "the key to learning in every learning area" (Ministry of Education, 2007, p. 12).

Opportunities to develop key competencies occur naturally in social contexts. People use these competencies in broader society to:

> live, learn, work, and contribute as active members of their communities ... The competencies continue to develop over time, shaped by interactions with people, places, ideas, and things. (p. 12)

Responsive pedagogy ensures that learning is connected to social interaction and responsibility.

"Key competencies" is not just a new name for essential skills. They include skills, but also emphasise how skills relate to knowledge, attitudes and values, and how skills can be used in interactions with others in various contexts (Ministry of Education, 2009). In a theoretical analysis of the key competencies commissioned for the Curriculum Marautanga Project, Margaret Carr emphasises their strong *dispositional* focus. They include attitudes, along with knowledge, skills and values (Carr, 2004). This focus on dispositions connects the key competencies initiative with the idea of "lifelong learning" (Hipkins, 2006).

If the children in the case studies had been in the school sector, we would see a potential connection to *The New Zealand Curriculum* through the key competencies. Lockie was developing in the areas of *relating to others*, *managing self* and *using language, symbols and texts*. For Alice, connections could be drawn to the key competencies of *participating and contributing* as well as *relating to others*.

Values in the curriculum

The New Zealand Curriculum and *Te Whāriki* are inspirational rather than prescriptive documents that promote a strong vision and values for learning. These curricula acknowledge that values will find expression in different ways in different schools and communities. Values will inform the philosophy and mission statement, the structures and practices, the environment and the relationships within any individual educational setting. Many of the values in *The New Zealand Curriculum* connect particularly well to responsive, relationship-based practice, as follows:

- *diversity*, as found in our different cultures, languages and heritages

- *equity*, through fairness and social justice
- *community and participation* for the common good
- *integrity*, which involves being honest, responsible, and accountable and acting ethically. (Ministry of Education, 2007, p. 10, emphasis added)

New Zealand has a bicultural and multicultural heritage, which influences the values that our society recognises. *The New Zealand Curriculum* states that:

> Through their learning experiences students will learn about:
> - their own values and those of others
> - different kinds of values, such as moral, social, cultural, aesthetic, and economic values
> - the values on which New Zealand's cultural and institutional traditions are based
> - the values of other groups and cultures.
>
> Through their learning experiences students will develop their ability to:
> - express their own values
> - explore with empathy the values of others
> - critically analyse values and actions based on them
> - discuss disagreements that arise from differences in values and negotiate solutions
> - make ethical decisions and act on them. (Ministry of Education, 2007, p. 10)

Key values create an ethos of respect, inclusion, accountability and taking responsibility, commitment to relationships, impartiality, being nonjudgemental, collaboration, empowerment and emotional articulacy (Transforming conflict, n.d.). These values support the development of a society in which people need to work, live and learn harmoniously and productively together. Children and young people are enculturated with these values in their own places of learning. Pedagogical decisions and implementation are thus more than educational practice—they are social mechanisms. If our curricula espouse restorative practices, then this presumably reflects a broader social desire for responsibility and accountability.

It is clear in the case studies of Lockie and Alice that values articulated in each setting influenced the outcomes. Values such as safety, honesty, respect, opportunity and positivity were articulated by staff and whānau, and underpinned pedagogical decisions, the development of relationships and the outcomes for the children. The focus on strengthening these competencies as they move on to school will ensure that Lockie and Alice, and other children for whom a sense of belonging is crucial, will be well supported.

Legitimation

The Ministry of Education describes *Te Marautanga o Aotearoa* (Ministry of Education, 2008) as the partner document of *The New Zealand Curriculum* (Ministry of Education, 2007). *Te Marautanga* was designed for Māori-medium settings, but it can be used in any New Zealand school. Rather than simply a translation of *The New Zealand Curriculum*, its development was based on Māori philosophies and principles. Glynn, Cavanagh, Macfarlane and Macfarlane (Chapter 3 in this book) discuss indigenous historical restorative practices, and there are links that can be discerned between restorative practice, Māori philosophies and principles and the curriculum. Because *Te Whāriki* (Ministry of Education, 1996) is a bicultural document and *The New Zealand Curriculum* makes a commitment to bicultural practice, effective pedagogical practice needs to be biculturally responsive.

Pedagogical practice should not just attend to traditional areas of learning. Such a view would position academic aspects of learning as more important than broader aspects, such as relating to others or communication. The curricula discussed in this chapter present a holistic approach to learning that acknowledges social interaction, and affirms the teacher as a critical agent in developing social responsibility, respect and restorative practice. Effective relationships are not just an additional benefit or outcome of learning. Academic learning is made stronger through effective relationships. When learners feel a sense of belonging and connectedness, they learn more effectively and are more confident about engaging in learning alongside others. As *The New Zealand Curriculum* states:

> While there is no formula that will guarantee learning for every student in every context, there is extensive, well-documented evidence about the kinds of teaching approaches that consistently

have a positive impact on student learning. This evidence tells us that students learn best when teachers create a supportive learning environment. (Ministry of Education, 2007, p. 34)

Responsive pedagogical practices are the legitimate business of teachers. The curriculum connects learning and relationships, behaviour and learning. Teachers can enhance educational outcomes through using evidence-based practices. The case studies in this chapter have provided curriculum-connected examples of pedagogical expertise in sociocultural strengths-based assessment, the contribution of individual and community members' voices, and systematic collection of relevant data.

Conclusion

This chapter has considered the curriculum as a means of transmitting social values and expectations. The New Zealand curricula for schools and early childhood education services are aspirational and affirmative. Teachers are viewed as people-centred, caring professionals. The broader relationship-based, responsive and restorative dimensions of curricula endorse what are ultimately the more important aspects of teaching. Curriculum documents position learners as competent and capable, and recognise that learning is a social activity. Effective pedagogical practice includes a consideration of relationships, respect and responsibility, as well as restorative practices. These considerations are the core tasks of all teachers, whatever the age of their students and across curricula. Responsive pedagogy exists *inside* the curriculum and is an essential part of teaching—it is not something "on top" of or additional to teachers' regular work or outside the curriculum. As illustrated by the case studies within this chapter, curriculum-connected responsive pedagogy can and does occur, including with and for the youngest of children.

References

American Psychological Association. (2010). *Publication manual* (6th ed.). Washington, DC: Author.

Bernstein, B. (1971). On the classification and framing of educational knowledge. In M. Young (Ed.), *Knowledge and control* (pp. 79–115). London: Collier-Macmillan.

Bourdieu, P. (1993). *Sociology in question*. London: Sage.

Broström, S. (2003). Understanding *Te whāriki* from a Danish perspective. In J. Nuttall (Ed.), *Weaving* Te whāriki: *Aotearoa New Zealand's early childhood curriculum document in theory and practice* (pp. 215–242). Wellington: NZCER Press.

Carr, M. (1998a). *Assessing children's experiences in early childhood: Final report to the Ministry of Education: Part two: Five case studies*. Wellington: Ministry of Education.

Carr, M. (1998b). *Assessing children's learning in early childhood settings* [a set of three videos and accompanying book]. Wellington: New Zealand Council for Educational Research.

Carr, M. (1998c). Taking dispositions to school: Keynote address to seminar on transition to school. *Childrenz Issues, 2*(1), 21–24.

Carr, M. (2001). *Assessment in early childhood settings: Learning stories*. London: Paul Chapman.

Carr, M. (2004). *Assessment in early childhood education: Keeping it complex, keeping it connected, keeping it credible*. A series of three papers based on keynote addresses presented at Te Tari Puna Ora o Aotearoa / NZ Childcare Association national conferences 2001, 2002, 2004. Wellington: Te Tari Puna Ora o Aotearoa / New Zealand Childcare Association.

Carr, M. (2010). *Learning in the making: Disposition and design in early education*. Rotterdam: Sense

Carr, M., May, H., & Podmore, V. N. (1998). *Learning and teaching stories: New approaches to assessment and evaluation in relation to* Te whāriki. Wellington: Institute for Early Childhood Studies, Victoria University of Wellington.

Carr, M., May, H., & Podmore, V. N., with Cubey, P., Hatherly, A., & Macartney, B. (2000). *Learning and teaching stories: Action research on evaluation in early childhood*. Wellington: New Zealand Council for Educational Research.

Dockett, S., & Fleer, M. (1999). *Play and pedagogy in early childhood: Bending the rules*. Melbourne: Thomson.

Drewery, W., & Winslade, J. (2005). Developing restorative practice in schools: Some reflections. *NZ Journal of Counselling, 26*(2), 16–32.

Hipkins, R. (2006). *The nature of the key competencies. A background paper*. Wellington: New Zealand Council for Educational Research.

Katz, L. (1999a). *Another look at what young children should be learning*. (ERIC Document Reproduction Service No. ED430735)

Katz, L. (1999b). *Balancing constructivist and instructivist curriculum goals in early childhood education*. (ERIC Document Reproduction Service No. ED435474)

Katz, L. (2003). The right of the child to develop and learn in quality environments. *International Journal of Early Childhood, 35*(1/2), 13–21.

Koenig, H. G., George, L. K., & Siegler, I. C. (1988). The use of religion and other emotion-regulating coping strategies among older adults. *The Gerontologist, 28,* 303–310.

May, H., & Podmore, V. (2000). "Teaching stories": An approach to self-evaluation of early childhood programmes. *European Early Childhood Research Journal, 8*(1), 61–73.

Ministry of Education. (1996). *Te whāriki: He whāriki matauranga mō ngā mokopuna o Aotearoa: Early childhood curriculum.* Wellington: Learning Media.

Ministry of Education. (2004/07/09). *Kei tua o te pae: Assessment for learning: Early childhood exemplars.* Wellington: Learning Media.

Ministry of Education. (2007). *The New Zealand curriculum.* Wellington: Learning Media.

Ministry of Education. (2008). *Te marautanga o Aotearoa.* Wellington: Learning Media.

Ministry of Education. (2009). *Key competencies.* Retrieved 20 October 2009, from http://keycompetencies.tki.org.nz

Nuttall, J. (2003). Introduction: Weaving *Te whāriki.* In J. Nuttall (Ed.), *Weaving Te whāriki: Aotearoa New Zealand's early childhood curriculum document in theory and practice* (pp. 7–16). Wellington: NZCER Press.

Perkins, D. N., Jay, E., & Tishman, S. (1993). Beyond abilities: A dispositional theory of thinking. *Merrill-Palmer Quarterly, 39*(1), 1–21.

Podmore, V. N., & May, H., with Mara, D. (1998). *Evaluating early childhood programmes using the strands and goals of* Te whāriki, *the national early childhood curriculum.* Final report on phases one and two to the Ministry of Education.

Reedy, T. (2003). Toku rangatiratanga n ate mana-mātauranga "knowledge and power set me free ..." In J. Nuttall (Ed.), *Weaving Te whāriki: Aotearoa New Zealand's early childhood curriculum document in theory and practice* (pp. 51–78). Wellington: NZCER Press.

Stanley, P. (2006a). A case against the categorisation of children and youth: Part 1: Theoretical perspectives. *Kairaranga, 7*(1), 36–41.

Stanley, P. (2006b). A case against the categorisation of children and youth: Part 2: Professional perspectives. *Kairaranga, 7*(2), 36–40.

Te One, S. (2003). The context for *Te whāriki:* Contemporary issues of influence. In J. Nuttall (Ed.), *Weaving Te whāriki: Aotearoa New Zealand's early childhood curriculum document in theory and practice* (pp. 17–5). Wellington: NZCER Press.

Transforming conflict. (n.d.). *Restorative approaches.* Retrieved 8 August 2009, from http://www.transformingconflict.org/Restorative_Approaches_and_Practices.htm

Part II:

Restorative Practices

5.

Restorative Practice in Action

Greg Jansen & Richard Matla

Case study: Joel

"Ms Green, Ms Green!" Joel called out, running up to his teacher in the school yard. "We still haven't had our chat thingy," he said as he pulled his scruffy, crumpled piece of orange paper out of his back pocket. Ms Green and Joel proceeded to have the "conversation" and repair the relationship that had been broken.

A typical encounter? What makes this one remarkable is not that a relationship was restored, but that the initial incident had occurred in week 9 of term 2, and Joel went to find Ms Green in week 1 of term 3—a whole five weeks later. The young man was following up with the teacher, and the restorative thinking plan, written five weeks earlier, was still crunched up in his pocket. He knew their relationship was damaged and that it needed to be restored …

Joel was no angel. He had been involved in a fair number of incidents in his time at school. It was often said that he could not organise himself out of a paper bag. Yet what he had come to understand was the importance of relationships, and the need to restore a broken relationship with a teacher he had a connection with.

Introduction

Restorative practices, restorative approaches, restorative measures, restorative justice, restorative pathways, restorative conversations— so many different names given to, in essence, very similar processes. Common to all is a desire to repair relationships that have been broken, to work together to identify who has been affected, what their needs are and who is obliged to repair the relationships affected, and to examine how to put things right and heal the relationships.

There are many different frameworks and many ways that people use the restorative process. For some it involves the full community conference, or the family group conference or te hui whakatika (traditional meetings to resolve conflict). For others, it involves short chats or impromptu conversations. However, no matter what the restorative approach used, it is the principles that are key and they remain constant. The way these principles are used may change depending on the culture of the environment and the setting, but the fundamentals—the philosophical underpinnings or the core principles—remain constant.

In this chapter we explore the continuum of restorative practices and the different ways they can be put into practice. These range from the way we develop relationships and resolve minor relationship breakdowns, to how we deal with large relationship issues—the major incidents. We explore restorative principles in a variety of settings—primary school, high school, an early childhood education setting, home and the wider community. We encourage you to ask how it can work for you in your educational setting, and we identify key indicators for developing a whole-school approach. This list is not complete, but instead aims to give examples of how restorative principles can be used in your situation. As Zehr (2002) states, "Restorative justice is a compass not a map" (p. 10).

The principles of restorative practice

From early childhood to secondary school settings there is a growing understanding that problems, conflicts and incidents are an opportunity for growth (Ashworth et al., 2008; Bolstad & Gilbert,

2008; Buckley & Maxwell, 2007). There is a desire to look at incidents as "learning pathways" as opposed to issues to be dealt with. There is an understanding that conflict breaks relationships and causes harm. This harm, including the needs of the affected community, has to be addressed. Zehr (2002) suggests three key principles of restorative justice:

- misconduct is a violation of people and relationships
- violations create obligations and liabilities
- restorative justice seeks to heal and put things right.

A commitment to repair and restore relationships is vital (Cavanagh, 2005, 2007). Restorative practices provide opportunities for this to occur.

Drewery (2003) proposes that "the single most important idea behind restorative practices is that respectful relationships between people are what really count" (p. 7). There are several definitions of and concepts linked to restorative practice, but the baseline for them all is respectful relationships. The restorative matrix, or social discipline window, devised by Wachtel and McCold (2001) and adapted from Glaser (1969), outlines the importance of working "with" as opposed to "doing it to" or "for" (see Chapter 1 of this book). As Wachtel and McCold (2004) note:

> The fundamental hypothesis of restorative practices is disarmingly simple: that human beings are happier, more productive and more likely to make positive changes in their behaviour when those in positions of authority do things *with* them, rather than *to* them or *for* them. For this reason, punitive approaches are the antithesis of restorative practices. The challenge is how we effectively work 'with' students, colleagues, managers and parents. (p. 1)

The questions in Table 5.1, which Zehr (2002) poses, remind us again of the subtle yet profound difference between restorative and punitive responses: the focus of punitive responses is on punishment, whereas the focus of restorative responses is on accountability, needs and healing.

TABLE 5.1 PUNITIVE vs. RESTORATIVE RESPONSES

Punitive response	Restorative response
What law/rule was broken? Who was to blame? What punishment is needed?	Who was affected? What are their needs? Who is obligated to put things right?
Response focuses on ... establishing blame (whose fault is it?) and delivering punishment and pain.	*Response focuses on* ... identifying the need created by harm and making things right.
Justice is sought through ... making people prove who is right and wrong.	*Justice is sought through* ... understanding, dialogue and reparation.
Justice is achieved when ... someone is proven guilty and punished.	*Justice is achieved when* ... people take responsibility for their actions, people's needs are met and the healing of individuals and relationships is encouraged.
Limits possibilities ... for full acceptance back into family, school or community.	*Maximises possibilities* ... for full acceptance back into family/school/community.

A model of restorative practices in education

Me āta tirohia ki te take.
The problem is the problem; the person is not the problem
(White, 1989).

As we explore the various ways in which restorative principles can be put into practice, it is vital we remember that we are working with the *person*. White (1989) asserts that it is critical to focusing on the problem, rather than confusing the person with the problem. We must work together to restore and maintain the mana of the people involved. Wachtel and McCold (2004) argue that:

restorative practice is the science of building social capital and achieving social discipline through participatory learning and decision making. The most critical function of restorative practices is restoring and building relationships. (p. 1)

In this section we introduce a model of restorative practices in education.. We have developed the model as part of our professional work on restorative practice with schools and teachers, and it integrates strategies from a wide body of literature. The model also illustrates that there are a number of valid but varied approaches that can be used when working restoratively.

Explaining the model

The Model of Restorative Practices in Education (see Figure 5.1) illustrates how restorative approaches can be applied across a school and the wider community. A number of factors determine where practitioners will be working within the model, but it is critical that they are aware of their position and the underlying reasons. Contributing factors in determining this include:

- the seriousness of the incident
- the time available
- timeliness
- the number of stakeholders
- preparation required
- the skill and confidence of the facilitator/s.

As Macfarlane (2007) indicates, while there is "difficulty of achieving a general consensus about what constitutes behaviour disorder, it is possible to identify a number of clusters of behaviour each of which has recognisible features" (p. 46). Macfarlane and Prochnow present a behavioural difficulty continuum, grouping behaviours into three main clusters: mild to moderate; moderate to severe; and severe to serious (see Chapter 2 of this book). Identifying the cluster the student incident belongs to helps with the choice of intervention style and the restorative approach.

The model in Figure 5.1 outlines the various types of restorative conversations and conferences, and identifies key factors for each approach. Although the essence and phases of restorative conversations and conferences are not identified on the continuum, they are common to all approaches. Remember, this is not an exhaustive list of approaches: it is an overview of the range of situations and incidents for which restorative processes can be used. The model in Figure 5.1 illustrates the range of approaches from informal to formal; for example, from the personal conversation to a full community

FIGURE 5.1 A MODEL of RESTORATIVE PRACTICES in EDUCATION
Source: Jansen & Matla (2009)

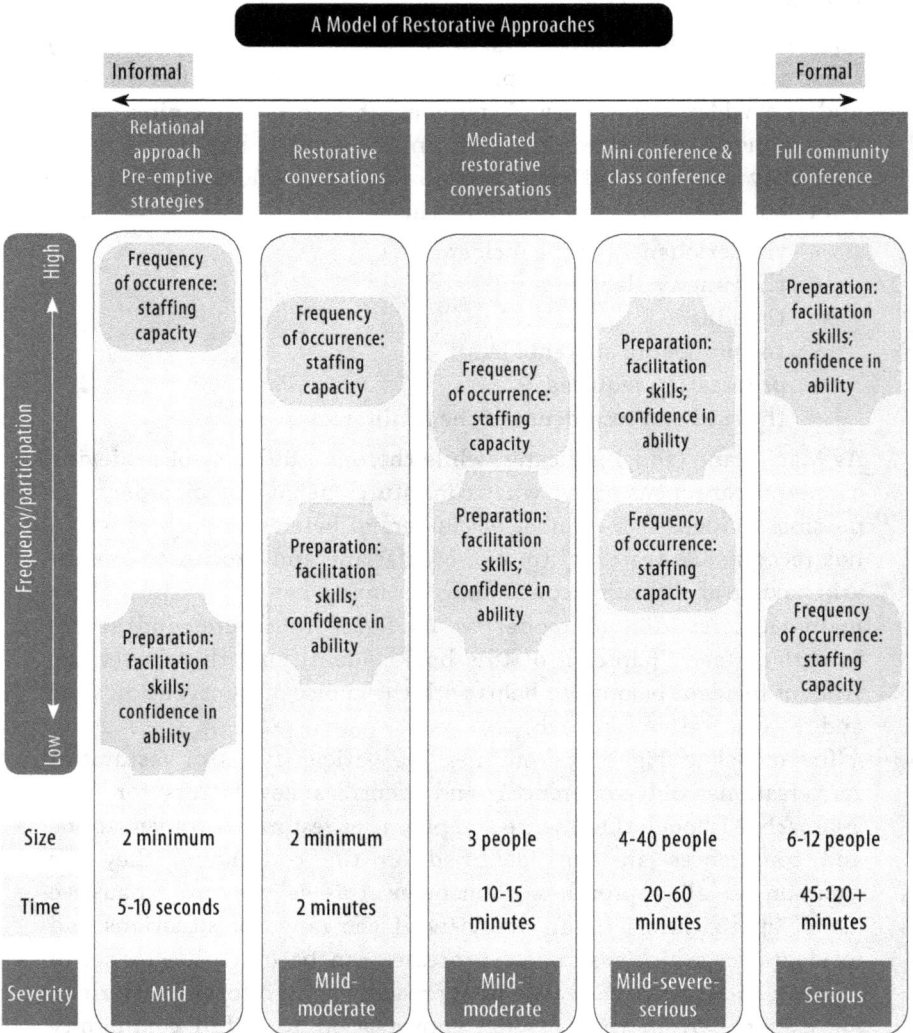

A Model of Restorative Approaches

Informal →→→→→→→→→→→→→→→→→→→→→→→→→→→→→→ Formal

Relational approach Pre-emptive strategies	Restorative conversations	Mediated restorative conversations	Mini conference & class conference	Full community conference
Frequency of occurrence: staffing capacity	Frequency of occurrence: staffing capacity	Frequency of occurrence: staffing capacity	Preparation: facilitation skills; confidence in ability	Preparation: facilitation skills; confidence in ability
Preparation: facilitation skills; confidence in ability	Preparation: facilitation skills; confidence in ability	Preparation: facilitation skills; confidence in ability	Frequency of occurrence: staffing capacity	Frequency of occurrence: staffing capacity

Frequency/participation: High → Low

Size	2 minimum	2 minimum	3 people	4-40 people	6-12 people
Time	5-10 seconds	2 minutes	10-15 minutes	20-60 minutes	45-120+ minutes
Severity	Mild	Mild-moderate	Mild-moderate	Mild-severe-serious	Serious

conference or te hui whakatika. The number of people involved, the time taken and the level of incident severity are all proportional to the formality of the conversation or conference. A low-level or minor incident usually involves as few as two people and takes only a short period of time— as little as two to four minutes.

Other considerations identified in the Model of Restorative Practices in Education include:

- *frequency of occurrence*—the frequency of restorative conversations/conferences
- *staffing capacity*—the number of staff in your school/centre who use restorative conversations/conferences
- *preparation*—this is critical to all restorative conversations/ conferences, and refers to the time and effort required to prepare for a particular conversation/conference
- *facilitation skills*—the facilitation skills needed for a conversation/conference, including questioning, paraphrasing, summarising, inclusion of all participants and use of silence
- *confidence in ability*—the facilitator's confidence needed for the conversations/conferences.

The key factors in Figure 5.1 are divided into two groups: frequency of occurrence and staffing capacity; and preparation, facilitation skills and confidence. The relationship between these two groups is inversely proportional: when the first group is high, the second group is low, and vice versa. To illustrate this point, the restorative conversation requires basic facilitation skills, a low level of preparation and only limited confidence in one's personal ability. This means that many of those among a large number of staff—if not all— can run such conversations, and the frequency will therefore be high. In contrast, a full community conference requires a large amount of preparation, a high level of facilitation skills and a high level of confidence. Full community conferences are used to respond to less frequent, more serious incidents. Their frequency is therefore low, and the number of staff capable of conducting such conferences will also be low.

There is no assumption that any particular dimension of the model is more worthy than another. The model is not a hierarchical continuum, and where the practitioner chooses to work within the model will depend on the extremity of behaviour, his or her skill and experience, the skill and experience of colleagues, previous situations involving the student/s concerned, the available resources and the policies and practices of the workplace.

Wherever the practitioner is working within the model, two key aspects prevail: the essence and phases of the restorative approaches.

The essence of restorative conversations and conferences

Whether you are having a restorative conversation or are participating in a larger conference, the essence and basic principles remain the same. The essence of the restorative approach comprises four steps.

1. *Tell the story*: What happened?
2. *Explore the harm*: Who do you think has been affected? In what ways?
3. *Repair the harm*: What do you need to do to put things right?
4. *Move forward*: How can we make sure this does not happen again?

Morrison (2007) calls this the story telling, the emotional engagement and the restitution. Chapter 6 of this book explores restorative conversations in more detail.

The restorative keystones: The common thread

At all levels of restorative conversations and conferencing, three "keystone" phases are essential to ensure the process is robust: the preparation phase; the participation phase; and the post-conference phase. These keystones work together to form a conceptual arch. If any single phase is missing or is poorly carried out, "cracks" will appear, affecting the ability of the arch to stand up, often leading to the loss of a genuine and effective process, as well as "crumbled" conversations and conferences. The keystone phases are summarised in Figure 5.2 and explained in more detail below.

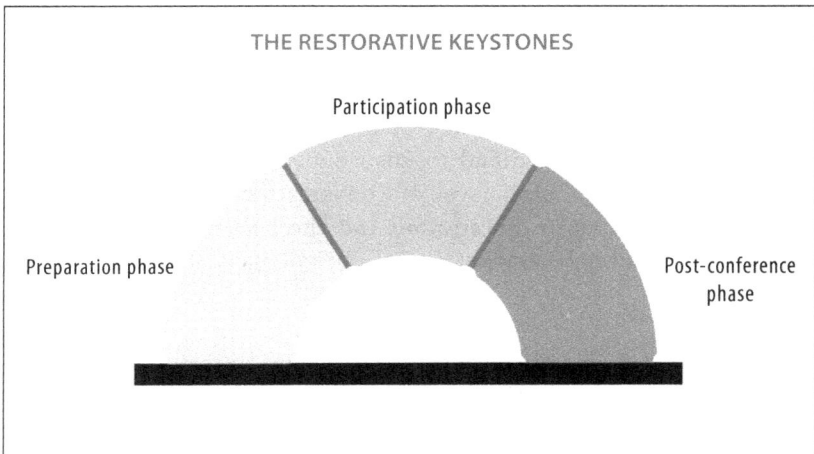

FIGURE 5.2 PHASES of the RESTORATIVE APPROACH
Source: Malta and Jansen (2009)

The *preparation phase* involves the ground work: establishing details of the incident; communicating with those affected; exploring who and how people have been affected; setting up the protocols and environment for the conference; and beginning to explore how things can be put right. During this phase all parties involved are prepared, know the process and are in a position to take part.

The *participation phase* involves the facilitation and running of the conversation or conference. It requires the active participation of all those affected by the incident. The process of this phase follows the essence of restorative conversations: **T**ell the story; **E**xplore the harm; **R**epair the harm; and **M**ove forward. Depending on the size of the conference, one or two facilitators may be needed or used.

The *post-conference phase* follows up the conversation/conference by monitoring the progress of the agreement or contract. It also provides opportunity for feedback and evaluation. "SMART" agreements are very helpful for maintaining integrity during this phase: **S**pecific; **M**easurable; **A**ttainable; **R**ealistic; and **T**imed.

From principles to practice—putting it into action

In the following section, each restorative practice approach from the Model of Restorative Approaches is briefly outlined, along with a case study. These case studies are of actual incidents, but the names and situations have been modified to ensure anonymity. It is important to remember that at each level of conversation or conference, the *essence of the restorative conversation* and the *phases of the restorative conversations* need to be evident.

The restorative conversation

Teachers and students are encouraged to engage in restorative conversations, both for preventing and for conducting early intervention in low-level classroom disruption. This approach models respectful dialogue and includes the language of restorative enquiry.

> **Case study: The impromptu conversation**
>
> Ms Black and Mr Arthur were walking down the corridor heading to the staff room for lunch. Mary saw Ms Black walking by and politely interrupted her conversation. "Ms Black can we please have that conversation now?" Ms Black excused herself, stood in the corridor with Mary and proceeded to have the restorative conversation, which involved asking the following questions: "So Mary, tell me what happened? Who was affected and how? What needs to be done to put that right? How can we make sure this doesn't happen again? What can I do to help you?" The conversation lasted around four minutes and finished with Mary thanking Ms Black for her time and helping to get it sorted.

This approach allowed the student to take responsibility for her learning relationship with her teacher.

> **Case study: What's the story?**
>
> Mr Neil quietly walked up to Logan and prompted him to be on task with a knowing tap on his book. Logan's off-task disruptive behaviour continued. Mr Neil again moved alongside Logan and quietly asked him if he needed help with an aspect of his work. Logan replied, "Na, sweet", and started to work. However, shortly after this he was off task again and disrupting others' learning. Mr Neil moved up alongside Logan again and encouraged him to stay on task. He

suggested that if he wasn't able to stay on task then he would have to either move seats or leave the class, because his behaviour was continuing to disrupt other class members' learning. After a short display of on-task behaviour, Logan became off task again and disrupted others. Mr Neil had no option but to follow through with his previous instruction. He sent Logan to wait outside the classroom, not raising his voice or causing a scene, but remaining calm and direct. When Mr Neil got a moment he stepped outside the classroom to a have a conversation with Logan. "So Logan, what's happening? Who is that affecting? What needs to happen to put things right? What do you need to stop doing, start doing and stay doing?"

After the brief conversation an agreement was reached. An apology was made by Logan for his behaviour to Mr Neil. Logan suggested that he sit somewhere different so that he was not so easily distracted. He rejoined the class, moved from where he was sitting and focused on the learning he had missed. The conversation outside the class took a total of three minutes and no further action was required. Following the lesson Mr Neil caught up with Logan again to check in and see how he was going with catching up on his work. It was decided that Logan would continue to stay in that seat because it helped him to concentrate.

The following day as the class arrived Mr Neil had a very brief check in with Logan—how he was, what he needed to remember for today's lesson and where he was going to sit—so that they could work together to support Logan's learning.

Despite often being very brief, the restorative conversation allows both the young person and the teacher to problem solve and develop solutions. The incident becomes a learning process and an opportunity to develop stronger learning relationships. In each of the restorative conversation case studies so far, the essence and the phases of restorative conversations are evident. The teacher is "gently relentless" regarding expectations while maintaining a "with" approach.

Mediated restorative conversations

Mediated restorative conversations are used for mild to moderate incidents, where the break in a relationship cannot be restored by a simple restorative conversation. The mediated restorative conversation involves three people: the two involved in the incident and a neutral facilitator. Either party is able to call for a mediated conversation. The approach is particularly useful for providing support, accountability and mentoring to the process.

Case study: "It hurt inside"

> I will apologise for what I did and say it won't happen again, and I will listen to Miss Black and respect her, ignore what others are saying and get on with what I am supposed to be doing, because after what she told me *I feel sad inside* and now I know how she feels. (13-year-old boy)

This response came in a letter to his dean the day after a mediated restorative conversation with his teacher and dean. The young man had repeatedly caused disruption in class, and the teacher felt that no progress was being made so she requested some support to restore the relationship. During the meeting the boy believed he needed to take responsibility for his behaviour and the break in the relationship. However, he preferred not to apologise during the meeting because he wanted to think about what he was going to say. It was agreed that he would meet his dean in the morning, before school, because he needed to meet with his teacher to give her both a verbal and a written apology before class. The student gave both his verbal and written apologies to the teacher, and the relationship was restored.

Ongoing support from the teacher and the dean ensured the boy was able to continue the positive patterns of behaviour he had begun. At a later date the boy asked the dean, "Can we have one of those conversation thingies with my mum, as I want to get things sorted out with her?"

This process provided an opportunity for the boy to hear the effect his behaviour was having on his teacher, without a "lecture" and pent-up frustrations affecting the outcome. He was able to hear his teacher's emotion, and it also gave space for the boy to reflect on his behaviour before responding with a more genuine apology.

Case study: The science class

Mr Frank, the science teacher, had had enough and Tony was sent out of the class. "But it wasn't me, it's not fair … you always pick on me," Tony protested as he left the room. Tony went to the restorative thinking room to reflect on what had happened, feeling frustrated that he had been unfairly picked on.

It became obvious that the teacher and student were not going to be able to resolve the issues by themselves, so the dean was informed. The dean talked with the boy and the teacher separately, listening to what had happened. It became clear that the boy's behaviour had caused a relationship breakdown with the teacher. However, the teacher came to see that he had jumped to conclusions regarding the boy's actions. A time was set during interval the following day for a mediated restorative conversation.

The dean facilitated the meeting. The boy was asked what occurred, who was affected and in what ways. The teacher was then asked the same series of questions. The teacher heard the boy's frustration and acknowledgement of his part in the breakdown of their relationship. The teacher then acknowledged that he had jumped to a wrong conclusion and apologised for this to the boy. The boy was surprised the teacher had acknowledged some fault. The meeting finished with both the teacher and the boy apologising, shaking hands and coming to an agreement about how to deal with the situation should it happen again.

The situation did not occur again and a good relationship developed between the student and the teacher. The staff later commented how good it was that there was an environment in which that process could take place.

This conversation allowed the teacher and student to both reflect on and acknowledge their part in the incident. While some teachers may be concerned that acknowledging their limitations to students could mean they lose some control over students, others know that in reality it increases teacher–student respect and adds depth to the learning relationship.

The mini conference

Mini conferences sit between the mediated restorative conversation and the full community conference, and they are run by a neutral facilitator. Mini conferences involve the community of people affected by the incident. They are a response to moderate to serious incidents when more than two people are involved. All the participants at the conference have an opportunity for input. When agreement is reached it is formalised, and support is planned for following up the outcomes and ensuring obligations are met.

Case study: Starting early

School had finished, and while a number of pupils were waiting for the bus to arrive, a tussle broke out by the gate. One of the eight-year-old boys jumped in and said, "Stop! Stop! We need to have one of those chats things we did in class the other day." At that point he started organising the boys to stand in a circle and began to discuss the incident with all those involved, much to the shock and surprise of the parents and staff standing around.

Case study: "Ms, Ms, we've sorted it out!"

The deputy principal recounted this story to a group of staff in the office.

> I was dealing with this bullying incident the other day with two groups of girls and the issue was escalating out of control. After a brief investigation I realised a mini conference was going to be required. I prepared for the conference with both sets of girls and began the conference. The sharing of the stories and who was affected by the behaviour took a little longer than expected and soon the bell rang. I had to go to class but I hadn't finished the conference. Unsure what to do, I checked with both sets of girls that we could pick up the conference the following morning and complete it then. I reassured myself that both groups of girls felt safe that the issues were not going to continue before the next morning. I was nervous, but decided to leave it.
>
> The following morning, I was on the gate and the girls ran up to me, saying 'Ms, Ms, Ms, hey, hey, you know that meeting we were going to have this morning? We don't need it. We all met up yesterday after school and continued the discussion you started yesterday. We realised that what we were doing was silly and taking each other's comments out of context. So we got it sorted and we're all sweet now!'
>
> Needless to say, I was surprised, but pleased, as these girls had been through the restorative process on a number of occasions, so it was great to see some of it having an effect.

At that point one of the office staff raised her head up above the partition, and commented that restorative practices used at school could be used out of school too. It was much more useful than a detention in preparing for later life.

It is human nature to want to make connections with other people. We need mechanisms and processes that allow us to hear each other and repair broken relationships. As the office staff member indicated in the last story, this process is far more useful in later life than the traditional punitive detention process.

Class conferences

Restorative approaches can be used in both a proactive and a responsive way. A proactive approach promotes positive dialogue within a classroom and involves discussing classroom dynamics and promoting learning. A responsive approach is used when a whole class is affected by hostility or conflict, and when learning is impeded and relationships are damaged. A class conference is sometimes called a "no blame conference". A neutral facilitator, teachers, support personnel and students meet in a circle and discuss the issues, explore the harm and develop solutions together. The case study below is an extract from a teacher's email.

Case study: "I could see, hear and feel the power of the restorative process"

Just thought I'd share with you what happened in a class conference yesterday in my Year 10 class. We have had a number of bullying incidents within the class (name calling, put downs, swearing etc.), and last Monday I had had enough so I organised a class conference.

Some background on the class: 13 males, six females; two students recently stood down for cannabis, two students with special needs and health conditions, a number of silly boys and one student who admits he would be in jail in Aussie if he hadn't shifted to New Zealand this year. Three members of class have already been taken out and shifted to another class this year—a real mixed bunch to say the least!

Yesterday, I felt 'The Power' of restorative justice during the conference. It is that sense you get when people are being open and honest, taking responsibility and even the most immature and 'tough' boys are opening up and listening. Twice during the conference one of the girls asked our arguably most uncomfortable behaviour-challenged boys to 'be quiet and stop being disrespectful', which was more effective than what Ms Mary and I had tried! I could see, hear and feel the power of the restorative process.

The no-blame conference allowed a dialogue for students to share how things were for them, and an opportunity for students to respond and take responsibility as well. One incredible outcome was the fact that students who previously bullied, particularly students with special needs, offered to support special needs students in other classes where the teacher aide was not available. This outcome is still continuing. Remarkable! While this conference did go very well, we were realistic and the class asked that we could have regular check-ins like the meeting, so that any issues that did arise could be dealt with before they became bigger issues.

Case study: "The seats are out, we are ready to go"

Mary, the teacher, ran across the courtyard, late back to class and unsure of what chaos she would find. She had been unexpectedly held up at the end of morning break. To her amazement, when she arrived in her classroom she noticed the desks neatly stacked up at the side of the room, the chairs all set out in a circle in the middle of the room and the students sitting there waiting. "Ms," one girl called out as Mary walked through the door, "we got the room ready, coz we've got that circle thing." Mary was pleasantly shocked. This was only the second time she had planned to run a circle time, but it was obvious that her students wanted another chance to discuss issues with one another in an organised way. The circle began, taking longer than expected. To her amazement again, the planned creative writing after circle time resulted in a much higher standard of work being submitted than previously, despite having only half the time available to complete it.

When we provide students with opportunities to learn through restorative practice, we all win. Students long for a place and a structure that enables them to listen to and share with one another, to resolve issues, to strengthen relationships and to build a class culture.

Full community conference

This conference involves the whole community of people affected by an incident of serious harm, including parents and family members of the victims and offenders. Full community conferences require careful preparation by a neutral facilitator. Agreements are recorded and kept as part of the school's tracking system. People are assigned responsibility for various aspects of the agreement. Following the conference, the participants share food and drink as a symbol of their agreement. In the following chapters the te hui whakatika process will be explained.

Case study: The flying chair

Jeremy picked up the chair and threw it across the front of the room towards Tim, hitting him in the side of the head and knocking him to the ground. The teacher had no idea what had happened. All she saw was a boy lying on the ground and blood coming out his nose.

An open-and-shut case? Maybe not. As those dealing with the incident dug deeper it became clear that the chair thrower, Jeremy, had been hassled for months by Tim. This had reached the point where he had had enough and snapped. Did that make the throwing the chair OK or not? The need to unpack the story and deal with the issues and the harm caused was evident.

As expected, the parents of both boys were very upset. A number of interim meetings involving all those affected (the boys, their parents, the principal, the teacher and the facilitator) were held before the full community conference. This conference, run in the evening, was a great success. Although tense at times during the meeting, all parties were happy with the outcomes and what each party was going to do to begin to put things right.

Did it work? Six weeks later the two boys were observed in class, sitting side by side, with Jeremy helping Tim with his work—a restored and enhanced relationship!

Reflective questions to analyse an incident such as this may include the following: Would you expect to see the two boys working shoulder to shoulder, helping each other in the same class, just weeks later? Would the parents feel heard and appreciate the way the incident was dealt with? Would they be able to stop and talk when meeting each other in the street? Would relationships be restored and strengthened?

A whole-school approach

Hubbard (2007) argues that:

> Restorative Practices need to be totally integrated into the school
> motto, school values, school polices, school procedures and attitudes
> towards people and 'school vocabulary' so all are consistent with
> each other. This connection between all links is explicitly explored
> and discussed daily—thereby the total is greater than the sum of the
> individual parts.

As illustrated in the restorative continuum (Figure 5.1), staff capacity
requirements depend on the severity of the incident. However,
it is critical that all staff be able to manage the first two stages: the
pre-emptive relational approach and restorative conversations.
When members of staff are working consistently in this manner,
opportunities for learning are increased.

Thorsborne and Vinegrad (2004) support the notion that restorative
practices cannot be a "clip on", but instead need to be the central focus
if sustained change is to be expected. Buckley and Maxwell (2007), in
their research on schools using a restorative approach, found that:

> the introduction of restorative practices for resolving conflict and
> serious disciplinary problems is effective in reducing exclusions but
> a fully restorative approach will have a wider impact in building a
> constructive and inclusive school environment. (p. 26)

Rogers (2003) proposes that people take up change at different rates,
and that restorative capacity and sustainability within a school
or community are dependent on how well this rate of change is
managed. Amstutz and Mullet (2005) share their understanding of the
restorative process using a "restorative practices yardstick". According
to this, a school is working towards restorative practices when:

- the focus is primarily on relationships, and rules are secondary
- the voice of the person(s) harmed is heard
- the voice of the person(s) who caused the harm is heard
- collaborative problem solving is used
- responsibility is enhanced
- there is empowerment for change and growth
- there is a plan for restoration.

Zehr (2002) argues that the biggest threat to restorative practices is not narrowmindedness, bigotry, vengefulness or egoism, but rather the "gradual creep" of restorative standards moving steadily away from their foundation. The concern is that programmes become restorative in name only. Appendix A and Appendix B are two self-assessment sheets that have been developed to maintain focus and help guard against "gradual creep". Appendix A, "How Restorative Am I?", is a self-assessment to help individuals identify strengths and areas of concern in their practice and reflect on the way they are working with students. Appendix B, "How Restorative Is Our School?", has been designed to allow the whole school to reflect on areas of strength and concern through the eyes of all involved—not just those in key leadership positions. It could also be adapted for use in early childhood education services.

When planning for a whole-school approach it is vital that the change is strategic, supported and sustainable (Starbuck, 2006; Thorsborne & Vinegrad, 2004). There are six key considerations when planning a whole-school approach to becoming a restorative school:

1. *Develop a vision, a team and a strategy.* It is vital to create a team, work *with* one another collaboratively and adopt a strategic approach. Any leadership team wanting to implement and sustain a restorative philosophy and practices in its school must have a clear vision, and an understanding of how this vision weaves into the fabric of the community.

2. *Value people and their time—encourage the heart.* People don't care how much you know until they know how much you care, which is as true when working with young people as when working with staff. Most teachers chose a teaching career because they wanted to educate young people and make a difference. However, along the way some lose sight of this. It is critical that we re-engage with the hearts of our teachers to reignite their passion to connect with young people.

3. *Walk the talk—model the way.* If we choose to use a restorative approach, we need to model restorative relationships with all members of the school community.

4. *Build the relational capacity of your staff and students— experiential learning.* As we work to build relational capacity, staff and students need to feel and experience strong relationships and the power of the restorative process. Confucius reportedly said, "I hear, I forget. I see, I remember. I do, and I understand."

5. *Develop clear, explicit systems and guidelines collaboratively.* As a school it is vital to have clear systems and guidelines developed in conjunction with the staff in order to provide a solid guiding framework for staff.

6. *Gather data—numbers talk.* By gathering data, changes can be monitored, which strengthens accountability and provides support and encouragement for staff and students. This reflects the current call for schools and teachers to increase the use of evidence-based decision making and practice (Hattie, 2003).

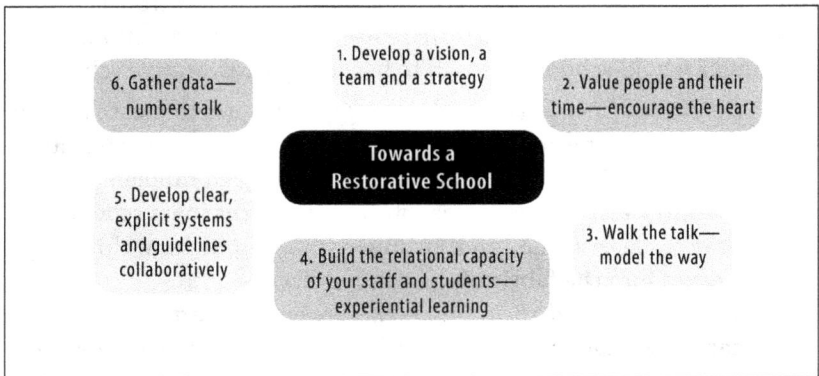

FIGURE 5.3 TOWARDS A RESTORATIVE SCHOOL

Source: Jansen and Matla (2009)

Conclusion

It has often been said that it is relationships, relationships, relationships that are key. Restorative practices that repair and reconnect strong relationships are vital, not only for young people while in the education system but also in life beyond school. By using a range of practical restorative approaches and strategies in our various educational settings, we embrace and empower ourselves as well as our young people. By working *with* one another to build, develop, maintain and restore relationships, we help students and ourselves to understand the effects of our actions on others, and we promote a culture of care and healthy communities. The focus is relationships, relationships, relationships.

References

Amstutz, L. S., & Mullet, J. H. (2005). *The little book of restorative discipline for school*. Intercourse, PA: Good Books.

Ashworth, J., Van Bockern, S., Ailts, J., Donnelly, J., Erickson, K., & Woltermann, J. (2008). An alternative to school detention. *Reclaiming Children and Youth*, 17(3), 22–26.

Bolstad, R., & Gilbert, J. (2008). *Disciplining and drafting, or 21st century learning?: Rethinking the New Zealand senior secondary curriculum for the future*. Wellington: NZCER Press.

Buckley, S., & Maxwell, G. (2007). *Restorative practices in education*. Wellington: Institute of Policy Studies and the Office of the Children's Commissioner.

Cavanagh, T. (2005). *Creating safe schools using restorative practices in a culture of care*. An ethnographic study conducted at Raglan Area School.

Cavanagh, T. (2007). *Focusing on relationships creates safety in schools*. Wellington: NZCER Press.

Drewery, W. (2003). *Restorative practices for schools—a resource*. Hamilton: Waikato University School of Education, Waikato University.

Hattie, J. (2003). *Teachers make a difference: What is research evidence?: Building teacher quality*. Auckland: The University of Auckland.

Hubbard, B. (2007). *Restorative practices Australia study trip*. Retrieved 15 July 2009, from http://rcrp.blogspot.com/

Macfarlane, A. (2007). *Discipline, democracy, and diversity: Working with students with behaviour difficulties*. Wellington: NZCER Press.

Morrison, B. (2007). *Restoring safe school communities: A whole school response to bullying, violence and alienation*. Leichhardt, NSW: Federation Press.

Rogers, E. (2003). *Diffusion of innovation* (5th ed.). New York: Free Press.

Starbuck, J. (2006). Introducing restorative justice into your school. *Primary Leadership Today*, 5, 4.

Thorsborne, M., & Vinegrad, D. (2004). *Restorative practices in schools: Rethinking behaviour management*. Buderim, QLD: Inyahead Press.

Wachtel, T., & McCold, P. (2004). *From restorative justice to restorative practices: Expanding the paradigm*. Paper presented at the International Institute for Restorative Practices conference, Bethlehem, PA.

White, M. (1989). The externalizing of the problem and the re-authoring of lives and relationships. Republished 1989 in M. White (Ed.), *Selected papers* (pp. 5–28). Adelaide: Dulwich Centre Publications.

Zehr, H. (2002). *The little book of restorative justice*. Intercourse, PA: Good Books.

Appendix A:
How restorative am I?

Source: Matla & Jansen (2009), adapted from Thorsborne (2009)

Take a moment to reflect on the way you deal with young people in your classes in the wake of incidents with students. Grade yourself on the statements using the scale below.

☐ ☐ ☐ = no   ■ ☐ ☐ = not often
■ ■ ☐ = usually   ■ ■ ■ = always

1. Do I remain calm during the dialogue? ☐ ☐ ☐
2. Do I truly listen, hear them out without interrupting? ☐ ☐ ☐
3. Do they feel listened to? ☐ ☐ ☐
4. Does the student understand why he/she is "in trouble"? ☐ ☐ ☐
5. Do they know what rule has been broken, and what the purpose of the rule is? ☐ ☐ ☐
6. Do we explore what the school values are around the issue? ☐ ☐ ☐
7. Does he/she come to understand the damage they have caused: Who has been harmed, and how? ☐ ☐ ☐
8. Do I talk about how it is for me? ☐ ☐ ☐
9. Do I take any responsibility for any part I might have played in what went wrong? Do I acknowledge that/ apologise? ☐ ☐ ☐
10. If there was an apology to me, do I accept it with grace? ☐ ☐ ☐
11. Is there a plan made, and have I offered to help with it? ☐ ☐ ☐
12. Is the relationship with the student/s repaired? ☐ ☐ ☐
13. Have I, at any stage, asked for someone I trust to observe my restorative practice and give me honest feedback? ☐ ☐ ☐
14. Do I try to handle most issues/incidents myself, or do I rely on others to "fix" things for me? ☐ ☐ ☐
15. Looking back on how I handled the situation, could I have done with some support? ☐ ☐ ☐

Look through your scores and use them to help you develop a plan to further strengthen your positive practice and improve areas of concern.

Appendix B:
How restorative is our school?
Source: Matla and Jansen (2009), adapted from Thorsborne (2009)

For a restorative approach to be highly effective, a full-school approach is vital. In building restorative capacity in your school, planning, ongoing professional development and sharing of best practice is essential. As you read the statements below, indicate a grade for your school.

☐ ☐ ☐ = not often   ■ ☐ ☐ = at times
■ ■ ☐ = usually   ■ ■ ■ = always

1. Do our students feel listened to? ☐ ☐ ☐
2. Do our staff feel listened to? ☐ ☐ ☐
3. Do our staff remain calm during dialogue with our students? ☐ ☐ ☐
4. Do our staff talk at our students? ☐ ☐ ☐
5. When issues/incidents arise, do our staff manage these themselves rather than relying on others to fix things for them? ☐ ☐ ☐
6. Are all of our staff (including support staff) aware of the restorative approach? ☐ ☐ ☐
7. Do our staff know where they can get more support/training? ☐ ☐ ☐
8. Do our staff at any stage ask for someone they trust to observe their classroom management practice and give them honest feedback? ☐ ☐ ☐
9. Do our staff take responsibility for any part they might have played in what went wrong, and is this acknowledged? ☐ ☐ ☐
10. Do we work with students and families to resolve incidents? ☐ ☐ ☐
11. Is the restorative approach used in our school a "clip on" or the central way of thinking and working? ☐ ☐ ☐
12. Are victims involved in the process of dealing with the issue? ☐ ☐ ☐
13. Does our school have a plan to continue to develop the restorative approach in our school? ☐ ☐ ☐

☐ ☐ ☐ = no   ◼ ☐ ☐ = not often
◼ ◼ ☐ = usually   ◼ ◼ ◼ = always

14. Do we inform our wider school community about the use of restorative practices in our school? ☐ ☐ ☐

15. Do we inform our student body about what restorative practices mean for them in our school? ☐ ☐ ☐

16. Do I remain calm during the dialogue? ☐ ☐ ☐

17. Do I truly listen? Hear them out without interrupting? Do they feel listened to? ☐ ☐ ☐

18. Do we both end up understanding the motivation/intention behind the behaviour? ☐ ☐ ☐

19. Does the student understand why he/she is "in trouble"? What rule has been broken? What the purpose of the rule is? ☐ ☐ ☐

20. Do I explain what the school values are around the issue? ☐ ☐ ☐

21. Does he/she come to understand the damage they have caused: Who has been harmed, and how? ☐ ☐ ☐

22. Do I talk about how it is for me? ☐ ☐ ☐

23. Do I take any responsibility for any part I might have played in what went wrong, and do I acknowledge that? Do I apologise? ☐ ☐ ☐

24. If there was an apology to me, do I accept it with grace? ☐ ☐ ☐

25. Is there a plan made? Have I agreed to help? ☐ ☐ ☐

26. Is the relationship with the students repaired? ☐ ☐ ☐

27. Have I, at any stage, asked for someone I trust to observe my restorative practice and give me honest feedback? ☐ ☐ ☐

28. Do I try to handle most issues/incidents myself, or do I rely on others to "fix" things for me? ☐ ☐ ☐

29. Looking back on how I handled the situation, could I have done with some support? Any ideas? ☐ ☐ ☐

Look through your scores and use them to help you develop a plan to further strengthen your positive practice and improve areas of concern.

6.

Restorative Conversations

Richard Matla & Greg Jansen

Case study: A heart to heart

Early in 2010 a New Zealand secondary school principal reflected on a conversation he had had with a student from his school over a decade earlier. He said he had never heard of restorative conversations, but what he said to this young man when he reported to his office about some reasonably serious misconduct was, "I want to have an adult conversation with you. Do you want to know what that involves?" To which the young man nodded.

The principal then said to him, "Well, in an adult conversation we will be very calm with each other, we will listen to each other's points of view, we will be very respectful and we will be extremely honest with each other. Do you want one of those conversations?" The young man readily agreed.

After the conversation with the young man they got to a point where he felt they were able to shake hands over the issue. As he reached out the young man pulled him close and they engaged in a hongi (pressing of noses to signal unity). Then the young man reached further and fully embraced the principal such was the depth of connection and power of this conversation.

The principal wiped back the mist from his eyes as he reflected on the enduring significance of this "heart-to-heart" conversation.

Introduction

This chapter looks into the detail of restorative dialogue in face-to-face conversations and conferences that take place in schools and early childhood education services. It also explores what restorative practices can—and indeed must—do to ensure that these dialogues are as effective as they can be. In 2009 a research project was carried out on restorative conversations involving focus groups of students, teachers and pastoral teams (Matla, 2009). A large part of this chapter reflects on the findings of this investigation, which posed the question, "What is required to make restorative conversations work?"

Restorative dialogues range from small statements or passing comments, to scripted approaches, through to full community conferences with a large number of participants. The focus in this chapter is on the conversations that take place between two individuals who have experienced a break in or harm to their relationship. Typically, in a school setting this would involve a teacher and a student, but peer-to-peer restorative conversations are being undertaken with increasing frequency.

The restorative conversation

The restorative conversation is an integral part of restorative practices in schools. It lies at the very heart of connecting with a student in order to seek to understand an issue or situation, reflect on it, find ways to repair harm done and reconnect those involved. These informal conversations can powerfully redirect behaviour, create a new understanding and build empathetic young people and schools.

Teachers are generally strong communicators with well-developed social skills, and as a profession they seek strong and healthy teaching and learning relationships with children and young people. They want their students to succeed, make good choices and learn. Systems that support this growth and development and enable students to "live well" with one another need to be strongly supported by educators. People—young people in particular—have a deep need to be *seen* and *known*. The depth and quality of student relationships within the school community are of great significance. With hundreds and often thousands of students congregating each day on individual school campuses around the country, the potential for damage and harm to relationships is considerable. Restorative conversations in schools create opportunities for rebuilding, strengthening and restoring relationships at the heart of a conflict through face-to-face meetings.

In the school setting, a restorative approach views misconduct not as rule breaking and a violation of the institution, but as a violation against people and relationships in both the school and the community. Using a restorative approach means that the harm done to people and relationships needs to be explored and repaired (Thorsborne & Cameron, 1999). There is growing evidence of positive outcomes from restorative approaches for both individuals and communities. Schools working in this way must endeavour to create the best possible conditions, pathways and environment for teachers and students in order to maximise the potential success of the restorative process.

Student–teacher relationships

Quality relationships

Students responding to a survey about what makes restorative conversations work (Matla, 2009) focused overwhelmingly on the quality of their relationships with teachers. Many teachers responded similarly in reflecting that the teachers' moods, approaches and willingness to engage with the students were important:

> Most teachers just go around the class and do their stuff, but she says 'How is your day going?' She is like a 'normal' human being! (Student comment, Matla, 2009)

Restorative conversations are integral to relationships within schools. As Chapters 2 and 7 of this book endorse, this is particularly significant for teaching and working with Māori students. The Te Kotahitanga programme (Bishop, Berryman, Cavanagh, & Teddy, 2009) is based on the premise that the single biggest determinant of the strength of the learning process for Māori and other students is the quality of the relationships within the classroom. Teachers are finding that strong relationships with students in turn support their engagement and learning:

> the new national curriculum document itself indicates that no longer are schools just a place where a student learns a subject then goes home to receive moral guidance and character development. Schools are, for increasing numbers of students, the most stable influence in their lives and are understandably a vital locale for accessing these broader elements of personal and social education. (Ministry of Education, 2007a, p. 12)

Jansen (2008) found that the depth of relationships established between teachers and students was directly connected to the effectiveness of the restorative process. However, the capacity and skills to build these connections were not universally found in all teachers or all schools:

> The building of the relationship is the talking with them ... but it's actually the skill of the teacher in the restorative chat; that is the crucial part. (Teacher comment, Jansen, 2008, p. 29)

It is increasingly apparent that, even with the best of intentions, teachers do not always possess the ability to relate effectively to students. Relating to students involves using a set of professional skills that need to be developed and practised. Ginott (1972) comments on the "ultimate power" of teachers to control outcomes of conflict. He found that it is a teacher's response that decides whether a crisis will be escalated or de-escalated, or a child humanised or de-humanised.

Connection before correction

Relationships have moved from being a by-product of the school process to being a vital raw ingredient. Restorative conversations provide an ideal vehicle for establishing, deepening and repairing connections, which in turn allow relationships to grow. Pranis's

(2005) work provides a framework for understanding the importance of establishing connections before any restorative work can be undertaken. Figure 6.1 provides an adaptation of this framework.

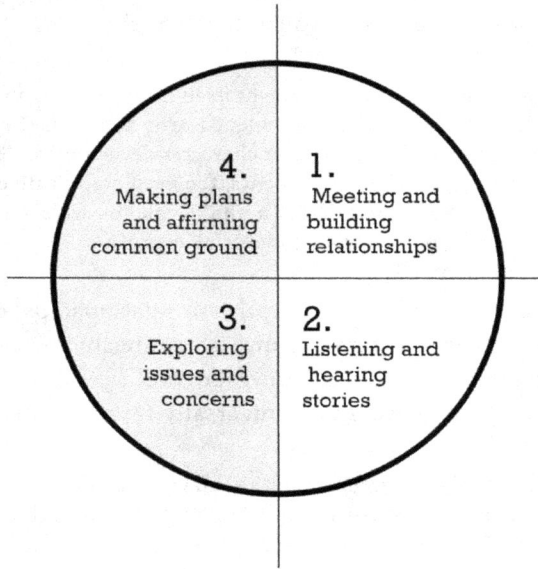

FIGURE 6.1 THE RESTORATIVE PROBLEM-SOLVING APPROACH
Source: Matla and Jansen (2009), adapted from Pranis (2005)

We are often inclined to move too quickly to the problem—see steps 3 and 4 of Figure 6.1 (exploring issues and concerns; making plans and affirming common ground)—spending most of our time on these aspects. This reflects a desire to deal rapidly with issues and their correction, rather than doing the groundwork and establishing trusting relationships. If we work instead through steps 1 and 2 of Figure 6.1 (meeting and building relationships; listening and hearing stories), connecting effectively and taking the time needed, we will build trust. If we establish relationships with trust, we are far more likely to arrive at truthful and durable solutions (Pranis, 2005).

The restorative philosophy is underpinned by the key principle that wrongdoing affects relationships. If relationships are shallow or insubstantial, the chance of restoration through participants' acknowledgement of the effect their actions have on others is weakened. There is a real need to strengthen relationships right across the school, and sound restorative conversations are a great way for this to happen. This sentiment is echoed loudly and clearly in feedback from students, who suggest that the relationships they have with teachers have a direct bearing not only on their enjoyment of classes but also on their engagement and achievement:

> If it's a teacher I really like and really connect with, then I will do all my work to the best of my ability. (Matla, 2009)

It is clear that some teachers still operate punitively. This not only antagonises students but also alienates them further from a system that should be about building people up and finding ways of moving forward together. When teachers lose sight of this and students are no longer talked *with*, but instead are lectured *to* and talked *at* (Wachtel & McCold, 2004) then the real power of the restorative process is lost.

Paradigm wars

Some educationalists feel confronted by restorative approaches. For these people, a paradigm shift in thinking is required. For those who have never questioned the effectiveness of punishment as a means to change behaviour, this is a real challenge (Thorsborne & Vinegrad, 2004). The restorative approach challenges the power base in some classrooms. Some teachers are unclear about the principles behind restorative practice, others lack confidence in its use and a determined few refuse to engage with the restorative philosophy at any level. There seems to be an internal battle for some teachers, who may struggle daily with conflicting paradigms:

> The basis of what is wrong is we have got a restorative system but we have still got a punitive mindset that is attached to it ... it's been broken down considerably because I don't think we are where we were ... I think we have come a long way but there is still a mindset of

needing to see a consequence and the consequence that is needed to
be seen is a punitive one. (School leader comment, Matla, 2009)

Students have reported that they felt teachers held grudges against
them, and that the issues were very personal rather than being about
their behaviour. Some teachers see the person as the problem and
struggle to see the problem as the problem. Braithwaite (1989) identified
this in describing the different types of shame. A wrongdoing student
often experiences "stigmatising shame" and labelling, rather than a
reintegrative experience, in which the focus is only on the wrongdoing.

However, it is also evident that many teachers feel confident and
secure in the process, appreciate the benefits for both learning and
relationships and are confidently undertaking effective restorative
conversations (Matla, 2009). One teacher went so far as to say she
found that punitive measures were "useless for relationships" (p. 25).
This bears out Morrison's (2007) finding that authoritative, human-
istic and democratic approaches favour both student and teacher.

Just as effective conversations leave students and teachers feeling
positive and engaged, ineffective conversations leave them feeling
alienated, disaffected and often more angry:

My restoratives [conversations] are threatening. (Student comment,
Matla, 2009)

In repairing harm and damage to relationships, it is absolutely
imperative that no further harm is caused. Restorative conversations
need to be conducted well or not at all.

Teacher buy-in

Adopting a restorative approach requires considerable teacher buy-
in, and some schools face real challenges in adopting this approach.
For teaching staff with long service records and those who favour
authoritarian approaches, restorative conferences challenge the
order of things—the hierarchy between pupils and teachers. Such
conferences can be seen as handing power to young people and
allowing young people to challenge the teachers' sense of authority. In

a restorative school everyone is on the same level. This conflicts with an authoritarian mindset (Rout, 2007).

Students place importance on systems being applied consistently and fairly. Jansen (2008) concluded that restorative conversations are open to all sorts of inconsistencies because of the great disparity in teachers' skill levels, confidence and genuine willingness to have relationship-based conversations with students. The willingness of teachers to involve themselves, at times deeply, in the restorative process often determines the outcome of a restorative conversation. The adult has (or should have) emotional maturity and control, and will have opportunities within the dialogue to model these characteristics. This helps to build a student's self-esteem and to move them forward:

> Sometimes, if I've got a real hard one [situation], I apologise first because there is something about that that's role modelling ... [It's] a really powerful thing for them to see someone ... come down to them in order to bring them back up to you ... maybe something to do with letting the child have some mana. (Teacher comment, Matla, 2009)

Teachers who reflect on restorative practices see the process as being as much about them and their own practices as it is about any students and their behaviour. Ginott (1972) came to what he called the "frightening conclusion" that he, as the teacher, was the decisive element in the classroom:

> It is my personal approach that creates the climate. It is my daily mood that makes the weather. As a teacher I possess tremendous power to make a child's life miserable or joyous. I can be a tool of torture or an instrument of inspiration. (p. 6)

School culture

If a school's dominant culture is one of rules and punishment, then students, teachers and parents are disempowered to resolve conflicts in a nonviolent way (Cavanagh, 2007). This disempowerment increases the potential for harm and violence to occur. Morrison (2007) echoes this, and suggests that "zero tolerance" responses offer nothing more than bandaids on deep wounds, potentially exacerbating situations for many young people. He calls them "downstream responses to problems that have their genesis upstream" (p. 50). Success in education is much more likely when schools, parents, whānau and the wider community work closely together. When this happens, the relationships are characterised by respect and valuing of one another's voices, identity and culture. Success is fostered by a genuine sense of partnership, whereby the school, family and community can apply their collective skills and energies, as well as their abilities to support, encourage and enhance the learning of children (Fancy, 2000).

Te Kauhua Māori Mainstream pilot (Ministry of Education, 2004) highlighted the significance of developing caring and collaborative consultative relationships between teachers and students, students and students, teachers and teachers, teachers and whānau, and school communities and whānau. The pilot indicated that these are the keys to enhanced outcomes for Māori student achievement.

When there is a lack of understanding between schools and communities, frustrations and difficulties are likely to arise (Fancy, 2000). Where communities, families and schools feel powerless to engage effectively with each other, a child's enthusiasm for learning and achievement can be reduced. Unhappy consequences can appear later when it is more difficult to do anything about them. All relationships need to be supported and healthy for a functioning, connected learning community to operate.

In his investigations into degrees of satisfaction with the implementation of restorative approaches into schools, Rout (2007) found that restorative practices changed the way people did their jobs and their attitudes towards their jobs. It was not uncommon to hear administrators say, "I feel more confident that I'm really getting to the root of the problem … I feel as though by doing this I make better connections between students and teachers" (p. 11). Rout concludes his research with the assertion that restorative practice is not an approach that ignores unacceptable behaviour, or "treats it softly":

> It goes to the heart of what makes unacceptable behaviour 'unacceptable'—the harm it does to others. For me, the restorative approach provides a holistic means of challenging unacceptable behaviour in a fair and supportive way that encourages 'caring and seeing with the heart'. (p. 34)

Linking to core education business

Any implementation of a new strategy, approach, initiative or set of expectations within a school setting must be linked to the core business of that school. This means considering what effect it will have on the teaching and learning and educational outcomes of its students. In creating these links, the strategy becomes valid, meaningful and relevant to teachers, and not just one more initiative piling on top of an already burdensome workload.

Restorative processes are an ideal vehicle for promoting learning opportunities for the key competencies in *The New Zealand Curriculum* (Ministry of Education, 2007b). The restorative conversation, at the very centre of practice in a restorative school, is a prime tool for developing the key competencies. Students become an integral part of the learning process rather than outside observers of it. Behaviour management should be as much a part of the educational process as any other type of learning within a school (Hansberry, 2009).

The flow-on effect of quality restorative conversations on the wider school is also significant. Starbuck (2006) suggests that, in time, as children see their teachers speaking to pupils in a respectful and trusting way, they will also begin to resolve conflicts in this way:

> Talk to them and maybe they are feeling frustrated or maybe they were feeling disrespected or maybe they were feeling anxious so in a way I feel like I'm teaching them to be in touch with emotions to get the empathy otherwise they won't get the empathy and to move beyond the apology. (Pastoral dean comment, Matla, 2009, p. 4)

It is reassuring for many teachers to know that what they have believed in and practised for years has a name, and indeed delivers outcomes that include high rates of school achievement, low rates of reoffending behaviour, a sense of belonging in a community, and emotional literacy (Thorsborne & Vinegrad, 2004). Teachers have often reflected that their busy schedules and workload pressures get in the way of their good intentions. Restorative practices are not quick-fix solutions, but it is clear that time invested early, concerning misconduct or violations against others, is time well spent and can head off many hours of work later on.

Effective conversations

In this section the discussion focuses on the essence of restorative conversations, key considerations for their practice, strategies for building capacity and what is required to make restorative conversations work effectively.

Scripting restorative conversations

The restorative conversation is an approach based on four essential philosophical questions posed in dialogue when using a restorative approach:

1. *Tell the story: What happened?* This is the preparation, the groundwork, the establishing of what actually went on, but also some of the history. What sorts of things were going through people's minds when this happened? What was going on for you when you did this?

2. *Explore the harm: Who has been affected, and how?* This establishes who may have been affected by the incident or event—the ripple effect and its effect on others. How have they been affected? What was it like for them? This question begins the process of developing empathy towards others involved.

3. *Repair the harm: What do we need to do to put things right?* This starts a process of understanding obligations and liabilities involving both victims and wrongdoers. What does the victim need in order to feel safe?

4, *Move forward: How can we make sure this doesn't happen again?* This enables individuals to grow from the situation, to set positive goals, look into "best self" attributes and establish who can provide specific support.

The scripted approach to restorative conversations is based around these questions. It varies according to the school context and the organisation of its structure, but, to be effective, scripts should contain these four elements. An example of a script is shown in Figure 6.2, with some additional questions or prompts to help get to the essence or the aims at each stage.

1. What happened?
(tell the story)

What were you thinking at the time?
What have you thought about since?
What did you have control over?
If there was a video camera on the wall what would it have seen?

3. What do you need to do to put things right? (repair the harm)

What else might need to happen?
How will this help? Tell me more about this.
When can this happen?
What exactly are you saying sorry for?

2. Who do you think has been affected? (explore the harm)

Who else has been affected?
In what ways?
Was this fair or unfair?
Was this the right or wrong thing to do?
Tell me more about that...

4. How can we make sure this doesn't happen again? (move forward)

What do you need to do? What can I do to help?
What are your goals to help you move forward?
What are you going to do to reach these goals?
What other support do you need?

FIGURE 6.2 A SCRIPTED APPROACH TO RESTORATIVE CONVERSATIONS
Source: Matla and Jansen (2009)

Script cards, chat cards, bookmark scripts and corridor conversation cards are all formats widely and creatively used by schools using restorative approaches. Teachers can carry these easily in diaries, pockets or plan books, and they act as useful prompts and guides for conversations:

> The script keeps things calm and stops you going into lecture mode ... the questions help you stay on the issue and not let things get off track. (Teacher comment, Matla, 2009)

Building capacity

If any of the key considerations of preparation, participation and post-conversation follow-up are not given due attention, the whole process is undermined and the assertion will be made that "restorative doesn't work". As we saw in the previous chapter, perhaps one of the single greatest threats to the effectiveness of restorative approaches in schools comes from what Zehr (2002) calls the "gradual creep" away from authentic restorative standards, and the subsequent danger of removing the possibility for change, restoration and growth. To avoid this, teacher professional development must continually inform current best practice.

Teachers need negotiation and mediation training—at times for use among themselves. A school's restorative journey can start in the staffroom with connected, functioning, relationship-focused teachers. Professional development that enhances teachers' relationships will also benefit the student body. Teachers working restoratively need ongoing training, dialogue, monitoring and support to develop and maintain their restorative skills. Behaviour management should be consistent in its restorative approach and should avoid further harm.

Even when schools have a restorative philosophy, in many cases issues are still being dealt with punitively by individual teachers (Matla, 2009), with little support given to students for changes in behaviour. Students are removed from rooms with little or no warning, creating further hostility:

> There are more and more people saying 'well I gave them an instant referral'. They just let things build up to a point where it's 'right you are out' immediately. So there is huge heat there. (Teacher comment, Matla, 2009)

Having a chance to calm down, or having the ability to remain calm in the face of confrontation, is absolutely vital if a situation is to be dealt with fairly, and if a restorative conversation is going to make any difference. A teacher of English summed this up well by saying, "calmness removes heat from a situation".

A pre-emptive conversation is an informal "on the move" conversation between a teacher and student that takes place within the teaching environment. It is very much rooted in the teacher's own pedagogy and management of issues before they escalate. The focus is on accentuating positive behaviours while gaining time to reflect and think about the negative behaviours before more harm is done. Giving young people an opportunity to reflect and make choices is a vital stage in behaviour modification. It helps to avoid rapid escalation to punishment that causes such anger and backlash from young people (Braithwaite, 1989).

Many teachers want examples of effective restorative conversations and also the opportunity to reflect on some ineffective examples. Until the process is experienced and "felt" it remains difficult to explain and use in practice. The same is true for students, parents and whānau, where there is considerable opportunity to model and demonstrate the process to wider school communities. This helps to ensure everyone has a consistent understanding of the process, expectations and obligations. Restorative conversations can be very brief or may involve a significant amount of time. More importantly, the attitude and desire behind the dialogue must be clear to all participants. Genuine restorative conversations require participants to step away from "busyness" and into the "moment". The power, significance and opportunities to be had in a conversation of possibly only a few minutes cannot be underestimated.

Key considerations

The following summary recommends some key considerations to help ensure that restorative conversations result in effective outcomes within a school setting. Eight priority areas are provided for ongoing development based on the desire to work *with* children and young people, and using the framework of Wachtel and McCold's (2004) Social Discipline Window (see Figure 6.3):

1. *Establishing and building relational capacity*—professional development specifically designed to build relational capacity in the teaching staff, and to build and sustain good teaching and learning relationships with young people.
2. *Pre-emptive strategies*—making every effort to de-escalate and redirect behaviour before it becomes more damaging.
3. *Understanding the essence of restorative conversations*—having a good understanding of the restorative philosophy, including the four key underpinnings of a restorative conversation, and staying true to it in practice.

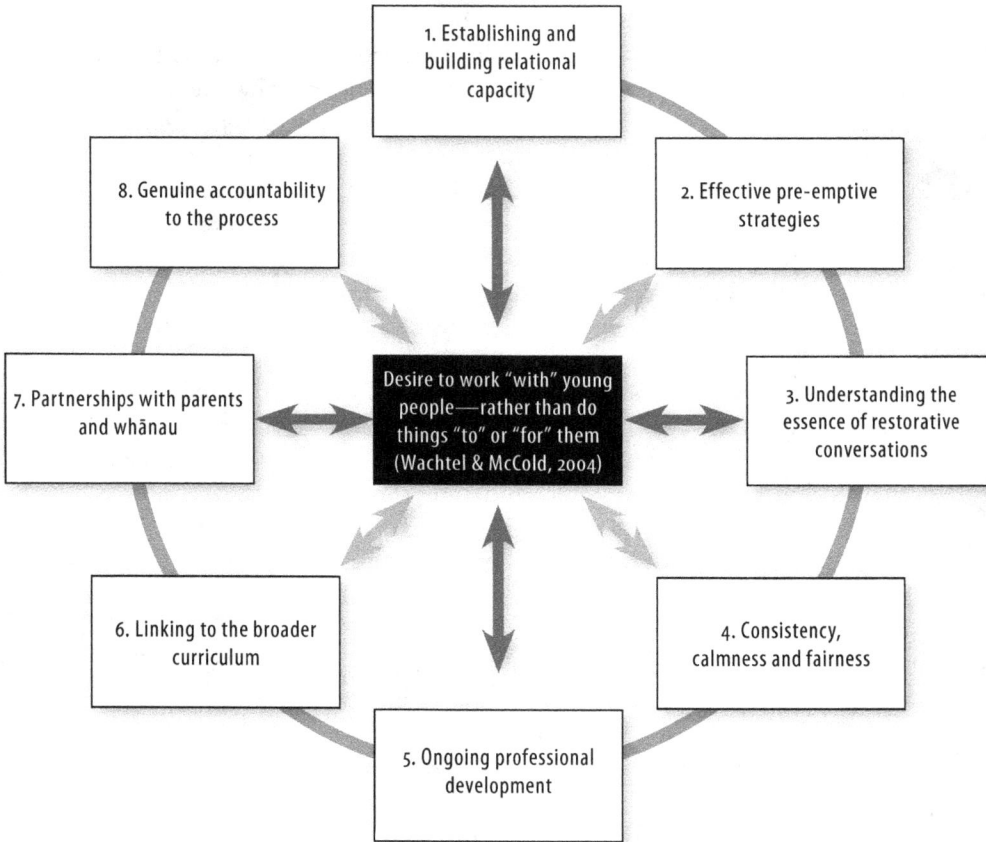

FIGURE 6.3 WHAT is REQUIRED to MAKE
RESTORATIVE CONVERSATIONS WORK?

Source: Matla & Jansen (2009)

4. *Consistency, calmness and fairness*—being committed to using the process fairly and calmly, and creating consistency in practice so that children and young people know where they stand.

5. *Ongoing professional development*—regular, practical professional development to help ensure restorative conversations and other approaches are consistent and effective. This is important for both teachers and students.

6. *Linking to the broader curriculum*—when the benefits to student learning and emotional development can be clearly established, teachers and senior educational managers have compelling reasons to work restoratively.

7. *Partnerships with parents and whānau*—involving parents and whānau in the restorative processes maximises the opportunities for long-term changes in behaviour.

8. *Genuine accountability to the process*—teaching staff are accountable for consistently following prescribed restorative systems, including pre-emptive strategies, restorative practices and follow-up supportive conversations.

Conclusion

Restorative conversations work effectively in school and early childhood education settings when they are well supported, and when the right environment and conditions are created. The benefits of using the process well reach far beyond repairing harmed relationships. The emotional development of children and young people is at stake. However, it is also apparent that there are inconsistencies in restorative practices. There is a real need for more support for teachers through ongoing professional development. Relationships between students and teachers remain central to effective conversations, and every effort to build and enhance these relationships needs to be made.

Restorative conversations require consistent application at all times, and those involved should be accountable. Students' innate sense of injustice is heightened by inconsistencies in practice. Ineffective restorative conversations are potentially worse than no conversation. If schools wish to sustain paradigm shifts in behaviour management, then they must address, in a fundamental way, the beliefs and practices of many teachers whose behaviour management is based on control and the use of punishment and other practices to achieve compliance (Thorsborne & Cameron, 1999). Pre-emptive and supportive restorative approaches are important for helping students to take responsibility for their actions and for avoiding a rapid escalation to punishment (Braithwaite, 1989).

Students are often criticised for not embracing the restorative process. This may well be the case, but education leaders need to ensure that teachers and senior managers are providing the best environment and processes in which successful, effective restorative conversations can take place. These are features that schools and early childhood education services have control over, and they have the ability to ensure their setting is a restorative context in all respects.

We must take each conversation seriously and see the opportunities for tremendous healing, development and growth of all those involved. Each conversation has the potential to turn people and events around (Macfarlane et al., 2003)—not frighteningly, but firmly and fairly. Each conversation should constantly search for ways of going forward and ways to develop new directions. Scott (2002) suggests that although no single conversation is guaranteed to change the trajectory of a career, a relationship or a life, any single conversation can. The heart-to-heart conversation is not *about* the relationship. It *is* the relationship.

References

Bishop, R., Berryman, M., Cavanagh, T., & Teddy, L. (2009). Te Kotahitanga: Addressing educational disparities facing Māori students in New Zealand. *Teaching and Teacher Education: An International Journal of Research and Studies*, 25(5), 734–742.

Braithwaite, J. (1989). *Crime, shame and reintegration*. Cambridge: Cambridge University Press.

Cavanagh, T. (2007). *Focusing on relationships creates safety in schools*. Wellington: NZCER Press.

Fancy, H. (2000). *Better relationships for better learning*. Wellington: Learning Media.

Ginott, H. G. (1972). Teacher and child. New York: Macmillan.

Hansberry, B. (2009). *Working restoratively in schools: A guidebook for developing safe & connected learning communities.* Buderim, QLD: Inyahead Press.

Jansen, G. M. (2008). *Restorative: Is it worth the time and effort?* Assigned project 2008. Christchurch: University of Canterbury, School of Educational Studies and Human Development.

Matla, R. E. (2009). *What is required to make restorative conversations work?* Assigned project 2008. Christchurch: University of Canterbury, School of Educational Studies and Human Development.

Matla, R. E., & Jansen, G. M. (2009). *Restore: Restorative conversations bookmark.* Retrieved from http://www.restorativeschools.org.nz/resources

Ministry of Education. (2004). *Te Kauhua Māori Mainstream pilot.* Wellington: Learning Media.

Ministry of Education. (2007a). *Links to the new New Zealand curriculum.* Retrieved 10 June 2009, from http://nzcurriculum.tki.org.nz/the_new_zealand_curriculum/key_competencies

Ministry of Education. (2007b). *The New Zealand curriculum.* Wellington: Learning Media.

Morrison, B. (2007). *Restoring safe school communities: A whole school response to bullying, violence and alienation.* Leichhardt, NSW: Federation Press.

Pranis, K. (2005). *The little book of circle processes: A new/old approach to peacemaking.* Intercourse, PA: Good Books.

Rout, S. (2007). *Using a restorative approach in secondary schools.* Unpublished paper.

Scott, S. (2002). *Fierce conversations: Achieving success at work and in life one conversation at a time.* New York: Berkeley Publishing Group.

Starbuck, J. (2006). Introducing restorative justice into your school. Primary Leadership Today, 5, 4.

Thorsborne, M., & Cameron, L. (1999). *Restorative justice and school discipline: Mutually exclusive?* Paper presented to the Reshaping Australian Institutions conference, Restorative Justice and Civil Society, Australian National University, Canberra.

Thorsborne, M., & Vinegrad, D. (2004). *Restorative practices in schools: Rethinking behaviour management.* Buderim, QLD: Inyahead Press.

Wachtel, T., & McCold, P. (2004). *From restorative justice to restorative practices: Expanding the paradigm.* Paper presented at the International Institute for Restorative Practices conference, Bethlehem, PA.

Zehr, H. (2002). *The little book of restorative justice.* Intercourse, PA: Good Books.

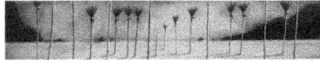

7.

Hui Whakatika: Indigenous Contexts for Repairing and Rebuilding Relationships

Mere Berryman & Sonja Macfarlane

Introduction

The sustained marginalisation of indigenous knowledge within colonial education systems has led to historical and entrenched disadvantage for many indigenous peoples, including Māori in New Zealand (Smith, 1999). In searching for more appropriate responses, Bishop (1996) and others (Berryman, 2008; Walker, 1987) contend that rather than search for solutions within the colonial culture that has traditionally marginalised them, Māori can locate solutions from within their own culture. The hui whakatika process (traditional meeting to resolve issues), which is underpinned by traditional Māori concepts of discipline, is one such approach that has been shown to achieve positive and enhanced outcomes for Māori. There is also a great deal of anecdotal evidence to indicate that this process is equally effective for non-Māori.

The roles and experiences of a non-Māori principal and a Māori resource teacher for learning and behaviour (RTLB) are presented as a case study later in this chapter. They have worked collaboratively with whānau members in schools to "repair and rebuild relationships" through the hui whakatika process. These professionals have found this process to be especially effective because it enables Māori cultural constructs and principles to be applied in order to develop culturally responsive and appropriate relationships of respect and trust (Ritchie, 1992). Their experiences illustrate how indigenous Māori solutions can provide relevant and effective responses, as well as enhancing the lives and experiences of all participants.

Links to the past

The Treaty of Waitangi (Te Tiriti o Waitangi), signed in 1840, still influences, to varying degrees, the lives of all contemporary New Zealanders. As our country's founding document, the Treaty promised partnership, power sharing and self-determination for both the nonindigenous (the nonindigenous European settlers—Pākehā) and indigenous Māori populations. However, many social commentators continue to report that interactions between these two groups have resulted in "... political, social and economic domination by the Pākehā majority, and marginalisation of the Māori people" (Bishop & Glynn, 1999, p. 50). Notwithstanding the challenging sentiments inherent in this statement, these dual aspects have (over time) perpetuated inequitable social, educational and economic outcomes for many Māori. Further, the historical marginalisation of Māori knowledge, language and culture continues to assert negative consequences on the status of Māori today, despite the recent renaissance of these cultural treasures (Bishop & Glynn, 1999; O'Sullivan, 2007; Smith, 1999). Clearly, contexts that maintain power imbalances, and enable cultural deficit explanations (victim blaming) for low performance only serve to pathologise Māori. Thrupp (2008) declares that these pathology interpretations maintain ongoing discourses about the Māori cultural minority status and therefore preserve power over what is determined to be pedagogy and knowledge in many classrooms attended by Māori students (Bishop & Berryman, 2006; Bishop, Berryman, Cavanagh, & Teddy, 2007; Bishop, Berryman, Tiakiwai, & Richardson, 2003; Shields, Bishop, & Mazawi, 2005).

Facilitating equitable power relationships between both treaty partners (i.e., where neither partner assumes dominance over the other) is one way of enabling social and cultural expression for Māori (Moeke-Pickering, Paewai, Turangi-Joseph, & Herbert, 1998; O'Sullivan, 2007). In more recent times this has involved redress and compensation for Māori in terms the historically unlawful confiscation of land. It has continued through government legislation which reflects the true tenets of the Treaty of Waitangi principles, along with successive educational policies and initiatives that have promoted (and not dismissed or maligned) the unique quality and status of Māori language and knowledge (Bishop & Glynn, 1999; Consedine & Consedine, 2005; Ministry of Education, 2008). Clearly, many past government educational policies which were aimed at assimilation, integration, multiculturalism and biculturalism, resulted in Māori sacrificing more and more of their own indigenous knowledge, educational aspirations, culture and language to the needs and goals of the mainstream. Sadly for many Māori, participation in mainstream education in New Zealand has come at a cost to their own culture and language (Bishop et al., 2003; Bishop & Glynn, 1999).

Kaupapa Māori solutions

Reclaiming Māori space and seeking to work with solutions that are informed by the wisdom of traditional Māori epistemology is "a way of decolonising the mind and is a critical part of recreating, restructuring a national and cultural consciousness" (Mead, 1997, p. 11). As Freire suggests, "just as the oppressor, in order to oppress, needs a theory of oppressive action, so the oppressed, in order to become free, also need a theory of action" (1996, p. 164). Kaupapa Māori (an understanding from within a Māori world view; ways that are Māori) theory suggests that reconnection with one's own heritage enables greater opportunity and ability to reclaim the power to define oneself (Bishop, 2005; Durie, 1997; Smith, 1997; Smith, 2008) and, in so doing, to define solutions that will be more effective for Māori, now and in the future.

A powerful example of where Māori have been instrumental not only in helping to define the challenges but also in delineating the solutions is family group conferencing. This revolutionary initiative is acknowledged as having started in New Zealand as part of the enabling of provisions in the 1989 Children, Young Persons and their Families Act (Raye & Roberts, 2007). The overrepresentation of Māori in government support systems and agencies motivated the New Zealand Department of Social Welfare to support a ground-breaking piece of legislation, which aimed to draw on the capacity of whānau Māori (extended family connections) to respond to problems related to events involving wrongdoing and conflict. Despite this legislation, and the ensuing use of family group conferencing being based on a report by respected Māori in New Zealand (Ministerial Advisory Committee on a Māori Perspective, 1988), the connections to Māori are no longer commonly acknowledged.

Whānau is now often described as "family", and the underlying principles of the Act, as discussed by Graveson (2008), are that:

- if the family can sort out the situation, then let them
- if the family lacks the capacity to do this, then let extended family and community assist them
- keep professionals and formal interventions out of the picture as much as possible
- only use formal interventions or experts as a last resort (adapted from Graveson, 2008).

Clearly, these principles fail to acknowledge the indigenous milieu of the Act. Restorative justice, like family group conferencing, is an approach that focuses on "putting things right" between all parties involved or affected by wrongdoing. It also seeks to address the problems that have resulted from unacceptable, unsociable behaviours by harnessing the necessary resources that lie within the traditional values of communities. Such initiatives have shifted the focus away from placing the spotlight on either the victim or the perpetrator, to identifying the solutions that lie within whole communities (Hooper, Winslade, Drewery, Monk, & Macfarlane, 1999). In New Zealand, restorative justice is understood by many to be strongly influenced by traditional Māori cultural values and preferred ways of responding to wrongdoing that emphasise restoration of harmony between the individual, the victim and within the collective (Macfarlane, 1998). With this in mind, the Restorative Practices Development Team from the University of Waikato set out a number of guidelines for restorative practices in schools, based on research outcomes aimed at reducing student suspensions (Restorative Practices Development Team, 2003). According to this team, the aims of restorative practices in schools are to:

- address the problem
- encourage understanding of the effects of the offence on all individuals involved and on the school community
- invite the taking up of responsibility (not necessarily only by the offender)
- avoid creating shame and blame
- promote the healing of hurt
- open up avenues of redress
- restore working relationships between those involved
- include everyone (including offenders) in the community envisioned by the process rather than dividing people into insider and outsider groups. (p. 11)

The Restorative Practices Development Team declares that achieving restoration requires that harm done to a relationship be understood and acknowledged, and that effort be made to repair that harm. In order for that restoration to happen, the voices of those affected by the offence need to be heard in the process of seeking redress. In addition, given the understanding that in pre-European times meetings to resolve issues, or hui whakatika, were conducted according to the protocols and customs of individual tribes, the Restorative Practices Development Team outlined the following processes of a restorative conference as "culturally appropriate" for use with Māori:

1. As appropriate, a conference will begin with karakia (traditional chants or prayers), and mihimihi (greetings and introductions), which acknowledge the presence and dignity of all in attendance.
2. "The problem is the problem; the person is not the problem" is written on the board or is spoken about.
3. What are you hoping to see happen in this hui? Each person has a chance to speak.
4. What is the problem that has brought us here? People tell their own versions.
5. What are the effects of that problem on all present (and others)?
6. What times, places and relationships do we know of where the problem is not present?
7. What new description of the people involved becomes clear as we look at the times and places where the problem is not present?
8. If there have been people/things harmed by the problem, what is it that you need to happen to see amends being made?
9. How does what we have spoken about and seen in the alternative descriptions help us plan to overcome the problem? People contribute ideas and offers of resources that help to overcome the problem.
10. Does that plan meet the needs of anyone harmed by the problem?
11. People are given responsibility to carry each part of the plan forward, and follow up is planned.
12. Karakia and thanks. Perhaps an offer of hospitality. (Restorative Practices Development Team, 2003, p. 20)

In order to better understand hui whakatika, the writers of this chapter worked with Māori elders. Together they identified pōwhiri (traditional formal rituals of encounter) as a cultural construct to better understand the need to form relationships when seeking to move into Māori spaces and to engage with Māori in activities such as traditional hui whakatika.

Pōwhiri

Spaces of encounter

Durie (2006) argues for the importance of the notion of "space" within formalised cultural rituals of encounter such as pōwhiri, whereby a realistic degree of distance is necessary at the outset until a relationship has been sought and formed. He contends that acknowledging a level of distance provides an effective arena for clarifying the terms under which parties come together and engage. Diminished distance may precipitate fear and panic, or lead to withdrawal, either of which would have a negative impact on the processes that are essential for building relationships and establishing engagement.

Understanding the concept of the "boundaries" within these spaces of encounter requires making the necessary distinctions between groups at the level of whakapapa (genealogical connections); that is, between the tangata whenua (hosts) and manuhiri (visitors); the living and the dead; men and women; the old and the young. These rituals of encounter highlight the importance of interdependence, and the interconnectedness of the roles and responsibilities of those who open the procedures through speechmaking and waiata to those who undertake all aspects of hospitality.

Appreciation of these distinctions enables mutually respected boundaries to be defined without pretence, and can provide a platform upon which respectful connections and subsequent engagement may emerge. Within these spaces, adhering to the domain of "time" means that being on time is less important than allocating, taking or expanding time in order to ensure that processes are completed properly.

Pōwhiri, or the less formal ritual of engagement (the mihi whakatau), are essential for building relationships and inclusive practices across and between tribal groups and other groups of people. They can also serve as metaphors for building relationships across groups of people and across world views (Berryman, 2008; Glynn, Berryman, Walker, Reweti, & O'Brien, 2001). Some of the key purposes of pōwhiri are to greet the icons and images that represent the tribal places and ancestors as well as the people present on the day, and to *represent* oneself in a way that "makes sense" within a Māori world view. The orators exchange formal greetings, and in so doing draw on their extensive knowledge of genealogy to establish extended family relationships and other important connections between the two groups. The orators recognise and respond to the mana of the other party by acknowledging their ancestors and any of their members who have died recently. They also greet the living elders and all those who are present on each side (hosts and visitors).

Complementary to these speeches are the songs. Many of them draw on traditional Māori knowledge, carrying information to ensure cultural values and information are passed on to the generations that follow, while others serve to maintain contemporary knowledge and events from both cultures. Only after this process has been completed do the two groups move together to exchange a hongi, where people approach close enough to acknowledge each other, press noses and share the same breath of life. Refreshments are then shared, and only then are the two groups free to interact socially and work together on common tasks such as solving problems.

Pōwhiri, therefore, provide a powerful analogy of the process of inclusion based on respect of differences. In so doing they provide us with guidelines for establishing relationships (Berryman, 2008; Glynn et al., 2001) based on mutual respect and trust, with Māori able to maintain self-determination within these spaces.

Building on relationships

For Māori, the processes of reconnecting, maintaining and extending relationships (whakawhanaungatanga—exercising collective responsibility through engaging in family-like relationships), active during pōwhiri, are also kept alive in stories and cultural rituals that are operational during interactions in many other everyday Māori cultural contexts. As well as being active during rituals of encounter, whakawhanaungatanga can also be active during the sharing of food, caring for one another's children and the sharing and ownership of possessions. The Māori concept of sharing property and the concept of time reiterate the notion that there are culturally linked ways of thinking, feeling and acting that are acquired through socialisation (Glynn, Wearmouth, & Berryman, 2006; Phinney & Rotheram, 1987). Both of these concepts exemplify Māori theory because they encapsulate a "Māori way" of doing things (Smith, 1995).

These practices highlight the particular and unique ways that Māori have of relating to one another, of viewing the world and of making sense of what they see. Put simply, there are Māori-specific patterns of thinking and Māori-preferred ways of doing. Durie (2007) posits that there are two main patterns or types of human thinking: centrifugal (outward thinking) and centripetal (inward thinking). Centrifugal thinking may be better understood by using the analogy of a telescope as it focuses on looking at the wider ecology. Centrifugal thinking can also be described as ecological, whereby understanding is gained through having a better awareness of the wider contexts and connections, where similarities convey the essence of meaning.

Conceptualisations that seek to include all of the people with whom one shares connections are fundamentally Māori, and inform the systems (processes and activities) used by Māori. Centrifugal thinking opens up potentially wide networks of support in which people understand their connections, and therefore their responsibility to care for and contribute to others.

Centripetal thinking, on the other hand, is reductionist and clinical in its focus, and can be likened to using a microscope. Understanding comes from the analysis of individual details and component parts such as inner thoughts and feelings. Centripetal thinking focuses on outside expertise determining the situation and then defining the roles and responsibilities of others. Informed by Western conceptualisations, centripetal thinking is fundamentally in direct contrast to how Māori interpret, make meaning and respond in their world.

A conceptual framework

For many Māori, the same rituals of engagement as those used during the pōwhiri can be used as a conceptual framework during other situations or contexts of encounter. Guided by notions of space, boundaries and time, as well as by roles and responsibilities, the phases of this conceptual framework broadly include:

- starting/opening rituals (which include respecting space and boundaries at the outset, and determining who speaks and when)
- clarifying and declaring who you are and where you have come from, building relationships and making initial connections
- clarifying and declaring intentions (which often includes raising the purpose of the meeting)
- coming together as a group
- collectively addressing the particular agenda or issue (kaupapa), which includes open and frank discussions, face-to-face inter-actions, reaching decisions and agreements, defining particular roles and responsibilities and taking the time that is required to do this
- seeking closure, which includes summarising decisions and agreements, and the uplifting of mana.

Pōwhiri, as a conceptual framework, is founded on and champions relationships as the foundation for the work of searching for and developing new and shared understanding (Smith, 2008). We have learned that hui whakatika incorporate Māori cultural principles and processes, contextualised within the same phases of engagement that are established through pōwhiri. The following four concepts from traditional pre-European Māori discipline also underpin hui whakatika:

1. *reaching consensus* through a process of collaborative decision making involving all parties
2. *reconciliation*—reaching settlement that is acceptable to all parties rather than isolating and punishing
3. *examining* the wider reason for the wrong, with an implicit assumption that there is often wrong on both sides—not apportioning blame
4. having less concern with whether or not there has been a breach and more concern with the *restoration* of harmony (Olsen, Maxwell, & Morris, as cited in McElrea, 1994)

These features are central to an effective hui whakatika. They ensure that those present listen to the concerns of all in ways that maintain the appropriate cultural protocols, and in ways that are responsive to the concerns and potential responses of all. As such, hui whakatika can continue to guide contemporary Māori and wider society when responding to issues of concern or conflict. This framework is now illustrated through the experiences of a non-Māori principal and a Māori RTLB as they work collaboratively with whānau Māori to "repair and rebuild relationships" through the hui whakatika process.

Case study: Hui whakatika

The principal of a decile 1 school, where 98 percent of the students are Māori, agreed to share the use of hui whakatika at his school.

> We've been using what they call hui whakatika for a number of years, because the most important thing, if kids have an argument or even a fight, if that occurs no one can undo what happened. We often regret and we wish it didn't happen, but we can't undo it so the most important thing to do is repair and rebuild the relationship between the kids who have had the disagreement or fight. Sometimes that takes time, other times you can do it very quickly.

He talked briefly about what was more likely to have happened in the past.

> Traditionally we would probably have used suspension ... you know that sort of approach. Have a formal board meeting. I can't remember when we had the last formal board meeting for suspension. We have had suspension in our school. We've moved away in the last two and a half years to try to not have them because [we have found] usually you can have a hui whakatika instead.

Then the principal described a time when the school had successfully used hui whakatika to resolve a situation involving challenging behaviour.

> We had one last year, a big kid at our school who was a big Year 8 and he was a bully. He was huge. He was the biggest kid in the school and he was bullying this other kid in his class. Anyway one day he went along and he pulled his [the other student's]

chair out and the kid fell on his tail-bone and he got hurt and then he picked him up by his neck and then he wrung his neck and laughed ... this kid was not a nice kid ... we thought this was getting to the serious stage so we arranged for a hui ... The teacher reported back to the DP [deputy principal] and he initiated it, and the RTLB facilitated it.

Both RTLBs based in the school [one Māori, the other non-Māori], whose involvement in the community was long standing, visited the families concerned. They explained the situation and invited all parties concerned to attend a hui whakatika, explaining that the intention of the hui was to address the situation by restoring both the relationship between the students and safety to the class and school. Given the serious nature of the incident, both families agreed to come. The principal explained how the hui took an interesting turn when the father of the victim came forward.

The father of the victim spoke to this kid and said, 'Mate, I know exactly where you are coming from, I know my son can be a bit of a smart-ass'— he didn't try and say his son was perfect—'but he doesn't deserve to be treated like that.' He said, 'I used to treat people like that', and I didn't know this, but this dad, the father of the victim, had been in and out of prison for quite a long period of time. He said, 'Look at this' [the father showed the boy his tattoos]. 'I did this when I was in [such and such prison] and I was doing exactly what you did. I thought it was okay. It wasn't.'

Then anyway... the bully started crying and the father said, 'Mate, you know I can see a lot of me in you and if you really need to take up an interest, I do a lot of hunting. If you'd like to come hunting with me you are more than welcome. Come up and stay at my place, but the most important thing I want you and my boy to get along.' And he wasn't suspended or stood down or all of that.

The principal was then asked to reflect on the outcomes.

What really affected the bully was he thought because the victim was probably the brightest kid in the school that he had come from a pretty easy background ... that he had a pretty privileged sort of life. This kid had not had this privileged sort of life, but the fact that the bully had a much more pleasant and spoilt life than the other guy, and he saw that, and he also saw that this father was forgiving. Those kids, they didn't end up being best buddies but they really gained a huge amount of respect and they were very pleasant to each other for the rest of the year and hopefully that will continue.

He reflected on another hui whakatika that had left a lasting impression on him.

I can remember one kid, his old koro [grandfather] was there ... he was the most emotional one [in the hui] because he was so gutted that his moko would do what he did. He was gutted and it was his own koro that really got through to that kid. It was just him crying and being a blubbery mess really that was the thing that was most powerful. It had everybody else teary-eyed to a certain extent. So it's okay to show anger and that, but if we do it in a controlled and supported way it's okay, it's okay to be angry with people ... it's what we might do sometimes when we have been badly hurt like this. But at the hui whakatika we're demonstrating and modelling to people too how we can ... like I can tell Mere that I'm pissed off with her without belting her or hurting her and all that. So the hui before the hui sort of sets the tone for that ... for what you want to say. You know you can go through it ... but we can go to the hui with a view to repairing and rebuilding the relationship.

He then talked about how these hui begin.

Well he [the Māori RTLB] would begin with a karakia, with a mihimihi to everyone, and then he would outline the kaupapa—it's actually quite formal the order of speaking. The hui before the hui have already been held and [it's] sort of agreed that if you are the perpetrator that at this hui you've gone there because you are willing, you wish to repair and rebuild. So you're not being forced here; if you don't want to go that way, we don't go that way, but in the hui whakatika you are there to repair and rebuild. So there is an admission of your guilt and an apology for your behaviour. It's not a punitive thing, it's not that. There could possibly be a consequence, an agreed consequence through consensus if they deem that necessary, but mainly the focus is on, let's repair and rebuild the relationship between the two parties ... and it's okay for mum and dad and the victim to be angry at the behaviour and that's part of it, that's a huge part of it. We want them to be emotional and show their hurt so that the perpetrator sees … I didn't just hurt Sally over there, I hurt mum and her nani and her uncle. They're all crying … and I feel bloody terrible.

Their guilt in doing wrong and witnessing that emotion is probably what's going to hopefully change their behaviour to make them think, 'If I do that there I don't just hurt that person, I can actually hurt a lot of people, and their own parents will be hurt as well'.

The principal was then asked to consider the implications of hui whakatika on others.

I honestly believe most people believe in hui whakatika or restorative practices because we know it works, but it's the time that it takes to do that and to get both parties to be willing participants. It's not for all, because some still believe the punitive approach works. [Some say] 'I got caned at school. It didn't change my behaviour. I just didn't do it in front of the teacher.' You know … you just make sure you didn't get caught.

He talked about the skills required to facilitate hui whakatika.

They've got to be a very good communicator; in our case you've got to be bicultural and bilingual. You know, really bicultural and bilingual. I think this really helps because we're 98 percent Māori. [Our Māori RTLB] is quite unique and he makes people of all cultures feel very safe. I think he has got that ability like he's very much aware of the people around here … I actually think that they appreciate his biculturalism. He makes them feel very comfortable."

He suggested that an RTLB such as this can be a valuable resource in the facilitation of hui whakatika.

He is very skilled at facilitating hui whakatika, or restorative hui, and he's getting better and better at it, he's more and more confident. We see that as a big part of their job as well because they have the time to have the hui before the hui to go see the parents … if you're going to have the hui with quite a few young people together it's actually very time consuming. You have to have the meetings before the meeting to make sure that we all understand and agree to the processes. So that's been a new role the RTLB have taken on and agreed upon by our cluster of schools. We're the only school that's regularly using them to date, but the other schools are at the beginning stages. That will grow and I'm sure, given time, they will be more widely utilised on a regular basis.

The principal spoke of a personal incident that had highlighted for him the importance of relationships.

It comes back to relationships. I can think of myself where I had a heated argument with another colleague, a person from a different school, and it was over nothing to do with school actually. Anyway we had this argument, we agreed to disagree. We both probably said things we shouldn't have and the next time we saw each other I said, 'Ooh sorry mate.' He said, 'Yeah, gees we got a bit carried away.' And that was the end of it, but we actually felt better because we are friends, we shouldn't have had that sort of argument, we're adults, but we did. We knew that saying sorry to each other was the right thing to do, and I think with our kids we've got to model all that. The adults must say sorry. If we don't say sorry and model that, we can't expect kids to do it.

I hope that when kids come into my office they know I'm not going to shout at them and I'm not going to rant and rave at them. They know that, even our most challenging kids, they'll happily come into the office with me because at least they know I'm not going to do that. They might not like me contacting mum and dad because I need to see them, but they know they don't see me as a threat to their safety and that's important. And they should feel the same with their teachers.

He concluded that during the transition to secondary school, relationships with students might be more vulnerable or more challenging for teachers to establish and maintain for various reasons.

We teach the kids for a number of years and I think that, as primary teachers, we realise that the relationship is really important. That I'm not going to engage this student unless I have a relationship with them and that's one of the advantages our system has where we teach them for 25 hours a week. One of the disadvantages: okay we may not be the specialist teacher like in science, we may not have the individual knowledge about the content of certain curriculum areas ... I agree with that ... or the expertise to necessarily deliver science well or maths as well as a maths specialist. I can see the pluses and minuses on both sides, but the one thing we do is we give ourselves time to form a relationship.

The principal specifically acknowledged that timetables might present challenges for secondary school teachers in terms of building relationships with challenging students.

Little 50-minute or 1-hour blocks you just don't have time to build on the relationship, you just don't spend enough time together. You don't get to know each other ... I know they're going to leave here and they're going through the terrible 14, 15 age group where most parents will tell you it's quite a testing time but even more reason to get to know each other because it is going to be a testing time.

Conclusion

Hui whakatika are neither widely understood nor commonly used in mainstream schools. However, the writers of this chapter have participated in a number of successful school and/or iwi-based hui whakatika. The Māori RTLBs in these schools sought to engage with Māori families in ways that are considered to be more culturally appropriate. They did this by drawing from *culturally appropriate* Māori ways of knowing and engaging within their work, and also by ensuring that their colleagues listened to and were *culturally responsive* to Māori families. In doing so, the Māori families were able to bring their own cultural experiences and expectations to the work being undertaken (Rangihau, 1977). These Māori RTLBs utilised and implemented their cultural expertise and knowledge; factors that were integral to supporting Māori students who were challenged by learning and/or behaviour.

References

Berryman, M. (2008). *Repositioning within indigenous discourses of transformation and self-determination.* Unpublished doctoral thesis, University of Waikato, Hamilton.

Berryman, M., Bateman, S., & Cavanagh, T. (2008). *Indigenous knowledge: Responses to contemporary questions*. A paper presented at the Traditional Knowledge conference, Te Tatau Pounamu The Greenstone Door: Traditional Knowledge and Gateways to Balanced Relationships, Auckland.

Bishop, R. (1996). *Whakawhanaungatanga: Collaborative research stories*. Palmerston North: Dunmore Press.

Bishop, R. (2005). Freeing ourselves from neo-colonial domination in research: A kaupapa Māori approach to creating knowledge. In N. Denzin & Y. Lincoln (Eds.), *Handbook of qualitative research* (3rd ed., pp. 109–138). Thousand Oaks, CA: Sage.

Bishop, R., & Berryman, M. (2006). *Culture speaks: Cultural relationships and classroom learning*. Wellington: Huia.

Bishop, R., Berryman, M., Cavanagh, T., & Teddy, L. (2007). *Te Kotahitanga phase 3: Whakawhanaungatanga: Establishing a culturally responsive pedagogy of relations in mainstream secondary school classrooms*. Wellington: Ministry of Education, Research Division.

Bishop, R., Berryman, M., Tiakiwai, S., & Richardson, C. (2003). *Te Kotahitanga: Experiences of year 9 and 10 Māori students in mainstream classrooms*. Final report to the Ministry of Education. Wellington: Ministry of Education.

Bishop, R., & Glynn, T. (1999). *Culture counts: Changing power relations in education*. Palmerston North: Dunmore Press.

Consedine, R., & Consedine, J. (2005). *Healing our history: The challenge of the Treaty of Waitangi*. London: Penguin Books.

Durie, M. (1997). *Identity, access and Māori advancement*. Paper presented at the New Zealand Educational Administration Society (An Indigenous Future) conference, Auckland Institute of Technology, Auckland.

Durie, M. (2006). *Foundations for psychological and social interventions with Māori*. Paper presented at the Compass Professional Development seminar, Auckland Institute of Technology, Auckland.

Durie, M. (2007). *Māori concepts of well-being: Interventions, processes and outcomes*. Paper presented at the Compass seminar, Hamilton.

Freire, P. (1996). *Pedagogy of the oppressed*. London: Penguin Books.

Glynn, T., Berryman, M., Walker, R., Reweti, M., & O'Brien, K. (2001). *Partnerships with indigenous people: Modifying the cultural mainstream*. Keynote address at the Partnerships in Educational Psychology Conference Centre, Brisbane.

Glynn, T., Wearmouth, J., & Berryman, M. (2006). *Supporting students with literacy difficulties: A responsive approach*. London: McGraw-Hill.

Graveson, C. (2008). *Restorative justice and police youth aid*. Paper presented at the Bridge Between Practice and Research symposium, Auckland University of Technology Restorative Justice Centre, Auckland.

Hooper, S., Winslade, J., Drewery, W., Monk, G., & Macfarlane, A. (1999). *School and family group conferences: Te hui whakatika (a time for making amends)*. Paper presented at the Keeping Young People in School Summit Conference on Truancy, Suspensions and Effective Alternatives, Auckland.

McElrea, F. (1994). The intent of the Children, Young Persons and Their Families Act—Restorative justice. *Youth Law Review* (pp. 4–9). Auckland: Youth Law Project.

Macfarlane, A. (1998). *Hui: A process for conferencing in schools*. Paper presented at the Western Association for Counselor Education and Supervision conference, Seattle.

Mead, L. T. (1997). *Ngā aho o te kākahu matauranga: The multiple layers of struggle by Māori in education*. Unpublished doctoral thesis, The University of Auckland, Auckland.

Ministerial Advisory Committee on a Māori Perspective. (1988). *Puao-te-ata-tu (day break)*. Wellington: Department of Social Welfare.

Ministry of Education. (2008). *Ka hikitia: Managing for success. The Ministry of Education Māori Education Strategy 2008 –2012*. Wellington: Author.

Moeke-Pickering, T. M., Paewai, M. K., Turangi-Joseph, A., & Herbert, A. M. L. (1998). Clinical psychology in Aotearoa/New Zealand: Indigenous perspectives. In A. S. Bellack & M. Hersen (Eds.), *Comprehensive clinical psychology* (Vol. 3, pp. 349–355). Oxford: Pergamon.

O'Sullivan, D. (2007). *Beyond biculturalism: The politics of an indigenous minority*. Wellington: Huia.

Phinney J., & Rotheram, M. (1987). *Children's ethnic socialization: Pluralism and development*. Newbury Park, CA: Sage.

Rangihau, J. (1977). Being Māori. In M. King (Ed.), *Te ao hurihuri: The world moves on* (pp. 165–175). Auckland: Methuen.

Raye, B. E., & Roberts, A. W. (2007). Restorative practices. In G. Johnstone & D. W. Van Ness (Eds.), *Handbook of restorative justice* (pp. 211–227). Portland, OR: Willan.

Restorative Practices Development Team. (2003). *Restorative practices for schools*. Hamilton: University of Waikato.

Ritchie, J. (1992). *Becoming bicultural*. Wellington: Huia.

Shields, C. M., Bishop, R., & Mazawi, A. E. (2005). *Pathologizing practices: The impact of deficit thinking on education*. New York: Peter Lang.

Smith, G. (1995). Whakaoho whānau: New formations of whānau as an innovative intervention into Māori cultural and educational crises. *He Pukenga Kōrero Koanga*, 1(1), 18–36.

Smith, G. H. (1997). *Kaupapa Māori as transformative praxis*. Unpublished doctoral thesis, The University of Auckland, Auckland.

Smith, L. T. (1999). *Decolonizing methodologies, research and indigenous peoples.* London and New York: Zed Books; Dunedin: University of Otago Press.

Smith, L. T. (2008). *Research and data collection and analysis among indigenous peoples.* Paper presented at the American Educational Research Association annual meeting, New York.

Thrupp, M. (2008). *Secondary teaching, social contexts and the lingering politics of blame.* Keynote address to the New Zealand Post Primary Teachers Association Conference, Secondary Teaching on the Move, Auckland.

Walker, R. (1987). *Ngā tau tohetohe: Years of anger.* Auckland: Penguin Books.

8.

Restoring the Individual

Sonja Macfarlane, Angus H. Macfarlane & Valerie Margrain

Introduction

This chapter outlines a restorative practice approach that was applied to an extremely serious situation at a school. The entire process, which included a hui whakatika kaupapa Māori restorative conference (as outlined in Chapter 9), was implemented as part of a suite of restorative strategies. The objective was to focus on restoring balance, harmony and mana by looking at ways of responding to the behavioural challenges that were presenting, looking at ways to prevent particular behaviours from re-emerging and then moving forward. Restoration was therefore implemented in its entirety, both as a way of responding to immediate concerns and also as a way of preventing (or minimising) those concerns.

The case study is presented in a behaviour report format. This format reflects a multidimensional, ecological and holistic approach to unpacking and making sense of all of the factors that influence behaviour across different contexts. Pseudonyms are used for the individuals and school referred to in the case study in order to protect confidentiality, and the dates have been altered. The case study describes Tori, a Māori boy aged 11 and in Year 7 at school. The reason for referral to special education support services (SE) was physical aggression (hitting, punching and pushing other students).

Behavioural history: School narratives

Previous school behaviour and intervention history

Anecdotal evidence recounted how Tori had been resorting to physical aggression when he started school at the age of five years. This coincided with the time that his biological father left the whānau home. Before Tori's referral to SE he had been excluded from two schools and suspended and/or stood down from all the schools he had attended between the age of five years and the referral date.

At the beginning of February 2003, when Tori was five years old, he was enrolled at Primary School A. In March 2004 he was excluded for "continual fighting and aggression". Prior to the exclusion Tori had been stood down once and suspended once. He was then enrolled at Primary School B until September 2005, when he was again excluded for "continual fighting, aggression and non-compliance". This latter exclusion was preceded by two stand-downs. Tori was then enrolled at Primary School C and remained there until the end of 2008 (Year 6). During this time he was stood down twice and suspended once for similar behaviours.

At the beginning of 2009 Tori was enrolled at his current school, St Benjamin's Middle School, in Year 7. Soon after this (early in term 1), the Resource Teacher: Learning and Behaviour (RTLB) service had been engaged for a period of 18 weeks prior to the referral to SE. Following are some of the strategies that were implemented during that time:

- *Incentives*—receiving computer time at the end of each day for achieving specific goals. This was initially successful and was enjoyed by Tori. However, inconsistent follow-up and application due to classroom rotations meant that it was not sustainable.

- *Self-management*—taking voluntary time out. This had limited success due to the fact that Tori was required to manage and recognise his own "signals" when he was unable to do so.
- *Social skills teaching*—participating in a small-group social skills programme with three other students. This had minimal success because Tori did not enjoy it and refused to attend after three sessions. Teachers noted no improvement as a result of attending these three sessions, and records indicated he had attended several social skills training programmes in previous years.

Tori was stood down for the last week of term 2 (2009) for physical aggression towards another student and verbal abuse of a teacher, which initiated the referral to SE.

Classroom context at the time of referral

At the time of referral to SE, Tori's class teacher was Ms Harwood. There were 32 students in the class: 19 girls and 13 boys. Twelve of the 32 students (about 38 percent) identified as Māori. The students sat at their own desks in mixed gender groups of up to six. The teacher determined the groups, and these were changed twice a term. Tori had been placed on his own at the back of the room, well away from the rest of the students. The classroom was tidy, well organised and brightly decorated with students' art, mobiles and work. However, the room was very crowded, making movement between desks and around the room difficult, with students frequently required to move their chairs in order to make way for someone to move past.

Ms Harwood endeavoured to run a tightly structured class. She believed in being firm with students and having high standards and expectations. She preferred whole-class teaching strategies and expected students to follow instructions, listen and complete all work requirements. She preferred not to run any individual or class reward or reinforcement systems, believing that the students were "too old for those types of things by now". Consequences were applied when students were noncompliant or breached the class rules. These included time out, writing lines during breaks, detention or going to the principal. Observation indicated that these class rules were negatively framed and not consistently adhered to by the majority of the class, and that the consequences were arbitrarily applied.

The class rules were as follows:

1. No physical violence.
2. No put-downs.
3. No stealing other people's property.
4. No talking when the teacher is talking.
5. No moving around the room without the teacher's permission.

Classroom culture

The teacher mentioned that the students had not bonded as a team: there were small and distinct subgroups within the class, which were often in conflict. The groups also appeared to change from time to time. Ms Harwood was very concerned about the lack of cohesion within the class and admitted to becoming increasingly frustrated about the apparent "negative tone". This was displayed most commonly in the form of "put-downs" by and between students, often escalating into more serious verbal or physical altercations.

Ms Harwood said that she liked Tori but found it very difficult to understand exactly what triggered his outbursts. They appeared to be unprovoked, but she conceded that other students occasionally made faces at him or muttered quietly in his direction, and that she usually did not hear what they said. Ms Harwood stated that she usually tried to ignore some of the more minor "outbursts". However, she mainly dealt with them by talking firmly and directly to Tori and then leaving him to calm down. If that did not work she sent him to the principal. She believed that many of the students in the class were scared of Tori and avoided him as much as possible.

Ms Harwood stated that since placing Tori on his own at the back of the class the outbursts had reduced a little, which had helped her to manage the class as a whole. However, the playground incidents were still occurring regularly. Ms Harwood had been keeping anecdotal data on incidents. Classroom incidents were more likely to occur on a Monday or a Friday, and were also more likely to occur in rotation subjects (technology, art or physical education) when Tori was with other teachers. Playground incidents occurred most frequently during lunch breaks, and on most days. Not all incidents resulted in physical aggression because teachers were sometimes able to intervene, thereby avoiding escalation.

Tori said he disliked most of the teachers at the school because he believed that they "pick on me". He thought Mrs Patterson (the deputy principal) was "pretty good", and his teacher, Ms Harwood, was "OK sometimes". When asked whom he would rather talk to out of all of the teachers, he said "Mrs Patterson". Tori also mentioned that he really liked the caretaker because he would "speak to me nicely" and "have a joke with me".

Functional analysis

A functional analysis was conducted in order to identify the events that were controlling the emission and nonemission of the behaviour of concern (physical aggression) in the school setting. Intervention strategies could then be designed to meet Tori's needs. Physical aggression in this context was defined as any response towards another person that could cause physical injury or pain. This presented as:

- hitting with a closed fist or slapping with an open hand
- hitting a person with an object that could harm them
- pushing and shoving such that contact resulted in the other person falling down or into another person or object.

It also included *attempting* to do any of the above. The functional analysis required data to be gathering data so that the *course, rate* and *severity* of the behaviour of concern could be clearly established.

a) The typical **course** of the behaviour of concern

An episode of physical aggression was typically preceded by various common precursors, particularly unsolicited personal comments directed by others at Tori. These caused Tori to adopt a stare ("eye-balling"), whereby he would glare at the other student(s). Eye-balling did not always lead to physical aggression but was usually followed by some verbal banter, initially mumbled, between Tori and the other student(s). This verbal interaction would then evolve into further name calling and personal put-downs by others directed at Tori's physical appearance ("Fatman", "Jabba"). In all observations, name calling was not initiated by Tori.

He would then move towards the other student(s) and push them out of his way. In one classroom incident where Tori was the recipient of name calling, he got out of his chair and walked behind the other student, who was sitting at a desk. He shoved the boy in the back, saying "Get out of the way dick, I wanna get past." The other boy remained seated, bounced the chair back further and then swung his arm back, hitting Tori in the thigh. Tori punched him on the back of the head and the other boy then stood up, turned and punched Tori on the upper body. Ms Harwood intervened by yelling at them to stop, and Tori became verbally abusive. He then refused to follow any further instructions. The principal was sent for and Tori was removed from the class.

In a recent playground incident, a verbal interaction between Tori and another boy culminated in Tori being call "Fatboy". He appeared to ignore it and shook his head. He then sat down on a bench. Ten minutes later when the other boy was not looking, Tori walked up behind him and shoved him in the back, calling him names. He then kicked him in the leg. The other boy then grabbed Tori by his clothing, at which point a duty teacher intervened to prevent escalation. Tori was sent to the principal and later received a detention.

*b) The typical **rate** of the behaviour of concern*

The rate of physical aggression was three times a week in class and four times a week in the playground. Tori's mother reported that physical aggression occurred at least once a day at home during the school week, and regularly many times more (six plus) during weekends.

*c) The typical **severity** of the behaviour of concern*

Most episodes of physical aggression lasted from 20 to 30 seconds. A typical course from onset of precursors to onset of aggression was five to 10 minutes. The worst injury to another person was a split lip. Most episodes involved hard pushing and shoving.

Whānau narratives and realities

Whānau/family information

Immediate whānau members included: Tori's Mum, Gina; Tori's sisters, Missy, aged 13, and Tairoa, aged 10; and his brothers, Joey, aged 9, and Bradley, aged 3. Tori's biological father had not been in contact with Tori or his other three children (Missy, Tairoa and Joey) since January 2003, just prior to Tori's fifth birthday.

For four years, until early August 2009, Tori had a stepfather (Dave) who lived with the family. During this time Dave and Gina had the youngest child, Bradley. Tori did not have a positive relationship with Dave. The two were regularly engaged in conflict and were, according to Gina, often involved in physical and verbal altercations. She also stated that all four older siblings were in continual conflict with each other at home (both verbally and physically). Gina stated that physical and verbal punishment had been administered most often by Dave, and occasionally by her, to all of the children. Since Dave had left she had been unable to manage Tori in this way any more because of his physical size. Gina also mentioned that Dave regularly administered physical and verbal "punishment" to her in front of the children.

Tori's mother worked a night shift (12 AM to 8 am) on week days at a plastics processing factory, which enabled her to be at home to care for Bradley during the day when the other children were at school. She would sometimes manage to sleep in the afternoon if Bradley had a nap, or would otherwise wait until Missy or Tori got home from school. Tori mentioned that he liked taking care of Bradley while his mother was sleeping.

Tori and Gina agreed that they regularly argued and were in conflict. However, Tori spoke with much warmth about his Nan (grandmother), who lived close by. On several occasions he mentioned how much he enjoyed spending time with her and wished he could do it more often. It was clear they had a very close bond, which provided both with a much-valued source of warmth and affection.

Te reo me ōna tikanga Māori (Māori language, cultural beliefs and practices)

Te reo me ōna tikanga Māori was important to all members of the whānau. However, for quite some time there had been a degree of disconnection in terms of involvement in extended whānau, hapū (subtribe or clan) and iwi (tribe) activities. Gina stated that this was "like having a dark cloud hanging over the whānau", adding that "part of us is somewhere else all of the time". She believed that reconnecting would be very beneficial for everyone in the whānau, including going back to their marae (traditional meeting place) more often, listening to and participating in te reo, waiata and kapa haka (cultural performing arts groups). Apart from Tori's Nan, they did not have any other extended whānau close by or within the takiwā (district). Tori expressed a strong desire to resume kapa haka—an activity in which he had previously participated and enjoyed. Te reo Māori was not spoken to any large degree at home, although Tori was able to understand and converse very well in te reo Māori.

Ecological analysis: Classroom

An ecological analysis was undertaken to identify those characteristics of Tori's "behaving environment" that might have been influencing his overall sense of wellbeing. The analysis was undertaken to determine particular variables that might have been in conflict with, or were a mismatch for, Tori, and that were specific to the physical, programmatic, instructional and interpersonal environments of the classroom, thereby fuelling the referral behaviours.

Physical environment

As mentioned, the classroom setting was very crowded due to the size of furniture and the space required for 32 Year 7 students. There was limited space for quiet, solitary work. However, the classroom was reasonably well set out. Placing Tori at a distance from the other students, which reinforced a perception that Tori "did not belong in the group", was preferred. Despite the fact that Tori stated that he preferred this situation, it was clear that he actually longed to be a valued part of the classroom whānau, to work with others and to be accepted.

He was often seen drawing attention to himself (noises, looks, occasional agreement with others) in order to establish some form of connection to the wider group. It was also clear that while Tori remained isolated from his peers he was unable to interact with them, practise any pro-social skills or observe appropriate classroom kawa (rules). It was noted that this isolation had led to a slight reduction in the rate of incidents, and was also offering a little respite for the teacher and other students. However, this situation was not sustainable, nor did it encourage others to modify their individual (and collective) behaviour. It did not create an accepting, inclusive and cohesive classroom culture.

Tori was able to see and hear the teacher from where he was seated. However, his location at the back of the classroom provided many opportunities for eye-balling to occur because Tori was required to look past/through other students at all times. This also provided opportunities for students' comments to be directed at Tori that were not within earshot of the teacher standing at the front of the classroom.

Programmatic environment

Tori enjoyed art, cooking and technology, and he had strengths in these areas. These subjects were not taken in his home classroom, but on rotation two afternoons per week (Monday and Friday). Incidents frequently occurred during these subjects due to the lower level of structure and greater freedom of movement. They provided more opportunity for inappropriate interactions—and inconsistent management strategies—to occur.

Instructional environment

Two levels of noncompliance were identified in response to teacher instructions:

1 *Low-level noncompliance* (defined as refusing to begin work, objecting to an instruction, defiance, walking away when asked to remain, or refusing to participate in an activity). This was viewed by the school as manageable, albeit irritating and time consuming. Teachers indicated that Tori's intermittent low-level noncompliance was no greater than that of many other students in his class, and was not therefore seen as a severe concern.

Instructions were *less* likely to be followed when:
- they preceded a subject or activity that he disliked or found difficult
- Tori was unsure of or did not understand what was expected of him
- he was in an unstructured environment
- he was with teachers other than his home class teacher
- he was confronted by a teacher after an initial refusal.
  Instructions were *more* likely to be followed when:
- Tori was in his home class
- they preceded a task of interest to Tori, such as art, project work or maths
- there was more structure
- there was less noise and fewer distractions
- instructions were delivered in a quiet tone
- instructions were given on a one-to-one basis
- instructions were given in small and frequent steps, with intermittent follow-up by the teacher.

Tori reported that being confronted by a teacher amounted to "dissing me" (meaning that he lost face) in front of his peers, and that he had to "back down". In one observed instance, Tori refused to comply with an instruction at an initial request. When confronted and reprimanded firmly by the teacher in front of his peers, his determination and resolve to be noncompliant strengthened and escalated into high-level noncompliance (defined below).

2 *High-level noncompliance* (defined as noncompliance following an incident of aggression or confrontation, during which Tori was highly aroused, would yell, swear and refuse to move or remove himself as directed, and the incident was intimidating to teachers and students). Tori was only extremely noncompliant following an incident of physical aggression with one of his peers, or if directly confronted by a teacher. In this situation the noncompliance was seen as severe. His heightened state of arousal meant that he was not able to be reasoned with until he had taken significant time out and calmed down. Because incidents of high-level noncompliance always followed an incident of physical aggression they were not seen in isolation.

Interpersonal/self-management environment

Within this environment a number of antecedents or setting events associated with a higher likelihood of physical aggression were identified. These were when:

- Tori was not under the direct supervision of a teacher
- he was in a classroom other than his home classroom
- he had less structure and routine
- he had more freedom of movement
- he was unsupervised in the playground
- Tori was engaged in eye-balling with another student
- another student called him names that focused on his size.
- It was also noted that there was a higher likelihood of physical aggression occurring in the afternoons, especially on Mondays and Fridays.

Conversely, the following antecedents or setting events associated with a lower likelihood of physical aggression were identified within the interpersonal/self-management environment. These were when:

- Tori was under the direct supervision of a teacher
- he was in his home classroom
- he had greater structure and routine
- he had less freedom of movement

- he was supervised in the playground
- Tori did not have to look through or past the other students (thus avoiding the potential for eye-balling with another student)
- other students refrained from provoking him by calling him names.

It was also noted that there was a lower likelihood of physical aggression occurring during the morning sessions.

A further analysis was conducted to identify the reactions and management styles that contributed to and/or ameliorated the issues and concerns described above. This also focused on the effects the behaviours might have had on the immediate social and physical environments, on the possible function(s) served by the challenging behaviours and on the possible events that might have served to maintain or inhibit their occurrence.

Within the classroom setting Ms Harwood appropriately used a nonconfrontational management style with Tori. She generally tried to distract, ignore or redirect him. She also positioned Tori and the other children carefully within the classroom to give Tori "space" and to allow him to "save face". However, by isolating Tori from the wider group, the covert message was that Tori did not belong. He was therefore provided with limited opportunities to interact appropriately with others. Closer proximity for Tori would have provided greater opportunities to strengthen the teacher–student relationship, as well as the student–student relationships. It would also have required other students to be accountable for, and to manage, their own behaviours so that a class culture which included everyone could develop. Finally, it would have enabled the teacher to notice and respond to particular precursors at a very early stage so that swift intervention could ensue.

Observations indicated that classroom rules, expectations and consequences for transgressions were applied inconsistently. The variable management of inappropriate student movement around the classroom was a concern. No reward or reinforcement systems—either individual, group or whole-class—were in operation for appropriate behaviours or low rates of challenging behaviour.

Tori was required to attend detention for the more serious incidents of physical aggression but was unperturbed by this or by many of the other consequences that functioned within the school system. However, he disliked being sent to the principal because it meant that his mother had to be contacted and was required to come in to school after 3 PM, when she would usually be sleeping. This situation frustrated her immensely.

Cultural analysis: Te Pikinga ki Runga

A cultural analysis was undertaken that focused on a set of culturally relevant holistic domains, needs and characteristics—physical (tinana), personal/self-concept (mana motuhake), relational (hononga) and psychological (hinengaro)—so that Tori's overall wellbeing could be better understood and managed. It was important to consider the status of Tori's overall wellbeing—his sense of "whole-ness". The kaupapa Māori framework *Te Pikinga ki Runga: Raising the Possibilities* (Macfarlane, 2009), along with a set of reflective prompt questions, formed the basis of this analysis (see Appendix A). The following discussion uses the cultural framework and questions from Appendix A to guide the analysis of behaviour, including influences, potential responses and protection of the individual.

Mana motuhake

Tori believed that no one really liked, cared about or understood him. He disliked school because the work was either "boring" or "too hard". He also believed that the teachers picked on him and blamed him for everything, even when it was not his fault. He therefore felt misunderstood. Tori disliked many of the students because "they call me names", "they tease me" and "they wind me up". He therefore felt aggrieved that he (rather than the other students) was most often apportioned the blame. Tori was not able to talk freely about what transpired during a debriefing session immediately after an incident.

Tori stated that his mum "thinks I'm a bit mental", and this appeared to reinforce his view that no one understood him. He admitted to blaming his mother for a lot of the unhappiness he experienced when Dave (his stepfather) was around, stating "she let him give us the bash".

Hinengaro

Tori was generally a verbally quiet boy who preferred not to talk freely to others or to instigate conversation. It was noted in all observations and interactions with adults that Tori preferred to talk as little as possible. In a one-to-one situation Tori was very quiet, and initially would not offer or instigate any conversation, preferring to respond to conversations instigated by others, and with the minimum of words. Feedback, observations and interactions with Tori indicated that he did not use full sentences freely. He did, however, become a little more communicative with each meeting, and began initiating small pieces of conversation during the last couple of visits.

Tori appeared to be distanced from his peers, both physically and socially, most of the time. He was very rarely seen to smile and often had a frown or sombre expression on his face. This was the case across both home and school contexts. His āhua (appearance) appeared to indicate lack of interest and lethargy, suggesting that he might be tired. With his peers he preferred to use body language and noises to communicate his needs or feelings. He would often stare or move slowly towards someone in order to let them know he was angry. He would make noises (whistle, cough, etc.) if he wished to communicate his views on a subject, but when he was enraged he would yell and swear at anyone who annoyed him.

Learning assessments administered by the teacher indicated that Tori was performing well below chronological age levels in all areas. The latest running record indicated that he was reading at 7.5–8 years. He was also a reluctant writer, who found legibility, sentence structure, spelling and syntax challenging. He appeared to tire easily during any period of sustained writing that exceeded three minutes. Tori enjoyed maths and was working at curriculum level 2. He had his own programme running and enjoyed working from the national curriculum level 2 textbook with supplementary work sheets. He had yet to master the recall of his times tables or basic facts, preferring to use his fingers to count as well as referring to his times tables chart when doing basic computations. Tori showed an interest and talent in the areas of art and creative design, food technology, computers and maths. He seized any opportunity to participate in these activities.

Tori found most tasks involving reading and writing very difficult or challenging due to an instructional mismatch between the activities provided and his learning needs. He was acutely aware of how his learning and performance levels were perceived by his peers. In order to divert attention away from his ability to complete his work, he would often use the time to do something he preferred—to daydream, or to avoid or pretend to do the work. Clearly he enjoyed maths because he was working from a textbook which was at a suitable level for him and the supplementary work sheets were fun and easy, enabling him to experience success.

Hononga

Tori had difficulty maintaining and sustaining lasting friendships. In the playground he gravitated to other quieter boys of his own age who were also regularly excluded from the main peer group. He was occasionally seen and heard proffering agreement with other more popular boys as a means of seeking approval. However, these advances were usually met with disdain and rejection. He was not allowed to have friends over at his house because of his mother's shift work and was rarely invited to anyone else's place. He did state that he had no real friends, but said, "I don't care anyway".

Tori said he was often hōhā (annoyed) with members of his family, except his little brother, Bradley, who he described as "cool". He said he was glad his stepfather had left because he was "mean to all of us", and that he had liked being at home a lot more since his stepfather had gone away. Tori said he would like to do more interesting things during the weekends because they were usually "really boring". He preferred to occupy his time after school and during weekends by playing on the Playstation 2 or watching videos. He preferred indoor activities to being outside. He enjoyed cooking and looking after Bradley. Tori's mother said that he regularly bullied his other younger brother (Tairoa) and his sisters. She stated, "He needs help I reckon". She mentioned that she would like him to go to a "stricter school where they would teach him about not bullying".

Tori regularly experienced challenges in the area of positive interpersonal interactions and skill development. He did not have any close or long-term friends; all of his peer relationships appeared to be transient. Interpersonal dynamics between Tori and his peers were strained most of the time, and his physical outbursts appeared to be isolating him further from his peers. The same could also be said of his interpersonal interactions with most of the adults in his life. He had therefore experienced unsatisfactory interactions over a lengthy period. This had led to Tori developing a negative self-concept and low self-esteem because of the high levels of social and relational rejection he continually encountered from others.

Tinana

Tori was a large boy in both height and weight. He was often the target of ridicule about his weight, and confided in the SE worker that he found this infuriating and distressing, stating, "It pisses me off". At one interview he stopped talking, put his head in his hands and began crying quietly. After he regained control he explained how upset the teasing about his weight made him, and how this was the main reason for him getting angry with other students.

In late 2006 Tori had been diagnosed with attention deficit hyperactivity disorder (ADHD). He took Ritalin (methylphenidate) for this and was on two slow-release tablets (40 mg) in the morning. He had been taking this prescribed medication for almost three years. This was administered at home before going to school. Other than that, Tori's general health was reported to be good. He had good vision and hearing, and no medical issues or allergies.

According to Gina, Tori was a fussy eater. He did not like vegetables and would only eat peas and potatoes from this food group. He preferred fish and chips, bread, noodles, pasta snacks, spaghetti and baked beans. Tori also disliked any form of physical activity or sport. He would often opt out during physical education (PE) and was an unwilling participant in most school sports activities. He was not participating in any out-of-school sport.

The forms of Tori's physical aggression have already been described. In the classroom he would also sometimes resist moving out of other students' way if they needed to get past him.

Analysis of meaning

A picture was beginning to emerge based on the data that had been gathered via observations and conversations with key people. Tori's physical aggression appeared to be his learned way of reacting to perceived threats in his environment and a way of expressing his anger. Physical aggression seems to have initially been a response to a lack of knowledge of alternative ways to solve problems, and perhaps still was to some extent. The school's efforts to teach Tori anger management and conflict resolution did not appear to have moved him from cognitive knowledge and awareness to implementing the skills as part of an established behavioural repertoire. Although Tori seemed to show some impulse control (in that he did not always respond with physical aggression), he was more likely to resort to physical aggression when there was a lack of external controls by way of routine (e.g., structure, content, proximity to others, positive role modelling, class-wide and peer support) or the presence of an adult in authority.

Opportunities to practise pro-social skills and appropriate ways of resolving conflict, and to make friends, would have served to increase Tori's self-esteem and self-concept. They would also have changed his perception of his environment from one in which he felt he had to be on guard or on the defensive and where he did not feel that he belonged. In addition, the challenges Tori faced in almost all curriculum areas at school were being exacerbated by his weak sense of overall wellbeing.

At home, the use of physical discipline in response to (or to indicate disapproval of) Tori's and his siblings' actions and behaviours had perhaps been modelled as a means of problem solving. Tori had therefore learned to resolve the conflicts he was having with his siblings and others in a similar fashion. In order for successful opportunities to be provided in the home context, there would need to be support and assistance for Gina. This support and assistance needed to be organised by the whānau and whānau whānui (wider family).

It was clear that Tori responded willingly to opportunities to receive unconditional love, affection and nurturing, as reflected in the way that he related to and felt about his brother Bradley and his Nan. However, there appeared to be few occasions when he was the recipient of such things. A key source of "nourishment", which had been missing in his life for quite some time, was his connection with his papakāinga—the whānau whānui, the marae, the reo and the tikanga.

Responding to Tori's personal/self-concept (mana motuhake), psychological (hinengaro), physical (tinana) and social/relational (hononga) domains provided very real opportunities for proactive and positive change.

Restoration

Planning and preparation

The process of restoration actually began on day one of this case (Monday, 20 July 2009), when conversations with key people (from both school and whānau) were beginning and relationships were being brokered. It was therefore critical to gain commitment and buy in from the school and whānau in relation to a shared vision for Tori. This vision provided the platform for uniting individuals from different locations into a collective and mutual objective. The vision was simply: "We want to support Tori so that he feels valued and is therefore able to participate positively at school and at home."

This was managed through maintaining respectful engagement and reciprocal conversations by listening to key pieces of information, identifying individuals' strengths and preferences, being non-judgemental, forging links between the school and the home and communicating in timely and appropriate ways. Once again, *Te Pikinga ki Runga* (Macfarlane, 2009) was used to guide the process. The focus here was on opening doorways—working in partnership by engagement, communication and collaboration with whānau.

All parties agreed on the following eight points:

- Tori's needs were paramount.
- Tori was a young person who had a right to experience success and happiness.
- Tori had special strengths and skills.
- The current situation was unsatisfactory but not insurmountable.
- Something constructive had to happen very soon.
- It was everyone's responsibility.
- Everyone had something positive to contribute.
- Working together would be the best way to achieve positive outcomes for everyone.

Once the collective vision and agreements were established, it was agreed that a restorative conference—a hui whakatika—would take place. This was scheduled for Thursday, 6 August, at 3.30 PM. The date and time were selected so that:

- Tori could attend
- teachers could attend without worrying about classes
- key observations and conversations could occur across contexts
- all the key people could be invited to the hui, with enough time for them to organise their schedules
- all attendees would be fully informed about (and comfortable with) the hui process
- Gina could arrange care for Bradley during the day, to enable her to sleep after her nightshift, and therefore attend the hui feeling refreshed
- Thursday afternoon's class could be structured for Tori so as to ensure a greater likelihood of success (computer time, art, maths and helping the caretaker formed the basis of this plan)
- time could be expanded if necessary.

Hui proper

The hui whakatika was held at St Benjamin's Middle School in a room that was regularly used for hui and reflected many of the cultural icons of the local iwi. It was large and comfortable, and the seats had been arranged in a circle for everyone. A whiteboard was set up and a guitar was also on hand. Gina and Tori opted to bring along whānau support, including Tori's Nan, a whānau kaumātua (tribal elder) from their marae and an older cousin. The school was represented by Tori's classroom teacher (Ms Harwood), the food technology teacher, the deputy principal, the principal, the caretaker and the school kaumātua. SE were represented by the special education adviser case worker and an SE kaitakawaenga (cultural adviser). In all, 13 people attended the hui.

The school kaumātua began the hui with mihimihi and karakia in order to clear the pathway for the rest of the hui. The whānau kaumātua responded in te reo Māori, declaring the family's willingness to contribute and participate. The SE kaitakawaenga then briefly outlined the kaupapa and the intended flow of the hui. He then began the process of whakawhanaungatanga, whereby everyone introduced themselves and made a brief comment about what they hoped to achieve at the hui. Everyone then had a cup of tea and something to eat.

When they reconvened about 10 minutes later, those attending listened to everyone's stories and perspectives without interruption. Although initially quiet and shy, whānau members began to contribute more as the hui progressed. The hui worked from a strengths-based approach, in which positive perspectives and thoughts were shared. Honesty was also a key component, and people were encouraged to share how they were feeling as well as what they thought might be a constructive response. It was clear that the tone and energy of the group became positive as everyone listened to each other's issues and frustrations. Many affirming statements were shared that challenged several previously held assumptions.

People started offering positive and supportive comments, which became solution-focused. They also began to see where they might need to take more responsibility for their own attitudes and actions. There was an obvious willingness to remain respectful of each other and committed to the kaupapa. A list of possible actions was then brainstormed and collated, to be reconstructed into a more formal plan at a subsequent meeting attended by everyone. Tori was asked if he wanted to contribute any further comments or offer any more suggestions. He turned to his Nan, smiled and raised his eyebrows beckoning her to speak at that point. It was clear that he was happy. His Nan just said that she was feeling very humbled and grateful to everyone for looking after "our boy". It was agreed that they would reconvene to formulate the intervention plan the following Monday (10 August) at the same venue and time. The SE kaitakawaenga then summed up, everyone was given a final opportunity to comment and the whānau kaumātua concluded with a karakia.

Formulating the plan

The planning meeting followed the same process as the hui whakatika. Members of the group agreed that having the planning meeting after the weekend allowed them some time to reflect on the things that had transpired during the hui. It also enabled them to gain greater impetus and resolve to move forward. Tori's wellbeing was a priority—his sense of self-worth, his self-esteem, his identity and his mana. It was therefore agreed that a two-pronged approach would be taken at school: a targeted support plan for Tori (Ministry of Education, 2011), and a whole-class plan to encourage shared responsibility and support for Tori. Support for the whānau would also target parenting skills and activities that enabled reconnections to be made with wider whānau and hapū. Supporting Gina through a process of whakanoa/whakatika (to make something safe again and to correct or put right in order to restore calm and bring balance) within the whānau helped to ensure that relationships would start to heal.

A formal schedule of reinforcement incorporating these and other incentives would be designed at school to provide motivation for the *whole class* to manaaki (support) Tori, as well as to determine particular motivators for Tori's individual successes. Fundamentally, this involved setting up a plan for the whole class which included rewards accruing for observable collegial support, help and encouragement being provided to Tori. Tori needed to feel that he was valued by others, both at school and at home. By enabling and empowering the other students to share in the benefits and rewards that would accrue for them through encouraging and supporting Tori, there would be no real advantage or incentive for them to continue the current pattern of provoking him. This in turn would provide Tori with an increasing number of opportunities to experience positive interpersonal peer interactions, and therefore to "practise" more appropriate ways of relating and responding to others. By adopting a whole-class approach, including peers as supporters in the intervention programme, Tori would not have to solve the current situation by himself: the responsibility would belong to everyone. Physical aggression would hopefully be minimised. Tori would also require an individual education programme (IEP), targeted at his learning needs and strengths, to enable him to begin to enjoy the progress he was making with his learning and his successes (Ministry of Education, 2011).

Te Pikinga ki Runga (Macfarlane, 2009) was used again to guide the IEP planing for Tori. Appendix B documents the intervention plan, including a focus on participation in the curriculum by targeting the key competencies from *The New Zealand Curriculum* (Ministry of Education, 2007). A motivational analysis was conducted to identify those events, opportunities, activities and incentives that Tori preferred and enjoyed, and that might be used effectively as positive reinforcement in a well-designed programme. A key aim was to prevent and/or ameliorate any potential for negative behaviours to occur. The intervention plan in Appendix B summarises entertainment and social/cultural factors that were identified by Tori as motivational for him, proposed support strategies and the involvement of key people within the *Te Pikinga ki Runga* framework.

Providing Tori with opportunities to develop appropriate pro-social skills and self-management strategies would take time and concerted effort. All the key people were being asked to change some aspects of their own behaviour to better manage Tori's behaviour, and such adaptations could prove to be challenging. The success of interventions would ultimately depend on the commitment, persistence and stamina of those surrounding Tori and their ability to work as a team.

Follow-up and review

At the follow-up and review meeting on Monday, 30 August 2009, feedback from all parties was extremely positive. Tori had been much easier to manage at home as well as at school. He was becoming more engaged in learning and in the social interactions and activities of the classroom. Gina had been using some positive strategies at home and, with the support of Nan and the external agencies, Tori had earned several small rewards.

At school Tori was more settled and positive, and he was becoming a true member of his class and school. Only two minor incidents had occurred at school since the hui whakatika, and school staff said that both incidents had been easily dealt with. In mid-September that same year the case was transferred back to the RTLB service over a two-week period for monitoring.

Gina and Nan stated that they felt valued having a greater voice and involvement in Tori's education, and felt that they were now in partnership with the school. They believed that many invisible barriers had been broken down during the hui whakatika. School staff also stated that they felt more inclined to approach the parents and seek their ideas and perspectives in terms of Tori's learning and education, something they probably would not have actively done before the hui whakatika.

Conclusion

The restorative practice approach that was implemented in response to this challenging situation proved to be a powerful and proactive response that benefited Tori, his whānau and the wider community. The approach upheld the notions of acknowledging mana, showing respect, realising potential, facilitating collaboration, activating reciprocity and achieving consensus. Trust was established among the support group so that a shared vision drove the collective kaupapa (or purpose). In response to a critical situation, restorative practice was clearly able to achieve a positive outcome. The evidence speaks for itself.

References

Macfarlane, S. (2009). Te pikinga ki runga: Raising possibilities. *set: Research Information for Teachers, 2,* 42–50.

Ministry of Education. (2007). *The New Zealand curriculum.* Wellington: Learning Media.

Ministryof Education. (2011). *Individual Education Programme (IEP) guidelines.* Retrieved June 24, 2011, from http://www.minedu.govt.nz/NZEducation/ EducationPolicies/SpecialEducation/FormsandGuidelines/IEPGuidelines

Appendix A:
Te Pikinga ki Runga framework and questions

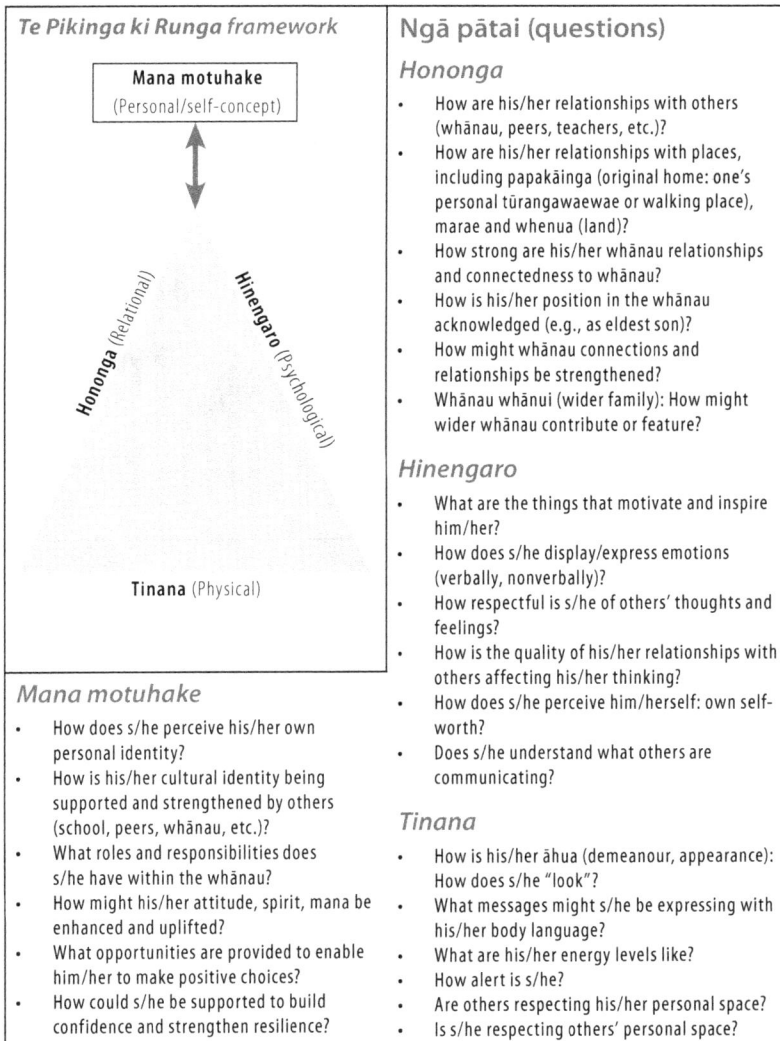

Te Pikinga ki Runga *framework*

Mana motuhake
(Personal/self-concept)

Hononga (Relational)

Hinengaro (Psychological)

Tinana (Physical)

Mana motuhake

- How does s/he perceive his/her own personal identity?
- How is his/her cultural identity being supported and strengthened by others (school, peers, whānau, etc.)?
- What roles and responsibilities does s/he have within the whānau?
- How might his/her attitude, spirit, mana be enhanced and uplifted?
- What opportunities are provided to enable him/her to make positive choices?
- How could s/he be supported to build confidence and strengthen resilience?

Ngā pātai (questions)

Hononga

- How are his/her relationships with others (whānau, peers, teachers, etc.)?
- How are his/her relationships with places, including papakāinga (original home: one's personal tūrangawaewae or walking place), marae and whenua (land)?
- How strong are his/her whānau relationships and connectedness to whānau?
- How is his/her position in the whānau acknowledged (e.g., as eldest son)?
- How might whānau connections and relationships be strengthened?
- Whānau whānui (wider family): How might wider whānau contribute or feature?

Hinengaro

- What are the things that motivate and inspire him/her?
- How does s/he display/express emotions (verbally, nonverbally)?
- How respectful is s/he of others' thoughts and feelings?
- How is the quality of his/her relationships with others affecting his/her thinking?
- How does s/he perceive him/herself: own self-worth?
- Does s/he understand what others are communicating?

Tinana

- How is his/her āhua (demeanour, appearance): How does s/he "look"?
- What messages might s/he be expressing with his/her body language?
- What are his/her energy levels like?
- How alert is s/he?
- Are others respecting his/her personal space?
- Is s/he respecting others' personal space?

Appendix B:
Intervention plan for Tori

Intervention Plan	Classroom motivation and positive reinforcement: *mana motuhake, hinengaro, hononga*	Setting up for success	Involvement of key people: *Hononga*
Name Tori **Ethnicity** Māori **Gender** Male **Date of birth** January 1998 **Age** 11 years **Class level** Year 7 **Referral to SE** 20 July 2009 **Intervention period** 20 July–14 September 2009	*Entertainment:* • Playstation 2 • watching a video • Timeout video parlour • computer time (games or Internet) • going to the pictures • listening to music • playing cards • playing tops	**The classroom:** *Hinengaro, hononga and mana motuhake:* • seat at front of class to reduce provocation/eye-balling) • seat in group of supportive peers • plan "buddy"/peer tutoring/co-operative learning activities • give a class responsibility that benefits the whole class	*Tori's mother (Gina):* • support/ideas outside of the whānau for parenting; strategies that will enhance Tori's mana, self-concept and identity • role modelling • reconnections with wider whānau and hapū; support for her and all the tamariki
Whānau • Gina (Mum) • Sisters: Missy (13), Tairoa (10) • Brothers: Joey (9), Bradley (3) • Nan	*Social and cultural:* • sitting with the rest of the class • helping to choose a class game or activity • helping the caretaker • helping by taking messages to the office	• have an individual education programme (IEP) • implement an individual behaviour programme (IBP) • class-wide reward/reinforcement plan	*Tori's Nan:* • Tori to spend more time with her • walking and meal preparation with Tori
Key competencies (He tikanga whakaaro):	• art (drawing or painting) • cooking • free time • leaving class early • spending time with his Nan • spending time with Bradley • spending time with his cousins • going to his marae • kapa haka	**The whānau:** *Hinengaro, hononga, mana motuhake and tinana:* • hauora (Māori health provider) support and involvement • Matua whāngai (agency set up to help families with issues around parenting and caregiving)	*School staff:* • Tori's classroom teacher to explore new ideas and approaches, including classroom management and programme adaptations • Mrs Patterson (DP) stated that she would be keen to provide mentor support for Tori • caretaker keen to have tasks for Tori to help him with at school
Manaakitanga *Relating to others* **Whanaungatanga** *Creating a culture of care* **Tātaritanga** *Making meaning* *Thinking* **Rangatiratanga** *Managing self* **Whaiwāhitanga** *Participating/contributing*		• Atawhaingia Te Pā Harakeke: a whānau/parenting support programme for Gina • marae: regular involvement • kapa haka for Tori • Nan walking with Tori each night • Nan and Tori to plan cooking times: menu, cooking and serving meal	*Peers:* • the class-wide plan would need to be explained, modelled and implemented • whole-class reward/reinforcement schedule put in place for observable tautoko (support), manaaki (care) and aroha (compassion) being accorded by peers to Tori • a positive classroom culture and environment would need to be a key goal for everyone

Linking culture home/school

Part III:

Enabling responsive pedagogy

9.

Leadership of Restorative Practices in Education

Jan Daley

Introduction

This chapter considers leadership concepts and change management theory in relation to the implementation of restorative philosophy, policy and practices in schools and early childhood education services. It is assumed that the responsibility for leading the vision and making major decisions about innovations rests with principals or head teachers. It is also assumed that some teachers will fill key roles in leading the implementation, and that all teachers will be involved in these school-wide innovations. Leadership is a systems-level action. Although the focus of this chapter is restorative practice, systems and actions that support the effective leadership of broader responsive pedagogical practice in educational settings are of course also crucial.

Readiness for change

Before discussing specific concepts of leadership, it is important to consider the conditions that support readiness for change. There needs to be a willingness from both the teachers and the organisation to embrace restorative practices and take on its new approaches. Apart from wanting to work constructively with students, teachers and educational leaders are likely to be motivated by evidence that links restorative practices with educational outcomes and the extent to which restorative practices are aligned with the curriculum.

Rationale for change

The desire to improve teaching, learning and achievement is often the impetus for adopting restorative practices. Schools and other institutions aim to enhance their learning environment and to build respectful and supportive relationships throughout their communities. The reduction in disruptive and challenging behaviour in classrooms is perceived to be a precondition of successful learning:

> Restorative justice offers the opportunity to address the complex issues which influence student outcomes and insists that schools become accountable for creating an authentic, supportive school environment. (Cameron & Thorsborne, 2001, p. 193)

Schools that are shifting towards restorative practices believe that positive changes in behaviour are rarely an outcome of punitive or retributive punishment. Instead, they believe wrongdoers need to accept responsibility for their actions and restore the damaged relationships with those they hurt. The restorative practices they are likely to use include restorative chats, circle talk, class conferencing, mini conferencing, the thinking room and mediation.

A compelling reason to move towards restorative practices is to reduce suspensions and expulsions of students for serious wrongdoing (Cameron & Thorsborne, 2001). A school may have become dissatisfied with behaviour management practices that appear to be ineffective in dealing with bullying, victimisation, conflict, violence, continual disobedience and defiance of teachers. They perceive that stand-downs, suspensions and expulsions, as well as time out and detentions, involve a rejection of the wrongdoers and are counter-productive to their engagement in learning. Rather than resolving the issues and restoring relationships, these disciplinary methods often lead to further misconduct and damage to relationships. When reducing suspensions is the prime reason for change, restorative practices may focus on formal conferencing for "high-end" offenders.

An underlying personal reason for some educators to adopt restorative practices is a desire to help transform civil society through education that equips students to live peacefully and to relate well to others. This motivation stems from the perceived values of restorative justice rather than the process of restorative practices (Wachtel & McCold, 2001). It views educational settings as microcosms of community and society: "To reduce the growing negative subculture … to successfully prevent crime and to accomplish meaningful and lasting change, restorative justice must be perceived as a social movement dedicated to making restorative practices integral to everyday life" (p. 129).

Liebmann (2007) commends the New Zealand youth justice system to other countries as an example of using restorative justice principles for dealing with youth offenders through the use of family group conferences, "virtually replacing an ailing, retributive welfare system, with large numbers of young people in residential institutions, with a restorative system that diverts most young people to community provisions" (p. 265). Through their participation in Child, Youth and Family conferences, many teachers have become familiar with how they work and would support similar use of them in schools.

Organisational culture and values

Organisational culture is a complex and dynamic concept, whereby assumptions and beliefs are shared yet operate subconsciously. The meaning and importance of a school's or an early childhood service's culture are elusive. A culture is there, it exists, it is taken for granted, but it is intangible, airy, vague and invisible. It cannot be prescribed in policy and procedures. It is commonly defined as "the way we do things" or "the way things are done around here". *Kiwi Leadership for*

Principals (Ministry of Education, 2008a) provides another simple definition: "What we value around here" (p. 18). McFadzien (2008) describes school culture as a product of how a school functions, combining values, attitudes and behaviours that pervade the different aspects of school life. They bring about a sense of unity of purpose that ideally has at its core the concept of creating a learning environment for the school community.

When establishing a school-wide restorative approach to behaviour management, it is important to consider the school culture that will incorporate the new ethos. Restorative principles in educational settings are not new. Educators have long promoted values such as respect, responsibility, care and concern for others, although restorative terminology might not have been used. Many schools use processes such as conflict resolution, peer mediation, peer support and peer mentoring that are now recognised as falling under the mantle of restorative justice. However, the further development of restorative practices involves a cultural change when the restorative language and focus on positive relationships is developed.

The values underlying restorative justice are also the traditional values that underpin socialisation practices in shaping behaviour in families and communities:

> The essence of the restorative approach is a collaborative problem-solving approach to misbehaviour. Restorative approaches simultaneously exercise high control and high support, confronting and disapproving of wrongdoing while supporting and acknowledging the intrinsic worth of the wrongdoer. (Wachtel & McCold, 2001, p. 121)

One teacher at a workshop noted that "restorative practices are nothing new to me, that's how I was brought up". His family model was one of disapproval and control of misbehaviour while maintaining respect in relationships.

McFadzien (2008) investigated how school culture develops and changes, the extent to which it can be planned strategically and the extent to which it evolves within the school community. He found the centrality of the principal to be pivotal—not only in strategy but also in shaping the evolving shifts. Any success in developing and changing the culture was determined by the uptake and support of the principal. He found that for teachers and principals, school culture is about "the way things are done", but for students and parents it is more about "how the school feels". This subtle mind shift should be considered when leaders and teachers are planning change initiatives:

> Repairing the harm necessarily forces us to learn from the experience that has led to the conflict and examine our attitudes, beliefs and behaviours that have contributed to it. This challenging of mindsets is where true culture change begins. (Blood & Thorsborne, 2005, p. 3)

Evidence-based practice

Having a rationale for restorative practices, and a desire to enhance the values inherent in building good relationships into the school culture, are prerequisites for successful change. Teachers also need reassurance that restorative practices work before committing to them. They want to understand the restorative philosophy and principles, and to know how restorative practices are operating successfully elsewhere. The research evidence is complex and complicated. Many studies are based on criminal justice systems and educational programmes for serious offenders. There is some research on high-end conferencing in schools but little on broader whole-school approaches. Findings are not easily generalised because of differing contexts and cultures, as well as differences in implementation strategies.

A substantial evaluation of the first two years of restorative practices in 18 pilot schools in Scotland (Kane et al., 2007) indicated that they "can offer a powerful and effective approach to promoting harmonious relationships in school and to the successful resolution of conflict and harm" (p. 6). The research from the primary schools and a special school indicated that they had:

- a strong focus on ethos and relationships in and out of classrooms and a generally broad view of RP underpinning specific practices;

- strong leadership and positive modelling of RP by principals and key teachers;
- a major contribution to the RP developments by class teachers and support staff;
- a focus on promoting restorative language in school inter-actions, using posters and cards with scripts;
- playground projects promoting positive relationships through games and activities supported by trained problem solvers and peer mediators;
- developed restorative conversations and classroom conferences; and
- social skills and cognitive reasoning programmes aimed at developing skills to prevent and restore conflict. (p. 9)

The findings for the secondary schools (Kane et al., 2007) were similar but reveal more diverse approaches. Some focused on specific students with challenging behaviour rather than on whole-school approaches. Secondary schools tend to start with conferencing for the high-end behaviour continuum as a way of dealing with serious wrongdoing and to reduce stand-downs and suspensions. These largely involved deans, guidance counsellors and senior staff members involved in pastoral care. While having positive outcomes, conferencing on its own has a limited impact on general behaviour management. Research has shown that conferences are far more effective for the students involved if they are part of a whole-school approach (Liebmann, 2007).

Kane et al. (2007) highlight the success of focusing on broad preventive and restorative whole-school approaches. Their evaluation incorporated data and views from teachers and students, including evidence of a reduction in playground incidents, discipline referrals, exclusion of students and use of external agencies. They stress that developments such as restorative practices do take time to establish and develop, but when introduced with commitment, enthusiasm, leadership and teacher training they have a positive impact on relationships in schools.

Research in Australia (Blood & Thorsborne, 2006) has confirmed that although restorative practices can work for individual students, they work better for those students when the restorative principles are embedded in the organisational culture, and where there are positive teacher–student relationships:

> While the effectiveness of this 'high end' restorative process in responding to harmful behaviour is no longer in doubt, what has become clear is that the use of conferencing itself is not enough to achieve the sorts of positive changes to school behaviour management policy and practice that it seemed to promise in the early studies. What the process of conferencing has highlighted for schools and practitioners is that efforts which focus only on reactive responses to wrongdoing have limited impact in achieving these changes. (Blood & Thorsborne, 2005, p. 2)

In New Zealand, Buckley (2007) researched a sample of 15 schools that were using restorative practices. He found that the philosophical principles were similar for all the schools: "trust, pride in the school, tolerance, striving for achievement, responsibility and respect for self and others" (p. 215). All the schools used nonexclusionary behaviour management strategies and achieved similar outcomes. These included better student engagement (as indicated by less truancy and absenteeism), greater achievement in all areas of school life, safer and more inclusive school climates, greater community and family participation in school activities and fewer suspensions.

Primary schools and secondary schools using a range of practices tend to integrate restorative principles, policy and practices into the whole-school behaviour management systems. The intent is proactive and preventive, in order to build positive relationships among all teachers and students. The overall aim is to change the school climate and culture to a more supportive learning environment. Leadership in these settings values the relational focus at the low end of wrongdoing, which involves resolving conflict in a respectful, inclusive and caring manner, acknowledging that this approach provides a foundation to prevent and reduce high-end wrongdoing.

Alignment with pedagogical initiatives

When considering new developments, education leaders must address concerns about staff workload and strive to align and integrate all developments to avoid initiative burnout. Restorative practices were just one of a range of simultaneous innovations in all of the 18 Scottish schools in the study by Kane et al. (2007). However, a willingness to reflect on practice and receptiveness to change were also evident in all these schools. It is significant that restorative practices were found to be compatible with other school approaches and initiatives.

The heart of restorative practices is improvement in relationships. This is also a key aspect of the direction that many schools are taking to improve student achievement. Hattie (2009), in his meta-analyses of research on student achievement, found that the key aspects of what works best for teachers to enable their students to achieve well are similar to what works best for all students. Most of these aspects depend on good working relationships between students and teachers. Research into Māori student achievement provides considerable evidence that reciprocal relationships and mutual respect between teachers and students are critical to student achievement (Bishop, Berryman, Tiakiwai, & Richardson, 2004).

The Te Kauhua Māori Mainstream Pilot Programme clearly shows that the development of caring, collaborative and consultative relationships in schools, school communities and whānau results in enhanced outcomes for Māori student achievement (Tuata, Bradnam, Hynds, & Higgens, 2004). The restorative principles align well with traditional Māori values and processes for dealing with wrongdoing because they aim to restore the mana of the one who has offended and of anyone they have offended. The process "signals respect and personal dignity, and the agency of the young person" (Drewery, 2007, p. 205).

The New Zealand Curriculum (Ministry of Education, 2007) recognises broad aspects of student mental and social development, particularly through the key competencies that enable people to live, learn, work and contribute as active members of their communities. The intention is that these competencies—*managing self; relating to others; participating and contributing; thinking; and using language, symbols and text*—should permeate the curriculum. Restorative practices could be an ideal vehicle for promoting these competencies. If schools can successfully link the introduction of restorative practices as a means of modifying student behaviour with a focus on the key competencies, "we may have an effective influence on student behaviour that develops a sense of morality, in considering the consequences of their behaviour, that is so often lacking in some young miscreants" (Collett, 2008, p. 14).

When school leaders decide that their schools are ready to make the move from retributive to restorative principles and practices, they begin finding out how to go about doing it. This is often through attending restorative practices training workshops; networking at workshops and hui; drawing on anecdotal evidence from colleagues who are already using restorative practices; and reading articles published in educational journals in New Zealand, Australia, Britain, Canada and the United States. The questions posed by principals who have used sabbatical leave to investigate this topic (Gattung, 2007; Stedman, 2008) are about understanding restorative justice principles, facilitation and leadership, staff training, administrative processes, impacts on staff–student and student–student relationships and on student achievement, buy-in of boards and staff, links with the new curriculum, and how stand-downs and suspensions integrate into the models.

Leadership concepts

In this section, concepts of effective leadership are considered in the context of schools and early childhood education settings. Examples of leadership approaches and styles are also provided.

Effective leadership

At a 2005 hui hosted by the Ministry of Education for secondary South Island principals and facilitators involved in the Ministry of Education Student Engagement Initiative (SEI), the principals discussed leadership approaches they had found useful in establishing and sustaining restorative practices in schools. The aim of the SEI is to reduce the numbers of students who are suspended, excluded or expelled and to reduce truancy in New Zealand schools (Drewery, 2007). One effect of the SEI has been to move away from retributive to restorative student behaviour management systems. The schools are building restorative principles into their classrooms and playgrounds, especially through the use of conferencing and restorative chats.

The principals identified that some form of distributed leadership is necessary for implementing restorative practices, because leadership is required from a team of key teachers, from others in leadership positions and from all the classroom teachers. The intention is to build a safe, caring, orderly and supportive school environment in which teachers can teach and students can learn—one of the key leadership dimensions identified by the iterative best evidence synthesis on school leadership and student outcomes (Robinson, Hohepa, & Lloyd, 2009).

An appropriate instructional or pedagogical leadership approach is required in order to focus on positive learning outcomes for students. An element of transformational leadership is also needed, because the aim is to reset the goals to enhance the learning environment, climate and culture of the school or other learning centre. In their quest to identify educational leadership activities that are linked to the achievement of valued student outcomes, Robinson et al. (2009) note that pedagogical leadership has a greater impact than transformational leadership. However, they also note that the two are converging as relationship skills become central to pedagogical leadership and transformational leadership is increasingly focused on pedagogy. The concept of servant leadership (see below) was also identified by the principals as incorporating moral purpose and inclusiveness in order to work towards positive changes in society.

Many theorists compartmentalise different leadership styles to encourage leaders to use styles that suit their context (Leithwood, Jantzi, & Steinbach, 1999), while others contend that educational leadership is too complex and dynamic to offer blueprints (Day, Harris, & Hadfield, 2001; Harris, 2005).

Leadership approaches and styles

There is a whole range of leadership approaches and styles, and each offers different strengths. The leadership concepts discussed in this section are:

- distributed
- instructional
- transformational
- servant.

These approaches relate to the leadership of innovations.

Distributed leadership

Harris (2005) describes distributed leadership as a form of collective leadership in which teachers develop expertise by working together, thereby maximising the human capacity within the school. Features include teamwork, participation, empowerment and risk taking. The theory behind distributed leadership is that leadership can potentially be attributed to all people in an organisation, and that all teachers can be leaders in certain circumstances. Such leadership increases leadership capacity and aims to promote strategies that increase the collective efficacy of teachers to improve student learning through people working individually and as members of teams (Fullan, 2007). Day et al. (2009) found that successful leaders distribute leadership progressively, and that trust is essential for the effective distribution of leadership.

A challenge for the leadership of restorative practices is to identify the best people to take the team leadership roles of staff training, managing a well-structured plan for operating the systems, monitoring and evaluation. The team is entrusted to lead professional learning communities to build and develop capacity throughout the educational setting:

> Teamwork, leading and following, and looking after others are a reflection of the culture, ethos and traditions in which shared leadership is simply an aspect of the way we do things round here. (MacBeath, 2005, p. 362)

Instructional leadership

Instructional or pedagogical leadership has a strong focus on teaching and learning through actions the leaders take to promote learning. Robinson (2008; Robinson et al., 2009) suggests that the closer that leadership focuses on the core business of teaching and learning, the more impact it will have on positive student achievement. This involves both promoting innovative pedagogy and providing a positive learning environment for all students, which may include restorative practices. This approach to leadership emphasises the behaviour of teachers as they engage in activities directly affecting the growth of students, involving regular discussion with teachers, providing reflection times and allowing time for regular professional learning (Bush, 2008; Southworth, 2002).

Transformational leadership

Transformational leadership is about establishing and maintaining the commitment of the members of an organisation to achieve the goals of that organisation. It relies on leaders and teachers sharing their values and interests. Establishing restorative practices requires a long-term vision and goals involving the whole educational community. Successful transformational leaders have a strong feel for the change process and lead by example, modelling shared beliefs, practices and values. Leithwood et al. (1999) describe eight aspects of transformational leadership: building school vision; establishing school goals; providing intellectual stimulation; offering individualised support; modelling best practice and values; demonstrating high performance expectations; creating a positive school culture; and developing structures to foster participation in school decisions (p. 9). This model could be useful as an implementation framework for restorative practices.

Servant leadership

The concept of servant leadership is based on an ethic of care and service, involving making sure the needs of people are served so as to enable students to grow appropriately for the greater good of society (Crippen, 2006). Cammock (2001) calls for leadership that encompasses a willingness to serve others and to make a difference; in other words, leaders with "soul". In his research on servant leadership, Youngs (2007) proposes that leadership practice arising from social activity fits well with developing an understanding of distributed leadership.

Leadership in early childhood education

There is considerable debate about the relevance of transferring notions of leadership from other educational sectors to early childhood education because of this sector's multifaceted nature. However, a distributed leadership approach is encouraged by some because it is best suited to the collegial and democratic early childhood education contexts (Thornton, Wansborough, Clarkin-Phillips, Aitken, & Tamati, 2009). In this context, Rodd (2006) argues that:

> leadership in the early childhood field appears more to be a result of groups of people who work together to influence and inspire each other rather than the efforts of one single person who focuses on getting the job done. (p. 17)

Jorde Bloom (2000) has connected metaphors of leading and guiding, nurturing and protecting, with feminist ideas of leadership. She states that "Leadership is virtually always viewed as guiding, co-ordinating, inspiring and motivating: never cajoling, forcing or imposing" (p. 71).

Findings from New Zealand early childhood education centres indentified and funded by the Ministry of Education as Centres of Innovation, demonstrate similarities in their definitions and enactment of leadership, with Thornton (2007) describing their use of courage, commitment and collaboration, within collaborative community-of-practice approaches to learning. The centres were established in 2000 as part of the 10-year plan for early childhood education. Teaching teams reflected on and investigated their innovative practices through action research (Meade, 2010). These centres are committed to providing quality services for the children; they articulate clear visions, values and beliefs; and they also demonstrate courage in rising to the challenges of sharing their innovations with others (Ministry of Education, 2009).

Leading change

Leadership roles are critical throughout the change process, including setting and sustaining the strategic direction.

Strategic direction

Commentary on restorative practices in educational settings is often contradictory. Some sources state that a paradigm shift is required, while others state that development is *not* a paradigm shift. This dichotomy requires some teasing out with regard to individuals, organisation and change management. It is certainly evident that some teachers will need to rethink their assumptions and attitudes before they are able to commit to and participate in new routines. Organisational shift may be connected to the philosophy or principles underlying behaviour management policies, the revision and development of procedures, as well as rebuilding the climate and culture. These all involve a long-term and ongoing vision, strategy and planning. However, for some people and some settings, the shift is quite small if the development aligns with individuals' and institutions' values, goals, attitudes, practices and culture.

Change management is dynamic and strategic, involving growth in relationships, vision and commitment. Fullan (2009) believes that:

> making change work requires the energy, ideas, commitment and ownership of all those who are implementing improvements. Shared vision and ownership are more the outcome of a quality change process than they are a precondition. (p. 11)

The ability of leaders to provide this implementation planning and strategic direction is critical for effective outcomes. The principal can then share the responsibility for strategy, and implementation with the lead team and teachers, and provide ongoing resourcing and support.

In early childhood education, innovative change is likely to succeed when there is a team leadership approach involving a supportive, committed and goal-oriented group of teachers (Rodd, 2006):

> Change should be understood by the leader as a people-oriented process which involves specific groundwork to prepare people to be receptive to change, action to implement change, and ongoing activity that stabilises change by the development of positive attitudes and behaviour. (p. 192)

Blood and Thorsborne (2005), drawing on their considerable experience of working with schools in several countries, advise that a three- to five-year strategic approach is needed. They have found that managing the emotional impact of change is as important as putting the new systems and practices in place. They comment on five overlapping stages of implementation in some detail:

1. *gaining commitment*—making the case for change and establishing buy in
2. *developing a shared vision*—preferred outcomes, common practices and language
3. *developing responsive and effective practice*—training, support, monitoring
4. *developing a whole-school approach*—realigning policy with practice, and transition
5. *professional relationships*—"walking the talk" and developing working relationships.

These implementation steps require an action plan outlining the vision and goals, the professional training for teachers, the systems to be put in place and the resourcing of ongoing support, monitoring and evaluation.

Sustaining change

The implementation action plan is just the beginning. Any behaviour management system has to be reviewed and adjusted over time to keep it relevant and vibrant. It is essential to have evaluation, reflection and ongoing training. Davies (2006) provides a strategy for sustaining change, such that strategically focused organisations try to:

- develop a culture of sustainability by building capacity and capability in new and demanding contexts
- balance the short-term targets with the long-term direction
- develop strategic measures of success around learning, teaching and culture
- be morally driven by values and beliefs to improve the lives of individuals and the community
- focus on learning as the core purpose of a learning organisation
- pay attention to strategic processes by involving teachers in conversation, commitment, enthusiasm, vision and leadership

- pay attention to the strategic approaches of creativity, reflection and solution focus
- be part of networked systems—professional collegial links to widen the scope of information gathering, collaborating and sharing
- develop sustainable strategic leadership across the school to grow and develop the leadership perspective and responsibility.

Operational considerations

Operational delivery and considerations are unlikely to succeed without the support of leaders within the organisation. These considerations include personnel, resourcing, training and student and school characteristics.

The restorative team

Middle managers are likely to be the facilitators or team leaders of restorative practices. Fitzgerald, Gunter and Eaton (2006) describe their role:

> Leadership then is the act of influencing and working with others in a highly collaborative, collegial and supportive environment that encourages risk and innovation and which places learning at the centre of all activities. (p. 40)

Duigan (2006) recognises the need to focus on leadership capabilities rather than competencies, acknowledging that capable people use their knowledge, skills and competencies confidently and with good judgement to respond to change.

However, the principal has a responsibility to set the direction and ensure momentum through ongoing interest, promotion and resourcing. The ongoing reflection and support between senior leaders and the facilitators is crucial to the success and momentum of implementing restorative practices. Building capacity relies on "inspirational leaders who get others to believe in what they can achieve themselves" (Hargreaves, 2005, p. 181). "A driven principal is vital" was the first indicator of success noted by one young teacher facilitator at the SEI hui. If leaders lose control of the oversight, then the vision, principles and practices are put at risk. One deputy principal returned from leave to find that in his absence a detention system had been added without consultation because a new teacher at the school had suggested it. The restorative room was doubling as a detention room, and the whole thrust of the restorative practices had been undermined and confused.

Resourcing

The challenges faced by the Scottish schools in the study by Kane et al. (2007) included:

- achieving a commitment to change
- a review of policy and procedures
- ongoing training and support of teachers
- enlisting parental support and communication with everyone involved after conferencing.

Some of these aspects have financial implications. When schools are unable to fully implement a restorative approach, they tend to settle for a mix of restorative options and stand-downs and suspensions, which is not ideal. In New Zealand, Buckley and Maxwell (2007) argue that a fundamental shift needs to occur for schools to see restorative practices as a whole-school management system. Funding limitations, particularly access to teacher training in restorative practices, are barriers to sustaining that shift.

Training

It is essential to provide some training for all teachers and in-depth training for a critical mass of teachers. Such professional development requires funding. Research and anecdotal evidence on what does not work or that hinders the successful implementation of restorative practices tend to focus on teacher resistance. Teachers' attitudes range from enthusiasm to scepticism, apathy and antipathy, and include those who believe they "already do it". Some individuals view the restorative approach as a weak form of punishment, not understanding what a mind shift it is for offending students (Buckley & Maxwell, 2007). Some call their processes restorative but they are really "thinly disguised punishment" (Blood & Thorsborne, 2006). It is likely that change in teachers' attitudes will follow Rogers' (2003) innovation curve, which categorises teachers into five groups according to the rate at which they take up change: innovators (2.5 percent), early adopters (13.5 percent), early majority (34 percent), late majority (34 percent) and laggards (16 percent). Ongoing evaluation of the practices and provision of training are needed to gradually bring all teachers on board.

A broader concept than the whole-school approach is the idea of communities of practice, whereby groups of teachers come to see themselves as being involved in a shared practice of teaching that transcends their own individual practices. As a result, they have an important stake not only in their own learning but also in the learning of their colleagues:

> They are ... the shop floor of the human capital, the place where the stuff gets made ... Teachers function as communities of practice when they share a common body of knowledge, when they work together and use it more effectively. Learning is the key. (Sergiovanni, 2001, p. 108)

Student response

It is important not to view restorative practice as a "quick fix" for all wrongdoing. Misbehaviour by students who habitually disrupt classes, cause conflict and break rules will not change with one application of restorative practice. Students need to experience ongoing educative restorative practices in order to improve their behaviour. It is also important to realise that even a "restorative school" may not entirely eliminate the need for punitive measures. Students with serious conduct disorders may need special consideration. Severely antisocial students who lack trust in other people are less likely to be able to empathise and may not be able to participate effectively in restorative conversations. Students who experience poor parenting, including generational behavioural dysfunction and abuse, are less likely to respond to restorative practices because they do not match their experiences in their homes and the wider community (Snyder, Cramer, Frank, & Patterson, 2005; Werry, 1997). However, there are also many stories of remarkable success for some of these students. Leaders need to balance positive, constructive approaches with evidence and realism.

The restorative school

Drewery (2007) and her colleagues have developed a description of the characteristics of a restorative school that can be used to shape a school's vision and underpin strategic planning. A restorative school is one that is:

- working for respectful relationships among all members of the school community
- focusing on encouragement and possibility rather than failure and deficit
- having teachers see themselves as being in relation to students and their parents, not as authorities over them
- having a focus on restoring order by restoring relationships rather than restoring authority when disciplinary offences occur
- including parents and visitors, who are welcomed as part of the school community
- ensuring the environment is one in which children and staff can enjoy their school life and have fun (p. 209).

There is a strong theme of community partnerships embedded in this description. As schools gain experience and success in the use of restorative practices, they are likely to want to involve parents and the wider community. Success leads to buy in from boards of trustees to sustain resources. Schools will work in with their wider community, perhaps operating as clusters of schools to ensure continuity of expectations and experiences as students move through the sectors. Parents will often ask the school to facilitate chats and conferences for their children for wrongdoing in the home and outside of school, thus extending the home–school partnership. Many schools will work co-operatively and creatively with community agencies, such as the police and social services, to provide compatible responses to the wrongdoing of young people. As an example, the city of Hull, England, is endeavouring to become a "Restorative City" (Mirsky, 2009).

Conclusion: A "to do" list

The leadership considerations for implementing restorative practices in educational contexts can be summarised as a "to do" list of three stages:

1. to prepare for this innovation and change
2. to collaborate on determining the restorative principles and leadership concepts that will drive it
3. to consider operational processes for ongoing development and sustainability.

The preparatory stage involves critical thinking, reading, networking and dialogue. It is essential to clarify the reasons for the proposed move to restorative practices. The possible extent of the practices for part or all of the school, and the desired range of restorative practices, should be established. It is helpful to talk with leaders from schools already using the restorative approach, to read some research papers evaluating the practices in other schools and to arrange for some key teachers to attend in-depth training in restorative practices. This should enable the identification of teachers to invite to be the initial restorative team leaders, or at least to facilitate work on bringing a team together. Consider the possible implications for the budget, facilitation of staff training and the facilities needed for the initiative, as well as the extent and timing of the changes to policies and procedures that may be required.

The collaboration stage should involve all teachers in professional dialogue and should reach out to the whole school community. The aim is to secure initial buy in for the proposed initiative. It is essential to collaborate with *all* teachers on how the ideas of restorative justice and practices could align with the shared vision, goals and directions for improving the school and developing its learning environment and culture. The alignment with other innovations, initiatives and professional learning of the teachers should be clarified. It may be useful to present a draft proposal to the board of trustees and student council, to open discussion with parents and students and to plan how to extend involvement with parents and the community over time.

The end point for this stage is to develop a three- to five-year draft strategic plan for implementation and sustainability.

The operational considerations require direction and ongoing support from the leadership, but the systems and procedures will be the responsibility of the restorative team and all teachers. Training for staff is essential, particularly to train all or at least a critical mass of teachers in restorative practices before going "whole school". There should be a budget for ongoing teacher training, team facilitation and facilities for conferencing. The policy and procedures for behaviour management and pastoral care will need to be revised and rewritten. It is important to include ongoing evaluation and monitoring, both to ensure continual improvement and to ensure that ad hoc changes that might undermine the principles cannot be made without full consultation.

This chapter has discussed leadership of the vision, strategies and task of enhancing or introducing a restorative approach and practices into schools and early childhood services.

It has demonstrated how leadership is critical to the successful implementation of restorative practices. Commitment "from the top" and within middle management ensures that the philosophy, policy and practices all align successfully.

References

Bishop, R., Berryman, M., Tiakiwai, S., & Richardson, C. (2004). *The experiences of year 9 and 10 Māori students in mainstream classes*. Wellington: Ministry of Education.

Blood, P., & Thorsborne, M. (2005). *The challenge of culture change: Embedding restorative practice in schools*. Paper presented at the Sixth International Conference on Conferencing, Circles and other Restorative Practices: Building a Global Alliance for Restorative Practices and Family Empowerment, Sydney.

Blood, P., & Thorsborne, M. (2006). *Overcoming resistance to whole-school uptake of restorative practices*. Paper presented at the International Institute of Restorative Practices, The Next Step: Developing Restorative Communities, Bethlehem, PA.

Buckley, S. (2007). Restorative practices in education: The experiences of a group of New Zealand schools. In G. Maxwell & J. H. Liu (Eds.), *Restorative justice and practice in New Zealand* (pp. 215–220). Wellington: Institute of Policy Studies, Victoria University of Wellington.

Buckley, S., & Maxwell, G. (2007). *Respectful schools: Restorative practices in education: A summary report*. Wellington: Institute of Policy Studies, Victoria University of Wellington and the Office of the Children's Commissioner.

Bush, T. (2008). *Leadership and management development in education*. Los Angeles: Sage.

Cameron, L., & Thorsborne, M. (2001). Restorative justice and school discipline: Mutually exclusive? In H. Strang & J. Braithwaite (Eds.), *Restorative justice and civil society* (pp. 180–194). Cambridge: Cambridge University Press.

Cammock, P. (2001). *The dance of leadership: The call for soul in 21st century leadership*. Auckland: Pearson Education, Prentice Hall.

Collett, T. (2008). Disorderly behaviour: Is the situation getting worse? *Education Today, 1*, 14.

Crippen, C. L. (2006). Servant-leadership: First to serve then to lead. *International Journal of Learning, 13*(1), 13–18.

Davies, B. (2006). *Leading the strategically focused school: Success and sustainability*. Los Angeles: Publications.

Day, C., Harris, A., & Hadfield, M. (2001). Challenging the orthodoxy of effective school leadership. *International Journal in Education, 4*(1), 39–56.

Day, C., Sammons, P., Hopkins, D., Harris, A., Leithwood, K., Gu, Q. et al. (2009). *The impact of successful leadership on learning outcomes: Ten strong claims: An NCSL/DFES funded study, 2006–2009*. Paper presented to New Zealand Educational Administration and Leadership Society, Christchurch.

Drewery, W. (2007). Restorative practices in schools: Far-reaching implications. In G. Maxwell & J. H. Liu (Eds.), *Restorative justice and practice in New Zealand* (pp. 199–213). Wellington: Institute of Policy Studies, Victoria University of Wellington.

Duigan, P. A. (2006). *Educational leadership: Key challenges and ethical dilemmas*. New York: Cambridge University Press.

Fitzgerald, T., Gunter, H., & Eaton, J. (2006). The missing link?: Middle leadership in schools in New Zealand and England. *New Zealand Journal of Educational Leadership, 21*(1), 29–43.

Fullan, M. (2007). *The new meaning of educational change*. Thousand Oaks, CA: Corwin Press.

Fullan, M. (Ed.). (2009). *The challenge of change: Start school improvement now*. Thousand Oaks, CA: Corwin Press.

Gattung, A. (2007). *Restorative justice programmes for students*. Sabbatical report to educational leaders. Retrieved 17 August 2009, from http://www.educationalleaders.govt.nz

Hargreaves, A. (2005). Sustainable leadership. In B. Davies (Ed) *The essentials of school leadership* (pp. 173–189). London: Paul Chapman.

Harris, A. (2005). Leading or misleading? Distributed leadership and school improvement. *Journal of Curriculum Studies*, 37(3), 255–265.

Hattie, J. A. C. (2009). *Visible learning: A synthesis of over 800 meta-analyses relating to achievement*. London: Routledge.

Jorde Bloom, P. (2000). Images from the field: How directors view their organisations, their roles and their jobs. In M. Culkin (Ed.), *Managing quality in young children's programmes: The leader's role*. New York: Teachers College Press.

Kane, J., Lloyd, G., McCluskey, G., Riddell, S., Stead, J., & Weedon, E. (2007). *Restorative practices in three Scottish councils: Final report of the evaluation of pilot projects 2004–2006*. Scottish Executive. Retrieved 8 August 2009, from http://www.scotland.gov.uk/Publications/2007/08/24093135/20

Leithwood, K., Jantzi, D., & Steinbach, R. (1999). *Changing leadership for changing times*. Buckingham, UK: Open University Press.

Liebmann, M. (2007). *Restorative justice: How it works*. London: Jessica Kingsley.

MacBeath, J. (2005). Leadership as distributed: A matter of practice. *School Leadership and Management*, 25(4), 349–366.

McFadzien, P. (2008). *School culture: Evolving naturally or planned strategically?* Christchurch: University of Canterbury.

Meade, A. (2010). *Dispersing waves: Innovations in early childhood education*. Wellington: NZCER Press.

Ministry of Education. (2007). *The New Zealand curriculum*. Wellington: Learning Media.

Ministry of Education. (2008a). *Kiwi leadership for principals: Principals as educational leaders*. Wellington: Learning Media.

Ministry of Education. (2008b). *Setting boundaries: Plan of action for addressing behaviour issues in schools and early childhood centres: Actions to 30 June 2009*. Wellington: Author.

Ministry of Education. (2009). *Centres of innovation*. Retrieved 15 July 2009, from http://www.leadece.minedu.govt.nz

Mirsky, L. (2009). *Hull UK: Towards a restorative city*. Paper presented at the Restorative Practices EForum. Retrieved 12 September 2009, from http://www.iirp.org

Robinson, V., Hohepa, M., & Lloyd, C. (2009). *School leadership and student outcomes: Identifying what works and why: Best evidence synthesis iteration*. Wellington: Ministry of Education.

Robinson, V. M. J. (2008). Forging the links between distributed leadership and educational outcomes. *Journal of Educational Administration*, 46(2), 241–256.

Rodd, J. (2006). *Leadership in early childhood* (3rd ed.). Maidenhead and New York: Open University Press.

Rogers, E. M. (2003). *Diffusion of innovations*. New York: Free Press.

Sergiovanni, T. (2001). *Leadership: What's in it for schools?* London and New York: RoutledgeFalmer.

Snyder, J., Cramer, A., Frank, J., & Patterson, G. R. (2005). The contributions of ineffective discipline and parental hostile attributions of child misbehaviour to the development of conduct problems at home and school. *Developmental Psychology, 41*(1), 30–41.

Southworth, G. (2002). What is important in educational administration: Learning-centred school leadership. *New Zealand Journal of Educational Leadership, 17,* 5–19.

Stedman, G. (2008). *Investigating restorative justice models and their application for use on primary schools.* Sabbatical report to educational leaders. Retrieved 8 August 2009, from http://www.educationalleaders.govt.nz

Thornton, K. (2007). *Courage, commitment and collaboration: Notions of leadership in the NZ ECE centres of innovation.* New Zealand Educational Administration and Leadership Society 2006 biennial conference: Leaders make a difference: Conference proceedings.

Thornton, K., Wansborough, D., Clarkin-Phillips, J., Aitken, H., & Tamati, A. (2009). *Conceptualising leadership in early childhood education in Aotearoa New Zealand.* Wellington: New Zealand Teachers Council.

Tuata, M., Bradnam, L., Hynds, A., & Higgens, J. (2004). *Evaluation of the Te Kauhua Māori mainstream pilot project: Research report.* Wellington: Ministry of Education.

Wachtel, T., & McCold, P. (2001). Restorative justice in everyday life. In H. Strang & J. Braithwaite (Eds.), *Restorative justice and civil society* (pp. 114–129). New York: Cambridge University Press.

Werry, J. S. (1997). Severe conduct disorder. *Canadian Journal of Psychiatry, 42*(6), 577–583.

Youngs, H. (2007). "There and back again": My unexpected journey into "servant" and "distributed" leadership. *Journal of Administration and History, 39*(1), 97–109.

10.

Modelling Restorative Practice in the Workplace

Margaret Thorsborne

Case study: Attitudes

The setting: a recent meeting I had with a school principal and a head of faculty, who were talking about their commitment to implementing restorative practices across their school community. The school has a history of high stand-down and suspension rates, and the two reported happily they had managed to rid themselves of a handful of troublesome Year 9 students which meant the school was a much safer place. The conversation ranged widely and one of them shared an anecdote about a long-serving staff member who still wielded a cane in the classroom (mostly for effect, they reassured me), but who regularly called his students "boofhead", "stupid" and "lazy". Another report about this teacher alleged that he called a student who had an acne problem "pizza face". They asserted that the kids loved this teacher.

I *could not* believe this. I wondered what performance management in the school looked like and even if there *was* such a thing. I did make the comment that the changes would demand a shift in attitude and behaviours across the adults in the school community. I was left thinking that the school had a long journey ahead of it, and as yet did not appreciate the depth of the issues the staff would need to tackle to create the sort of climate they wanted: friendly and safe, with high expectations of both learners and teachers. The focus of implementation efforts would need to, in the end, be on the quality of relationships between staff and management, and between staff and staff as well as relationships in classrooms and playgrounds.

Introduction

As I travel the length and breadth of New Zealand and meet with management and staff in schools already committed to implementing restorative practices, I am often asked if I think the restorative practice approach might be used to deal with staff matters. The main issue that troubles the implementation teams is how best to tackle the performance of staff who struggle with or refuse outright to adapt their practices to the "new" restorative practices paradigm. There is also the tentative question, "Could this be used for staff conflict?" The answer of course is unequivocally "yes". It simply *has to* if the school is striving for a whole-of-school community culture change. Responsive and relationship-based pedagogical approaches, such as restorative practice, work for all of us—adults, teenagers, children, teachers, parents and senior managers.

In this chapter the key ingredients of a healthy workplace are considered, along with how these mesh with the key values of restorative practice, particularly respect, honesty, humility, interconnectedness, participation, empowerment and hope. The range of issues that arise among the adults in a school community is discussed. A case study demonstrates how a restorative process, here called a workplace conference, was used to address a case of serious workplace bullying. Use of the circle process to improve communication and build social capital, and a comprehensive continuum of practice/processes, are recommended as effective systems to support workplace health.

Healthy workplaces

Barth (2005) endorses the importance of constructive workplace relationships, as follows:

> One incontrovertible finding emerges from my career spent working in and around schools: The nature of relationships among the adults within a school has a greater influence on the character and quality of that school and on student accomplishment than anything else. If the relationships between administrators and teachers are trusting, generous, helpful, and cooperative, then the relationships between teachers and students, between students and students, and between teachers and parents are likely to be trusting, generous, helpful, and cooperative. If, on the other hand, relationships between administrators and teachers are fearful, competitive, suspicious, and corrosive, then these qualities will disseminate throughout the school community. (p. 8)

Is such a state of harmony and co-operation easy to achieve? All of us who have worked in a variety of schools during our careers will know that these organisations (and the smaller teams or faculties within them) range from healthy, to middle of the road, to downright toxic in terms of the relationships between the adults. It is important to acknowledge here that the style and quality of leadership play a vital role in creating the culture of individual educational settings, which in turn defines the quality of relationships.

Much of my work as a consultant involves providing restorative interventions for workplaces beset by high levels of conflict, or dealing with formal complaints and grievances—people behaving badly. Throughout these cases, without fail the emotional fall-out for the staff we interview is reported in terms of toxic levels of anger, fear, distress and shame. How people can function effectively in such a climate is a mystery to me, and of course if this persists over time people do get sick, their performance drops and there are mounting costs to the organisation, the *least* of which is the cost of the consultant!

The work of Kelly (1996) in defining the ingredients of a healthy marriage can be extrapolated to relationships in a workplace. Kelly's ideas builds on the work of Tomkins (1962, 1963, 1987, 1991, 1992), who outlines a theory of human motivation now known as Affect and Script Psychology (ASP). It is not my intention to describe this theory at length, except to say that the affect system is fundamental to our survival as human beings with highly complex brains. Kelly (2009) argues that the core principle of ASP is that human behaviour is motivated by, among other things, a desire to be connected with others. Our (brain) wiring is such that we are motivated to do what makes us feel good and to avoid or stop doing things that make us feel bad.

Kelly suggests our behaviours from very early in life are guided by a blueprint of four "rules":

1. We do all we can to maximise positive feelings that make us feel good (maximise positive affect).
2. We eliminate or reduce the situations that make us feel bad (minimise negative affect).
3. We build awareness of our own feelings so that we can do 1 and 2 better.
4. We do more of 1, 2 and 3 by developing the power and skills needed to achieve them.

It is this underlying set of rules, preprogrammed in our brains from birth and operating like an internal computer program that never turns off, which leads us to want to be in relationships with other people.

If we are to apply this idea to the development, maintenance and/or repair of relationships in the workplace, then this blueprint might be adapted to develop the following guidelines:

- Create a climate in which it is acceptable to be open and honest and to talk about how we *feel*. This is called the *mutualisation of affect*.
- Find ways to validate, listen to, take seriously and respect others' negative views or feelings and refrain from "blowing people off". When we are truly listened to and taken seriously, and feel understood and valued, the negative effect is minimised.
- Discourage harmful workplace policies, practices and behaviours that diminish others, such as disrespect, bad manners, unfair

treatment of students, their families, colleagues, dishonesty, bullying and abuse. Minimise instances of behaviour that generate a negative effect.

• Encourage interesting and satisfying work and work practices that promote mutually satisfying relationships, and give clear direction that provides staff with clarity and a sense of security. Maximise the positive effect (Thorsborne, 2003).

It should be clear, then, that the whole philosophy underpinning restorative practice is built upon a solid foundation of being human, and of living and working together in such a way that allows us to connect in healthy ways. It is our biology—the way we are wired—no less.

Ancient restorative practitioners in all parts of our world, while not having the benefit of advanced knowledge about brain development and function, must have had, at some deep level, an understanding of what worked to keep our "herds" connected. If we examine some of the fundamental values that underpin the restorative paradigm, and convert these into explicit behaviours for adults and children in our school communities, we can see that these value-driven behaviours are designed to maximise positive feelings, minimise negative feelings and increase the likelihood that our connections with each other are safe. When impediments to these connections occur (all of us, adults and children alike, make mistakes), the restorative process can be activated to help bring healing.

The requirement for clarity about which behaviours are needed is echoed in the work of Corrigan (2005), who lists three major needs for us as professionals in the school community:

1. interesting, challenging and meaningful work
2. a clear sense of purpose for the work we do, including a focus on the whole child
3. clarity about what behaviours to express (e.g., mutual respect).

This third point is crucial. The school leadership must be explicit about how staff are to behave towards learners and towards each other. This is where, in my experience, restorative practice can guide us to see what these forms of behaviour are—what they sound like and feel like.

However, it is also the area of greatest friction. Restorative practice demands an authoritative rather than an authoritarian approach. For some, this alternative way of *being* with each other, and particularly with students, rubs against the grain. Yet because schools are places where young people reside, both as a collective and as individuals, getting to know them and to like them are prerequisites. From an implementation point of view, if the school has clarity about its espoused values, and those values align with restorative values, this is a great platform for organisational change.

I am always interested to note the state and style of relationships between the adults in a school community. In so many schools, adults are keen to embrace the restorative approach to deal with student incidents, but falter at the hurdle when it comes to resolving difficulties around relationships between staff and/or performance issues. Barth (2005) describes four main styles of relationships among staff within a school:

- *Parallel play*—teachers work in isolation from each other, are shut off in their classrooms and have little interaction: "We're all in this—alone." This can also describe the isolation of the school itself from other schools close by, where principals seldom co-operate or collaborate in any educational matters.
- *Adversarial*—teachers are in conflict with one another or management, and this conflict leaks into classrooms and corridors. Parallel play is much safer! Adversarial relationships are influenced due to the issue of competition for scarce resources. This is particularly true in relation to enrolments and the resulting funding that goes with having more or fewer students enrolled.

  For both parallel play and adversarial relationship styles, the enormous wealth of experience that educators have (craft knowledge), is held close and not shared.
- *Congenial*—teachers have personal and friendly relationships that are interactive and positive, valued highly and make the day worthwhile. It is here that we often make an effort around

birthdays and farewells, car pooling or taking each other's playground duty if something comes up. These relationships are *nice* and *friendly*, but this may not go far enough to challenge some of the prevailing less-than-helpful behaviours in order to develop a robust, *respectful climate* in the school community.

- *Collegial*—the hardest of all to establish. Barth looks for the following indicators of collegiality when he is visiting a school:
  - educators talking with one another about practice
  - educators sharing their craft knowledge
  - educators observing one another while they are engaged in practice
  - educators rooting for one another's success.

For collegial relationships to exist in any school, a climate of trust needs to have been established so that robust, respectful dialogue can happen. There also needs to be a strong direction and modelling from the leadership about the need to eliminate or minimise those behaviours that erode trust and goodwill. These are exactly the ingredients needed to create healthy workplace relationships.

The best examples of collegial relationships in New Zealand schools that I have seen include:

- professional learning circles that have been established in some schools, based on the priorities these schools focus on in a given school year
- agreed/negotiated observation, feedback, coaching for practice development and performance management
- highly structured regular meetings in faculties between the head of department or syndicate leader and the teacher in relation to practice
- high-quality internal professional development sessions.

Some schools have adopted an emphasis in their performance appraisals on positive, respectful relationships with peers and students. Some schools have gone as far as recruiting staff— including principals—who have adopted or are willing to adopt restorative practices as a skill set and who hold restorative values.

Staff relationship breakdown in schools

When we interview staff in a faculty or team as part of preparing for restorative intervention, the stories we hear reveal a depressing picture of the health of these relationships that have often been neglected for weeks, months and sometimes years. The causes are often multiple, but predictably include poor relationships, poor processes and systems and poor accountability, although it is often hard to separate the causes as they tend to overlap and contribute to each other.

Poor relationships

Unhealthy and dysfunctional relationships among staff usually have a range of contributing factors to do with an individual's "relationship" behaviour, including:

- poor social/communication skills—poorly developed emotional intelligence
- psychiatric/mental health disorders—there are staff who may or may not have been diagnosed with difficulties such as bipolar disorder, clinical depression or drug and alcohol issues
- lack of aligned values between people and the organisation— especially in relation to deeply held values about the best way to raise children, the purpose of discipline and the use of punishment
- lack of integrity—not being able to trust people to do what they commit to and/or who don't walk their talk
- lack of acknowledgement and encouragement—the need for affirmation is as important for adults as it is for children.

Poor processes and systems

Limitations can be apparent within many aspects of organisational processes and systems and these can have a huge impact on relationships between people. These include:

- *inadequate systems*—this applies to any system in the organisation, but in particular to the school's behaviour management system (often abused). Finding solutions to discpine issues is not data driven

- *decision making that is not consultative enough*—there may be an authoritarian approach, where decisions are made top down and staff are expected to fall into line
- *poor problem solving*—this may be related to poor social and communication skills, or may simply be a failure to think through desired outcomes before launching into a strategy and/or a failure to use the data
- *lack of clarity about roles and responsibilities*—this issue is particularly important during the reorganisation that restorative practice requires (e.g., the changing role of the dean or deputy principal from the person who punishes a student on behalf of a teacher, to someone who facilitates the repair between the teacher and the student; or teachers not understanding that relationship problems in a classroom are primarily their responsibility)
- *poor selection and recruitment*—so often we can be hoodwinked by glowing references, an impressive CV or a sterling performance in an interview, but sometimes the selection pool may not have been deep enough.

Poor accountability

In Chapter 9, the importance of leadership in creating a desired school culture and climate was considered. Following are some of the leadership issues that have a particular impact on workplace health and wellbeing:

- *Lack of a link between organisational strategy and restorative practice*—this is an issue about leadership again (the vision for the school, its values and the benefits that restorative practice can deliver in terms of overall educational strategy). The failure to make this link leaves restorative practice as some sort of optional add-on.
- *Not holding people accountable*—schools are very keen to hold students accountable for the impact of their behaviour, but the sting in the tail of restorative practice is that the adults first and foremost must be accountable for theirs. No wonder students address us with cries of "Unfair!"

- *Not making the tough decisions*—although most of the senior management in a school are very decent, likeable people, it takes a certain kind of toughness to confront a staff member who may not be rising to the new restorative behavioural norms. As a result, schools can run the risk of being populated by professionals who should have been moved on long ago, or at least should have been called on to address their underperformance.
- *Inadequate performance management*—it would be a rare school that has effective meetings on a regular basis between staff and their line managers (e.g., faculty and syndicate heads meeting with their teaching staff) to discuss issues of performance relating to pedagogy and/or relationship management. Performance *must* be linked to organisational strategy, and if that includes restorative practice then it must be measured, and staff must be properly supported so that their skills improve to a level where the desired educational outcomes become possible (Thorsborne & Borrows, 2009).

Using restorative processes for problem solving

Restorative practices used with students can also be used between staff. Chapter 5 of this book discusses restorative strategies, including pre-emptive strategies, restorative conversations, mediated restorative conversations, mini conferences and class conferences, and full community conferences. The hui whakatika process is described more fully in Chapter 7. While all of these approaches can support staff-to-staff relationship resolution, this section focuses on the contribution of workplace conferences and circles. A model of intervention is then applied to staff relationships.

Workplace conferences

No one, single restorative process can solve the range of issues outlined above, but the interview process used before an intervention can provide vital information about recurring themes. The facilitated process (be it a workplace conference, circle or mediation) can also help staff and management to understand what lies at the heart of the relationship breakdown that is causing the angst. The process of reaching an agreement allows participants to collectively develop a plan to address the issues and shape a better future. Sometimes the plan needs to be a long-term one and may involve coaching key parties to behave more effectively. Sometimes the systems may have lain at the heart of the problem, so the plan needs to focus on more effective systems.

In workplaces, the restorative conference becomes a *workplace conference*. The same rules apply—bringing people together who are affected by an incident or series of incidents so that a shared understanding of the impacts can be reached, before a collective decision can be made about how to move forward. There are some significant differences of scale that make the workplace conference a rather more complex process, although the philosophy remains the same. The workplace conference is usually the process chosen after other processes have failed. As a result, it usually deals with the longer term, chronic issues and harms. Adults are much less forgiving than young people: the process may take anything up to half a day or a whole day, and follow-up is usually more complex and needs to occur over the long term. Change of behaviour in adults must be supported by appropriate scaffolding in the form of coaching, mentoring and, possibly, therapy. The changes required must be hung on a performance framework that is determined by the vision, values and goals of the organisation. They cannot be achieved in a vacuum.

Sometimes an intervention may be requested to resolve a relationship breakdown between two staff members, and in these cases mediation is often requested. If this deterioration has occurred over a long period of time (which it usually has), then the fallout will have "infected" other staff who work closely with the staff members involved in the conflict. If the resolution process only involves the two staff, the others don't get to tell either of them how the problem has affected the wider group. For that reason, the restorative process is useful because it demands that we identify the *community of people* affected by the problem, and they are the ones who can help to craft the solutions.

The following case study in a high school involves one such situation. The case illustrates the long-term damage caused when senior management failed to adequately manage workplace harassment and the diminished performance of a staff member. This was a particularly challenging case, because the person responsible was very powerful and highly influential among some of the staff. It was also challenging because of the sheer length of time his behaviour had gone unchecked—some 10 years.

Case study: Workplace harassment

A female head of department (HOD) in Social Sciences had been harassed by one of her staff, an English teacher who worked in both faculties. They had worked together for some 10 years, and over time he had sought to erode her authority, publicly criticised her during staff meetings and in the staff room and recruited new staff to his "side". He was also unco-operative with examination preparation and marking. This harassment had occurred against the backdrop of a constantly changing administration regarded by staff as lacking strength and leadership.

When a new female (and highly competent) principal was appointed to the school, the HOD finally shared her concerns with her. It was not the first time the English teacher had turned his attention on another staff member. Recent history was littered with tales of people he had targeted who had left, some seriously emotionally damaged. It became clear to the principal that she could no longer allow this situation to continue, and she broached the conference idea with key parties: the HOD, the deputy principal (who had been a target in the past, but had survived), the assistant principal (who had attempted to coach the teacher to adopt gentler ways), the head of the English department (who also supervised this teacher—he worked across two faculties), the HOD's husband (who also worked at the school as a teacher), a district inspector (who had received a number of complaints over the years) and another English teacher. The HOD was initially extremely reluctant to participate. She felt extremely vulnerable and very frightened. She had also started having disturbing dreams of death and injury to herself and her children, who were students at the school. In the end she had convinced herself that the English teacher would shoot her at school one day.

No pressure was put on her to participate in the conference, but she was assured that the conference would proceed whether or not she participated. There were enough people there who were familiar with the issues and how she was feeling to represent her interests. On the day she did choose to take part, and her story was very powerful.

The English teacher was very contemptuous of her fears and distress during the conference, until the point when he finally realised that she was in fear of her life. He maintained that all he had ever done was act in the best interests of his students—that she was not a good teacher and that students hated her and were fearful of her. During the conference other participants contradicted his own assertions that he was highly competent and therefore a better teacher than the HOD. He was certainly appealing to some students, but he was lazy, badly organised, had problems with assessment and was deeply divisive among staff, actively recruiting new staff, who formed cliques in the staff room. The district inspector also shared his view of the teacher's competence, referring to the thickness of the file on him at head office. The HOD, in contrast, was highly respected by students once they got to know her, and there was pressure each year to enrol in her subjects.

It didn't "click" with the English teacher that the issues were being taken seriously until the HOD told him she was on the verge of taking out a restraining order because she feared for her life. He finally acknowledged that he had done some serious harm to her, and more widely to other staff. He did apologise in a genuine way, and for a small moment in time seemed to understand the depth of harm he had done. During a break in the day he disclosed to another participant that he had been badly bullied at school and had learned to cope by growing a thick skin. I suspect that he struggled to understand why the HOD could not cope with his treatment of her, as he had learned to do himself at school when he was young. He had certainly regarded her as weak and unless he had the benefit of long-term therapy to address his own harms, his attitude would have persisted beyond the conference. This illustrates how difficult it can be to overcome a lifetime of beliefs and behaviours and why getting adults to change behaviour is a real challenge.

The conference itself was long and very difficult. The levels of anger, distress, humiliation and fear made for a very emotionally exhausting day. The teacher finally agreed to stop his harassment of the HOD in all its forms, and to stop his divisive and damaging behaviour in the staff room and at staff meetings. The group did not ask for his employment to be terminated or for him to be transferred elsewhere. They simply wanted him to stop the bullying.

In the wake of the conference, the district inspector reported on the process and outcomes to his superiors, who were keen to sack the teacher outright, overriding the conference participants' agreement. This was a major concern for the conference participants and the school at the time. They rightly asked, "Why did we go through such a difficult process to have our decisions overridden?" With some negotiation between the school, the union and the science teacher's legal representative, he was transferred instead to another school, where he was placed under close supervision by a strong male principal. It was believed that the recovery of all affected parties would be compromised by his continued employment at the first site.

The HOD took extended sick leave on worker's compensation, and underwent extensive psychiatric treatment for post-traumatic stress disorder and depression. While the conference itself was difficult for her (indeed for everyone), it was the *accumulation* of years of distress, fear and humiliation (that becomes the emotional territory of victims of workplace bullying) that contributed to the need for her extended sick leave and treatment. After a graduated return to work she is now at work full time (Thorsborne, 1999).

While the reader might ask "Why wasn't he simply sacked?", there are a couple of issues that need exploring that may answer this question. Sacking a staff member from a public sector institution is a long, difficult, costly and deeply divisive process that leaves enormous emotional damage in its wake. This damage still needs to be addressed, particularly as getting rid of someone does not heal relationships. It was important to conference participants that this teacher did not lose his job. The second issue is about one of the guiding principles of restorative justice/practice: that of *encounter*. In other words, the people in the problem are the people who best understand the problem and therefore should be involved in the problem solving. So the conference, from a restorative perspective, was the appropriate approach. Pragmatically, though, transferring the teacher to another school was a sensible long-term option, because the problems were so deeply rooted and had such a long history that a return to trust and respect between the teacher and the HOD was an unrealistic outcome.

Although this case was at the extreme end of the restorative con-tinuum, there have been many other examples of a less serious nature that have responded well to the workplace conference process. The trick is to implement them quickly as soon as problems become apparent, before the scar tissue of disgust, distress and humiliation becomes too thick, and to follow the rules concerning the comprehensive preparation of all participants for such a process.

Circles

Another intervention that can be used both preventively, and as a response, when an issue is having an impact on relationships, is the circle. The modern circle process has evolved from old preserved practices from native North American traditions. Like the workplace conference, the circle process is highly structured and underpinned by strong values developed by the group itself, honouring such things as dignity, participation, equality and emotional expression. A talking piece is used, passed from person to person, and it is only when the object is held that a person can speak. Basically, the circle is a process that allows people to tell their own stories (Pranis, 2005).

Circles bring people together to have honest and sometimes pain-ful dialogue about difficult issues and experiences, in a climate of respect and genuine concern. The process assumes that people want to be connected to others in ways that are genuine and good, and this expression of thoughts and feelings in a context of caring matches the values that underpin restorative justice. The process can be used for a variety of purposes: talking through an issue; reaching an understanding about a conflict situation and how it is affecting everyone; healing when someone (or more than one person) has suffered trauma or loss; support for someone going through a difficult patch in their life; community-building circles to create bonds and build relationships among people who have come together for the first time; conflict resolution circles, where a plan is built through consensus; reintegration and reconciliation; and last, but not least, for celebration and sharing the joy of accomplishment (Pranis, 2005). Both the workplace conference and the circle process require trained facilitators.

An intervention model for staff issues

Morrison (2007) proposes a three-tiered model of intervention for student behaviour based on a model that is used to frame approaches to public health. In a tiered approach, the health of the general public at a preventative level would mean that we embrace healthy habits which lead to good health (careful eating, lots of exercise, innoculations). At the targeted level (the second tier), particular strategies are developed to deal with issues like diabetes, high blood pressure, obesity, and at an intensive, third level, it would mean dedicated and formal responses to acute health issues (like an epidemic of swine flu). This model can be applied easily to staff relationships. Interventions at the primary or universal level (i.e., for everyone) act as a defence or immunisation strategy that will hopefully prevent or minimise the likelihood of conflict arising in the first place. Secondary or targeted interventions are used when relatively small conflicts arise. This would usually require a skilled intervention by a third party, such as a head of faculty, team leader or school counsellor. Tertiary or intensive intervention is appropriate for the most serious and problematic issues, and is used to respond in cases such as grievances and formal complaints. It might be necessary to employ an external consultant (or at least someone from another school or Ministry office) for this level of work, either because the parties do not trust the school officials to manage the process without bias, or because they see management as the cause of the problem.

Figure 10.1 shows a hierarchy of responses to staff conflict and behaviour issues, ranging from reactive (the top two tiers of the triangle) to the proactive work that needs to underpin these approaches to problem solving. This bottom or universal layer becomes the bedrock on which the restorative processes are built. The work that has to be done in a school to build and maintain collegial relationships cannot be underestimated in its scope, or indeed complexity. If one considers the factors that contribute to relationship damage among adults in the school, as discussed earlier in this chapter, the responsibility for quality leadership and management is especially significant. As part of this, the solutions depend on the mindset, skills and willingness of people in key positions to do the hard work of relationship development, maintenance and repair. However, all staff must share in this as responsible and respectful colleagues, reflecting responsive pedagogy in all facets of their work.

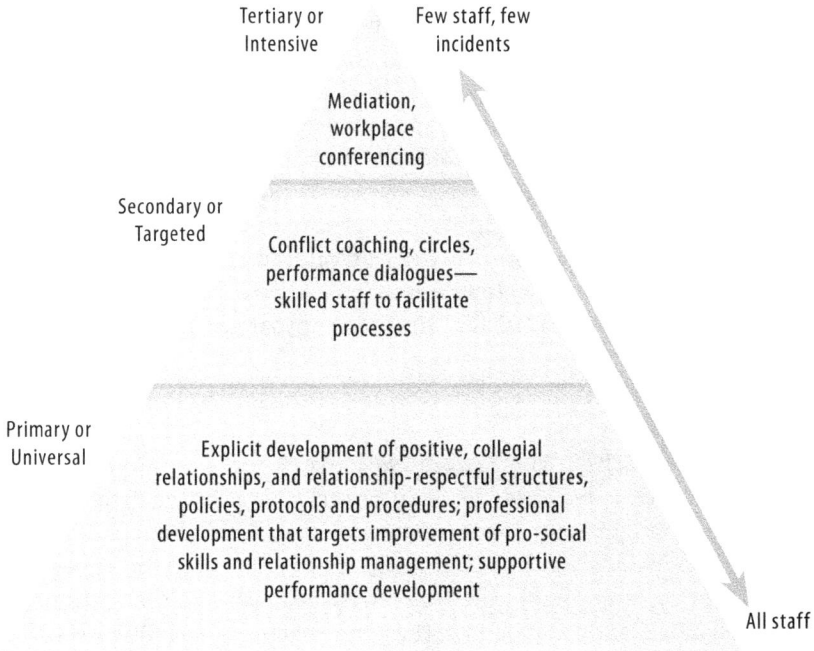

Tertiary or
Intensive

Few staff, few
incidents

Mediation,
workplace
conferencing

Secondary or
Targeted

Conflict coaching, circles,
performance dialogues—
skilled staff to facilitate
processes

Primary or
Universal

Explicit development of positive, collegial
relationships, and relationship-respectful structures,
policies, protocols and procedures; professional
development that targets improvement of pro-social
skills and relationship management; supportive
performance development

All staff

FIGURE 10.1 A WHOLE-SCHOOL APPROACH TO RELATIONSHIP
MANAGEMENT

Source: Adapted from Morrison (2007)

If this difficult though satisfying work is done in teams, faculties and the larger staff group, then difficulties can be tackled promptly and thoughtfully. At the universal level, energy and commitment to develop trust and respect and co-operation in collegial relationships is a must. At the targeted level, the school can put together a team of people who have specialist skills who can then offer a range of processes. For example, conflict coaching can be provided for staff wanting one-on-one support to resolve an issue with another staff member and they want to handle it themselves. If an issue arises within a team or faculty and there are strong feelings that need to be aired, a circle process might be used. Alternatively, some staff and faculty/team meetings might use the circle in preparation for decision making or problem solving. It is important that staff in positions of line management responsibility are provided with meaningful training in conflict resolution and performance management.

In spite of the best efforts of leadership and management, high-level conflict or other harmful behaviours or incidents occasionally happen at the intensive level. Appropriate processes, such as mediation and workplace conferencing, can then be offered to the parties involved. In a restorative school climate it would be rare for people to refuse to participate in such positive, healing approaches to problem solving (Morrison, 2007).

Conclusion

Schools embark on the restorative journey for a number of reasons. Sometimes it is because the Ministry of Education has suggested the approach might help them with worrying data about stand-downs and suspensions, and other indicators of poor student engagement. Some schools embrace the philosophy because it closely aligns with their values, and they believe their approach to discipline needs to be adjusted so that these values are not compromised. Others take up the challenge because it is simply a very good idea and one that will, in the long term, improve academic outcomes for students. Whatever the motivation, the journey is a long one that needs a carefully thought through strategic plan with strong, supportive leadership.

The restorative philosophy places the relationship at the heart of the educational experience. We know that learning in classrooms is more likely to be successful when the relationships between teacher and learner (and his or her family), and between the students themselves, are healthy, mutually respectful and a source of enjoyment, challenge and partnership. The emphasis in schools so far has been to get these relationships right.

Schools are also workplaces for adults. What works best between adults and students also works for adults in their relationships with each other. If schools intend to implement restorative policy and protocols, they must pay close attention to the quality of staff relationships. If these are not positive—if there is little trust between management and staff, and if there is a history of unresolved conflict, poor structures and processes—then the staff will "smell a rat" and say, "Why should we change our approaches with kids when our relationships with each other and our own wellbeing don't seem to matter?"

To change the behaviour of the students in our classrooms and playgrounds we must change our own behaviours: adults first. To sustain the change process we must look to our own relationships with our colleagues. These should be a source of deep and mutual satisfaction. This does not happen by accident. Our relationships must be built, nurtured and repaired when disconnections occur. We have to walk our talk with each other.

References

Barth, R. (2005). *Improving relationships.* 11th annual William Charles McMillan III Lecture, Grosse Pointe Academy, Grosse Pointe Farms, MI.

Corrigan, J. (2005). *Final report and executive summary: Group 8 High Performing Schools Program* (GR8HPSP). Retrieved 1 November 2009, from http://www.gr8education.com

Kelly, V. C. (1996). Affect and the redefinition of intimacy. In D. L. Nathanson (Ed.), *Knowing feeling.* New York: W. W. Norton.

Kelly, V. C. (2009). *A primer of affect and script psychology.* Workshop presented at the Widening our Lens, Connecting our Practice, 2nd International Conference on Restorative Practices, Vancouver, BC.

Morrison, B. (2007). *Restoring safe school communities: A whole school response to bullying, violence and alienation.* Sydney: Federation Press.

Pranis, K. (2005). *The little book of circle processes: A new/old approach to peacemaking.* Intercourse, PA: Good Books.

Thorsborne, M. R. (1999). *Beyond punishment—workplace conferencing: An effective organizational response to workplace bullying.* Paper presented to the Beyond Bullying Association's Responding to Professional Abuse conference, St John's College, University of Queensland, Brisbane.

Thorsborne, M. R. (2003). Integrity. In C. Barker & R. Coy (Eds.), *The seven heavenly virtues of leadership* (Chapter 4). Brisbane: McGraw Hill AIM.

Thorsborne, M. R., & Borrows, S. (2009). *Beyond CR process: Working under the waterline in dysfunctional workplaces.* Workshop presented at the Widening Our Lens, Connecting Our Practice, 2nd International Conference on Restorative Practices, Vancouver, BC.

Tomkins, S. S. (1962). *Affect/imagery/consciousness, 1: The positive affects.* New York: Springer.

Tomkins, S. S. (1963). *Affect/imagery/consciousness, 2: The negative affects.* New York: Springer.

Tomkins, S. S. (1987). Script theory. In J. Aronoff, A. I. Rabin, & R. A. Zucker (Eds.), *The emergence of personality.* New York: Springer.

Tomkins, S. S. (1991). *Affect/imagery/consciousness, 3: The negative affects—anger and fear.* New York: Springer.

Tomkins, S. S. (1992). *Affect/imagery/consciousness, 4: Cognition—duplication and transmission of information.* New York: Springer.

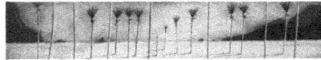

11.

Responding to Challenging Behaviour: Heart, Head and Hand

Jane Prochnow, Angus H. Macfarlane,
& Ted Glynn

Introduction

The Ministry of Education announced a shift in managing student behaviour (Ministry of Education, 2009a) in the *Positive Behaviour for Learning Action Plan* released in December 2009 (Ministry of Education, 2009b). The aims of the plan include training and supporting parents, teachers and schools, but in this chapter we deal with the major implications for teachers in classrooms. Training for teachers under this action plan focuses on building relationships with students, developing and strengthening classroom management skills, teaching social and problem-solving skills, as well as reducing aggression, conflict and noncompliance (Ministry of Education, 2009c). The school-wide positive behaviour support envisaged in the plan essentially advocates both preventing problem behaviour and consistently managing problem behaviour when it does occur. In light of the Ministry of Education's initiative, we discuss the educational strategies and options available to teachers and administrators when preventive measures to reduce challenging behaviours and encourage positive behaviour do not appear to have been effective.

The idea for this chapter evolved from the presentation of a paper by the first two authors of this chapter, Jane Prochnow and Angus Macfarlane. It concerned the need for both assertiveness and warmth in classroom management, and the need to take into account the classroom environment—specifically, the social and cultural contexts of the classroom. We devised a set of reflective questions that teachers can use to search for cultural biases within their own classroom practice which might be serving to trigger events before (antecedents) and/or unintended consequences following challenging or disruptive student behaviour. We suggested, for example, that marginalisation and belittlement of students may provoke or exacerbate challenging and disruptive behaviour, or student withdrawal and disengagement from classroom activities.

The authors' presentation argued that teachers' implementation of culturally responsive, understanding, positive and culturally relevant pedagogy would prevent most challenging behaviours from occurring in the classroom. Not surprisingly, during question time one hopeful teacher, who indicated that she carefully and warmly followed the preventive suggestions we had discussed (along with other preventive strategies), asked, "What do we do when preventative practices are included as part of the classroom processes but challenging behaviour still occurs?" Teachers all over New Zealand might ask a similar question. For example, what happens when the special education case worker and the Resource Teacher: Learning and Behaviour (RTLB) have done their best, the teacher aides have done their best, the researchers have collected their data and given their advice and the student with the difficult behaviours is still in the class, challenging the patience and professionalism of the teacher every day? Short of exclusion, what *do* we do?

We discuss these questions here by focusing on a teaching approach that accepts each member of the class as important, worthy and having something worthwhile to contribute. We believe that the classroom environment should enable each student to be accepted for who they are, to feel that they belong and to accept some responsibility for their actions, reactions and behaviours.

The presentation also emphasised our belief that the best way to teach and practise warmth and assertiveness is encapsulated in a powerful analogy introduced by Sergiovanni (1994). In this analogy, the *heart* is about the values and beliefs underlying our philosophy towards teaching and inclusive classroom management. The values and beliefs are founded on building relationships among students and between teachers, peers and parents. The *hand* is about the action taken to restore damaged relationships and to put things right. Restoring damaged relationships is one of the sets of practices (strategies, skills, decisions and interventions) we employ to create and maintain warmth, and to assert learning and behaviour management in the classroom. The *head* is about thinking and reflecting—on our personal theories of practice, on giving and receiving feedback to change behaviour and on developing self-awareness—and about self-directed monitoring of our own behaviour and helping students to do the same. Part of self-awareness involves taking responsibility for our actions, thinking about who is affected by our actions and behaviours, what their needs are and what is needed to put things right to restore damaged relationships.

Overall, this chapter addresses three issues:

- the need to examine New Zealand classroom practice and classroom environments, with a focus on both preventing misbehaviour and creating or restoring relationships
- the need to address the behaviours of both the teacher and student within the classroom environment, as well as how these behaviours affect teacher–student relationships
- the need to engage students who exhibit severe and challenging behaviour in constructing restorative strategies and practices they can fully understand, and within which they can have a sense of agency and responsibility.

Context

Providing positive behavioural support for students through a three-tiered system, as occurs in New Zealand, has been recommended internationally for a decade or more (Horner & Sugai, 2000; Office of Special Education Programs Center on Positive Behavioral Interventions and Supports [OSEP-CPBIS], 2000). The New Zealand school system has accordingly adopted what is essentially a three-tiered system of services and interventions. The first tier comprises preventive class-wide and school-wide support to assist teachers with general high-frequency but low-intensity behaviour management strategies. The second tier involves specialised interventions for at-risk students whose behaviour is of low-to-moderate intensity, with help from RTLBs or from other categories of support personnel.

The third tier involves specialists from the Ministry of Education (Group Special Education), and focuses on providing intensive and structured support for teachers of those students with severe emotional and/or behavioural problems. Although the percentage of students in the third tier is quite small, usually between 1 percent and 5 percent, this small number can account for over 50 percent of the behavioural problems in schools, because the students' behaviour is resistant to low-intensity preventive measures. The behaviour of each one of these students can occupy most of the teacher's attention and disrupt learning opportunities for the entire class, and can at times create an unsafe environment for other students and the teacher. More importantly, severely challenging and disruptive behaviour patterns may also single the student out as not "belonging" in the class. This can be exacerbated if the student comes from a minority ethnic and/or socioeconomic background and is located in a majority/mainstream classroom or school context. Isolating the student often begins a process of segregation, which can ultimately end in complete exclusion (Ferri, 2009).

In New Zealand, as in other Western nations, an important requirement in the deployment of strategies and interventions is that they should be preventive, positive and based on research-validated practices (OSEP-CPBIS, 2000). However, there is also an additional and equally important requirement: the development and implementation of strategies and interventions that are culturally responsive. This implies the need to take into account the values, knowledge bases, lived experiences and preferred cultural practices of the students, their families and communities.

This requirement is far from being met at the present time, and a major reason is the lack of effective communication and collaboration between schools and their communities. As a result, there is a very low level of input from members of those communities in designing and evaluating the preventive and restorative practices that schools deploy with their children.

In the increasingly heterogeneous classrooms of New Zealand, the growing number of students with intense and challenging behaviour poses a serious threat to maintaining class-wide and school-wide support structures and strategies that are *positively* focused. This is particularly challenging to teachers at those times when resorting to punitive responses seems to be both quicker and easier. Fortunately, and to their great credit, many effective teachers have rejected the use of punitive responses, or at least are very reluctant to resort to them. There is a growing appreciation that punitive teacher responses help teachers in the short term because they provide an immediate, albeit temporary, respite from the continuing intensity of challenging and disruptive student behaviour. However, punitive responses do not teach or model positive behaviours, rarely decrease target behaviours in the long term, often create a pervasive, hostile environment affecting all students, disrupt learning and do not transmit any concern, understanding or caring for the learner being punished.

However, students displaying severe and challenging behaviours are likely to have experienced repeated punishment. They are also likely to have felt rejection and disapproval from adults and teachers frequently enough in the past to be minimally affected by continued punitive responses to their behaviour. The punishment and rejection they have experienced has made them experts at displaying the kinds of behaviours that signal disengagement and dissociation from school and teachers, and that signal their *not wanting to belong* in their classroom and school.

Prevention and relationships

Restoring these students to engagement in the classroom requires building an honest, respectful and trusting relationship, which in turn requires that both the student and the teacher behave differently towards each other. This process is likely to require teachers to access new knowledge and understanding, which are emerging from three streams within the large and growing literature on ways of responding to challenging behaviour in schools. The three streams are:

- the literature on behaviour support and evidence-based practices (e.g., Gresham, 2004; Horner & Sugai, 2000; Turnbull et al., 2002)
- the literature on culturally responsive pedagogies of relationships in classrooms (e.g., Bishop, Berryman, Cavanagh, & Teddy, 2007; Ladson-Billings, 1995, 2006; Macfarlane, 2004, 2007)
- the literature on the need for teacher–student relationships to be focused on building a caring, rather than punitive, culture within classrooms (Gay, 2000; Noddings, 2002; Valenzuela, 1999).

The challenge for teachers and other educational professionals is to appreciate that approaches such as relations-based inclusive teaching (*the heart*) are based on sound theoretical models that "make sense" to students as well as teachers (*the head*). They are also focused and specific enough to be confidently and effectively implemented (*the hand*) by students, teachers and school management personnel. One such theoretical model that "makes sense" and is easily implemented in practice is the restorative conversation.

Thorsborne and Vinegrad (2008) consider that most conversations in restorative approaches to challenging behaviour in the classroom centre around three questions:

- What happened?
- Who has been affected?

- How have they been affected, and what needs to be done to make things right again?

Using these questions works well with defined or particularly serious incidents, where the wrongdoer and victim can be easily identified. However, the cyclical and entrenched nature of disruptive and challenging behaviours in the classroom can sometimes make it very difficult to clearly identify wrongdoer and victim, or to understand what happened, who has been affected and how they have been affected. It is possible, for example, that the student displaying challenging behaviours is also a victim in the class. Students who hurt others have often been hurt themselves, deeply and frequently.

Once student behaviours and interactions with peers and teachers have become entrenched, chronic and resistant to change, it can be very difficult to identify causes for the behaviours. The negative cycle in which chronic behaviours are operating frequently obscures the original causes of the behaviours, such that no one may know any longer or remember what caused the behaviours. In these situations, uncovering the original causes of the behaviour becomes less important than stopping the cycle, decreasing the behaviours, examining the harm done to all affected, taking responsibility for repairing the hurt and establishing relationships that will prevent recurrence of the cycle (Thorsborne & Vinegrad, 2008).

We suggest a process for examining the antecedents and consequences of challenging student behaviour in the classroom in order to support teachers to respond appropriately and effectively to it. The process begins by examining the social interactions that are occurring (students–students, teacher–students, students–teacher). We then ask questions such as: What is the nature of those interactions? This involves looking for possible triggers and causes for the behaviours, as well as possible consequences and other factors that might be maintaining these behaviours. As teachers we might also ask questions such as, What do my observation and reflection tell me? How can these behaviours be prevented? How can this damaged relationship be restored? To what extent is my behaviour contributing to this damaged relationship?

Student academic achievement is related to teacher management practices (as embodied in both antecedent and consequent teacher behaviour) more than to any other teacher practices (Brownell et al., 2009). This finding highlights the importance of teachers knowing and understanding a range of effective behaviour management procedures and having sufficient experience to use them appropriately. We need to leave behind the tempting argument that because so much student behaviour stems from causes and factors that lie outside the classroom and school, we have little or no agency or responsibility for addressing them (Prochnow, 2006).

We also need to forgo the attraction of finding any single intervention that will work for the majority of students with severely disruptive and challenging behaviours. Such intense and challenging behaviours demand individualised interventions that are designed (a) with the use of a functional analysis of the individual learner's behaviour, and (b) to restore the relationship with the student, rather than being selected on the basis of their being familiar to the teacher or on the basis of the teacher's willingness to use them (Gresham, 2004). Selecting interventions using these latter criteria alone may result in their not being fully implemented, or carefully monitored, and thus less likely to be fully effective. Nelson et al. (2009) found that learner behaviour change was directly related to the extent to which interventions were (correctly) implemented.

From the perspective of responsive and restorative approaches to behaviour change, our primary focus needs to be on behaviour and what it means. Initially, we try to determine and understand what a student's behaviour might be communicating to the teacher (or to others) about the state of their relationships, and about their feeling of not being included in and not belonging to the classroom. It is important to understand what challenging or disruptive behaviours mean both to the student and to the teacher.

This is addressed in part by carrying out a functional analysis of the antecedents and consequences of the behaviour. This important step in functional analysis of the behaviour is necessary to establish what may be triggering or maintaining the behaviour; in other words, what function the behaviour serves for the child (Lane et al., 2007). We then examine the behaviours by forming a hypothesis to help us to explore the likely *purposes* of the behaviour, rather than just what is simultaneously occurring with the behaviour. We may also need to carry out a functional analysis at the macro level (beyond the classroom) to explore what wider purposes the challenging and disruptive behaviours might serve for the student (Horner, 1994; Sugai, Horner, & Sprague, 1999; Van Acker, Boreson, Gable, & Potterton, 2005).

We might also ask further questions incorporating our hypothesis, such as: Do the behaviours serve the function of *avoidance* for the particular student, allowing the student to *escape* from academic, social or physical interactions or tasks? Is the student trying to avoid academic failure, avoid making any effort, to escape from being belittled and marginalised or to avoid having to comply with rules or demands that he/she sees as demeaning or embarrassing? On the other hand, we might ask: What is the student *gaining* from this behaviour? Is the student gaining adult or peer attention? Control over the teacher? Power over peers within the classroom, or within the community? Is the student gaining peer esteem? Is the behaviour displayed an attempt (perhaps misguided) to be included within the class, or to be included within a disruptive subset within the class?

The following checklist of questions can guide the teacher in reflecting on the child's and the teacher's own behaviour:

1. Which behaviours are the most difficult and need to change first?
2. What purpose do these behaviours serve? Escape? Attention? Reward?
3. Has there been a breakdown in relationships between teacher and student, or between student and students?
4. What reinforcers and/or interactions maintain the behaviour?
5. What part do I (the teacher) play in maintaining the behaviours?
6. What part do the school structure or classroom contexts play in maintaining the behaviours?
7. Is cultural awareness actively practised in the class and school?

8. What positive behaviours could serve the same function as the difficult behaviours?
9. Can the student perform the positive behaviours?
10. Does the student have the ability to engage with the academic material in the class?
11. Is the material appropriate for the academic level and age of the student?
12. Are the family/parents/caregivers involved?

With restorative approaches, as with responsive behavioural approaches in general, both the questions we ask and the answers we get need to be based on clear and focused descriptions of the student behaviour, the goals for repairing harm, the procedures implemented and the outcomes reached. Restorative approaches also need to identify and describe the opportunities provided for staff input, feedback from professionals as well as teacher and administrative commitment (Safran & Oswald, 2003). It is easy to lose track of behaviours, the goals set and the procedures implemented when the language used in reporting and discussion is vague, encompassing and imprecise.

However, even where the requirements for clear and precise description are met, there will be specific incidents of challenging or disruptive behaviour where students may not know, or will not communicate, what is wrong. This is particularly true if they feel they have been treated unjustly, or feel they do not belong in the class or school. Where a particular relationship has been damaged, a student may simply become locked in a vicious downward cycle of punitive, hostile, aggressive avoidance and esteem-damaging interactions with their teacher, peers and even parents. Knowing who should be accountable for the immediate incident may not help us to understand and improve the current situation, or to reduce a student's feelings of exclusion or betrayal. These objectives can be addressed through engaging in a restorative conversation.

Preparing for a restorative conversation with the student (and possibly with others involved) thus requires both a close understanding of the social and cultural context within the classroom, and searching for likely triggers and reinforcers of the challenging or disruptive behaviours. The student's behaviour should also be observed carefully in the classroom environment (or wherever the offending behaviours are occurring) to explore its relationship with the behaviour of others, and its relationship with task demands, time of day, spatial arrangement of the classroom, schedule changes and any prescribed medication that may (or may not) have been administered. In order to understand the challenging behaviour at the macro level, facilitators need to engage in conversations not only with the student but also with the teacher and the parents, inviting them to share their understanding of what the disruptive and challenging behaviours might mean in the various contexts in which they interact with the student.

After a functional analysis has helped us to determine the conditions under which behaviours are more and less likely to occur, we can begin to develop strategies that are either *preventive* (reduce the likelihood that the behaviours will occur) or *interventive* (introduce an explicit attempt to respond to the behaviours when they occur). Intervention strategies are most effective when developed with input from the student, so that the student's needs can be addressed and new behaviours established, while taking account of the needs and behaviour of others within the social and cultural context of the classroom and school.

Once a hypothesis has been developed about the possible macro functions of challenging or disruptive behaviour, many restorative conversations can be guided by the teacher (e.g., where the behaviour is of mild to moderate intensity). A discussion facilitator may be involved where the behaviour is more severe and destructive, and where it is necessary to include not only the student and the teacher but also other participants, such as a specialist case worker and a parent. However, after an examination of the classroom context, teacher and peer interactions, a functional analysis of behaviour and an examination of the appropriateness of curriculum tasks for this student have been completed, the onus for changing chronic behaviour will ultimately lie with the student, in co-operation and collaboration with peers, the teacher and specialist/s.

Self-monitoring may well be an outcome of a restorative conversation or meeting, and it has the advantage of creating awareness in the students (and teachers) of their own behaviour and its impact on others, as well as perhaps building empathy for those wronged and a commitment to put things right. Students who have come to accept their part in actively engaging in restorative negotiations will be less likely to view themselves as "us" being dominated by "them" in relation to the teachers or school (Brantlinger, 2009). Reducing feelings of isolation and domination is an important step in students feeling able to participate fully in a restorative conversation or conference.

Case study

The following case study presents an example of a scenario between a Year 10 Māori student, Mahina, and her feisty drama teacher, Julia. The case study is authentic, and used with consent, although pseudonyms have been used to protect the identity of the participants.

Case study: Mahina and Julia

Their interaction begins with some sharp exchanges about Mahina's coming late to class and her sullen nonparticipation in the lesson, versus Julia's great enthusiasm for wanting all her students, but particularly Mahina, to enjoy the lessons she has prepared with such care, and to love drama as much as she does herself.

J: Oh, wow! Here comes Mahina. Make your entrance Mahina. Take a bow.
We're all waiting for you ...

M: Geez. Who would hurry to get to this class? Must have nothing better to do. Don't bother waiting for me Miss. I'd be bored anyway.

J: Mahina! Can't you just arrive on time and get into our work for the day?

M: Not my work Miss. Your drama queen stuff. I don't care. Why should I?

J: Don't get smart Mahina. You are late, and I am disappointed with you.

M: Get over it. As if I matter. You just worry about your drama stuff.

J: Mahina, I've put a lot of time into getting this play ready. Now you're being very rude to me.

M: So? Get over it.

The sharp exchanges soon escalate into some demeaning taunts and rude comments from Mahina about Julia, and frustration and anger from Julia that her well-prepared lesson is being hijacked by Mahina. She feels deeply hurt and resentful towards Mahina. She reminds Mahina firmly about the penalties for arriving late, and for verbally abusing staff members, and gives a firm and clear command for Mahina to stop. Mahina backs down but is still resentful, as is indicated by her refusal to look Julia in the eye.

J: Mahina, don't you even care about this class?

M.   Na. It's dumb. And so is your idea of acting. Hah!

J: Mahina. You were late for this class. Now you are cheeking me. You can be reported to the dean for being late. And you are in big trouble for answering back and being so rude. Do you really want that?

M: Yeah. Na. I mean—I'm sorry Miss. OK?

As Julia struggles to get control of herself and the situation, she realises that further confrontation with Mahina in class is not going to be helpful to either of them. She remembers her school's policy about having a mini restorative conversation to find out what might have been driving Mahina's behaviour, and thinks about how the whole exchange has had an impact on both of them. She gently moves a little closer to Mahina and quietly invites Mahina to have a brief conversation at the end of the lesson. Mahina agrees to join her.

J: Mahina, can we have a talk together about all this at the end of class?

M: Yeah. Na. I s'pose so Miss. I'll wait up.

The remainder of the lesson proceeds uneventfully. When Julia and Mahina meet together soon afterwards it becomes clear that they had been talking past each other, and that each had been misinterpreting the behaviour of the other. Through exchanging several honest statements about their real feelings and expectations, they are able to resolve their difficulty and gain a deep respect for each other.

J: Thank you for waiting for me, Mahina. I didn't like it when you were saying those things about me. I felt sad about it because I think you are a great young actor.

M: You think so Miss? You reckon?

J: Of course I do. I was waiting for you to start off reading the part of Whaea Moke in our new play for the competitions.

M: Really Miss? Do you think I can do it?

J: Why do you think I was pushing you?

M: I thought you were picking on me cos I was late and you wanted to shame me out in front of my mates.

J: No, Mahina. I just wanted you to get into the part and make a great job of it, as I know you can.

M: I didn't know you thought about me for the part Miss.

J: Well I did. And I see I was a bit silly to think that you already knew that.

M: And I was dumb to think you were just hassling me, Miss. I do want the part. It's a neat play.

J: Thank heavens Mahina. Let's pick it up again tomorrow shall we?

M: Sweet as, Miss.

Julia meets a fellow teacher, Alan, and tells him how she is particularly pleased to find that by engaging Mahina in a restorative conversation early after the event she does not have to follow on and implement a more formal level of restorative conversation with Mahina in the dean's office. This more formal form of restorative conversation might require facilitation by a third party, and the writing of notes and explanations that would be entered into the school records.

J: Hey Alan, guess what? I nearly got into strife with Mahina today over her role in the new play. We nearly went off the rails, but we just held it together. I tried doing one of those mini restorative conversations straight after class and it worked! Now she and I are friends again, and I don't have to go down to the Deanery and set up that formal 'facilitated conversation' thing!

A: Wow. Amazing. I wish I could bring it all together like that. Good for you.

At the next scheduled drama lesson Mahina arrives on time and greets Julia quite happily and enthusiastically, even offering her some help with the lesson.

Conclusion

This chapter has offered a different understanding of the possible causes of and solutions to severe and challenging student behaviour within classrooms and schools. The understanding incorporates strategies drawn from a functional analysis of behaviour and from culturally responsive pedagogies. The strategies involve teachers careful examining and reflecting on their own behaviour in order to better understand how this may be contributing to the challenging student behaviour they encounter, and how changing their own behaviour might contribute to reducing or minimising this behaviour. The strategies also seek to involve students themselves in finding ways to improve their behaviour.

Functional analysis strategies help teachers to understand the communicative intent of students' challenging behaviour and the meaning this behaviour might have for students. An antecedent–behaviour–consequences analysis, for example, might establish that a challenging behaviour provides a student with a means of escape from the negative cycle of punitive disciplinary strategies, or with a means of avoiding engagement in social and cultural contexts that marginalise and belittle the student, but it also offers him/her no sense of identification or belonging. Students' challenging behaviour usually carries powerful messages to teachers. Culturally responsive pedagogies provide teachers with ways to acknowledge and affirm that every student has valid knowledge and experience to bring to the classroom, and to create opportunities for all students to contribute that knowledge and experience. Such pedagogies also help construct a classroom culture and environment that are safe and supportive for everyone.

Restorative conversations are one particular culturally responsive pedagogical strategy that shifts the teacher away from an exclusive focus on punishing the perpetrator of harmful behaviour to a focus that incorporates the restoration of harmony and positive relationships. Restorative conversations centre around identifying what harm has occurred, who has been harmed and how they have been harmed. It then seeks to invite the wrongdoer into the process of repairing the harm and restoring the damaged relationships. The series of exchanges reported between a Year 10 Māori student, Mahina, and her drama teacher, Julia, illustrate the successful deployment of a restorative conversation carried out by an astute classroom teacher as soon as possible after the occurrence of challenging behaviour. This example shows how a strained and threatened student–teacher relationship was repaired and restored before it caused further harm to either party.

References

Bishop, R., Berryman, M., Cavanagh, T., & Teddy, L. (2007). *Te Kotahitanga phase 3: Establishing a culturally responsive pedagogy of relations in mainstream secondary school classrooms*. A research report to the Ministry of Education. Wellington: Ministry of Education.

Brantlinger, E. (2009). Impediments to social justice: Hierarchy, science, faith, and imposed identity (disability classification). In W. Ayers, T. Quinn, & D. Stovall (Eds.), *Handbook of social justice in education* (pp. 400–416). New York: Taylor & Francis.

Brownell, M. T., Bishop, A. G., Gersten, R., Klingner, J. K., Penfield, R. D., Dimino, J. et al. (2009). The role of domain expertise in beginning special education teacher quality. *Exceptional Children, 75*(4), 391–411.

Ferri, B. A. (2009). Doing a (dis)service: Reimagining special education from a disability studies perspective. In W. Ayers, T. Quinn, & D. Stovall (Eds.), *Handbook of social justice in education* (pp. 417–430). New York: Taylor & Francis.

Gay, G. (2000). *Culturally responsive teaching: Theory, research, and practice*. New York: Teachers College Press.

Gresham, F. M. (2004). Current status and future directions of school-based behavioral interventions. *School Psychology Review, 33*(3), 326–343.

Horner, R. (1994). Functional assessment contributions and future directions. *Journal of Applied Behavior Analysis, 27*, 401–404.

Horner, R. H., & Sugai, G. (2000). School-wide behavior support: An emerging initiative. *Journal of Positive Behavior Interventions, 2*(4), 231–232.

Ladson-Billings, G. (1995). Toward a theory of culturally relevant pedagogy. *American Educational Research Journal, 32*(3), 465–491.

Ladson-Billings, G. (2006). From the achievement gap to the education debt: Understanding achievement in U.S. schools. *Educational Researcher, 35*(7), 3–12.

Lane, K. L., Rogers, L. A., Parks, R. J., Weisenbach, J. L., Mau, A. C., Merwin, M. T. et al. (2007). Function-based interventions for students who are nonresponsive to primary and secondary prevention efforts: Illustrations at the elementary and middle school levels. *Journal of Emotional and Behavioral Disorders, 15*(3), 169–183.

Macfarlane, A. (2004). *Kia hiwa rā! Listen to culture: Māori students' plea to educators*. Wellington: New Zealand Council for Educational Research.

Macfarlane, A. (2007). *Discipline, democracy and diversity: Working with students with behaviour difficulties.* Wellington: NZCER Press.

Ministry of Education. (2009a). *Shift in managing student behaviour.* Media release, 7 December 2009. Retrieved 1 January 2010, from http://www.minedu. govt.nz/theMinistry/AboutUs/mediaCentreLanding/mediaReleaseIndex/ ShiftInManagingStudentBehaviour.aspx

Ministry of Education. (2009b). *Positive behaviour for learning: Action plan, 2010– 2012.* Wellington: Author.

Ministry of Education. (2009c). *Positive behaviour for learning: Summary of initiatives.* Retrieved 7 January 2010, from http://www.minedu.govt. nz/theMinistry/EducationInitiatives/PositiveBehaviourForLearning/ SummaryOfInitiatives.aspx

Nelson, J. R., Hurley, K. D., Synhorst, L., Epstein, M. H., Stage, S., & Buckley, J. (2009). The child outcomes of a behavior model. *Exceptional Children, 76*(1), 7–30.

Noddings, N. (2002). *Educating moral people: An alternative to character education.* New York: Teachers College Press.

Office of Special Education Programs Center on Positive Behavioral Interventions and Supports (OSEP-CPBIS). (2000). Applying positive behaviour support and functional behavioural assessment in schools. *Journal of Positive Behavior Interventions, 2*(3), 131–143.

Prochnow, J. E. (2006). Barriers toward including students with difficult behaviour in regular classrooms. *New Zealand Journal of Educational Studies, 41*(2), 329–348.

Safran, S. P., & Oswald, K. (2003). Positive behavior supports: Can schools reshape disciplinary practices? *Exceptional Children, 69*(3), 361–373.

Sergiovanni, T. (1994). *Building community in schools.* San Francisco: Jossey-Bass.

Sugai, G., Horner, R., & Sprague, J. (1999). Functional assessment-based behavior support planning research-to-practice-to-research. *Behavioral Disorders, 24*(3), 253–257.

Thorsborne, M., & Vinegrad, D. (2008). *Restorative practices in schools: Rethinking behaviour management.* Bundaberg, QLD: Inyahead Press.

Turnbull, A., Edmonson, H., Griggs, P., Wickham, D., Sailor, W., Freeman, R. et al. (2002). A blueprint for school wide positive behavior support: Implementation of three components. *Exceptional Children, 68*(3), 377–402.

Van Acker, R., Boreson, L., Gable, R. A., & Potterton, T. (2005). Are we on the right course? Lessons learned about current FBA/BIP practices in schools. *Journal of Behavioral Education, 14*(1), 35–56.

Valenzuela, A. (1999). *Subtractive schooling: U.S. Mexican youth and the politics of caring.* New York: State University Press.

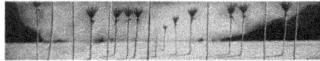

12.

He Tapuwae mō Muri: Footsteps to Guide the Future

Valerie Margrain & Angus H. Macfarlane

Introduction

Responsive pedagogy is influenced by competing challenges within the education landscape. Chapters 2 and 3 of this book discuss the significant increase in the frequency and intensity of challenging behaviours in classrooms and the public demand that schools and early childhood education services be safe places for all students. Furthermore, teachers and educational leaders are increasingly aware of the importance of exercising inclusive policies and practices, accepting diversity and applying human rights and UNCROC (the United Nations Convention on the Rights of the Child) principles (Ministry of Youth Development, 2008). Restorative practice is one example of a responsive pedagogical approach that can support schools and early childhood education services to both resolve and minimise issues, rather than rejecting individuals or passing problems on to someone or somewhere else.

In this chapter we reflect on the key principles of responsive pedagogy for teachers engaging with challenging behaviours. First, we review the principles for effective implementation, using the acronym "tapuwae" (footsteps):

- Teaching
- Aims
- Partnership
- Universality
- Wisdom
- Accountability
- Evidence-based practice.

We then consider how responsive practice could and should develop within schools and early childhood services to support teachers to engage with challenging behaviours. We precede our discussion with a philosophical reminder that, regardless of the setting or age, problems, conflicts and incidents can increasingly be recognised as opportunities for growth (Ashworth et al., 2008; Bolstad & Gilbert, 2008; Buckley & Maxwell, 2007). Incidents provide learning opportunities and deepen our understanding of the complexities of interpersonal relationships.

He tapuwae

In Chapter 1, the following whakataukī was introduced:

> He tapuwae o mua, mō muri.
> Pathways from the past, to guide the future.

The content from Chapters 1 to 11 can be aligned to the acronym "tapuwae", through the following seven principles for effective implementation of responsive pedagogy:

- the need for explicit Teaching of constructive strategies to support effective relationships and interactions
- clear Aims and expectations for students, teachers, organisations and communities

- working in Partnership with people—respectful and relation-ship-based practice
- acknowledgement of the Universality of cultural responsivity and restorative philosophy in early childhood, primary, secondary and tertiary education, the wider community and society
- Wisdom in the selection and timing of practices
- Accountability to students and to the wider community and society
- use of Evidence-based practice.

We will now discuss each of these principles in turn.

Teaching

In this section we argue that although there may be a strong "heart" and willingness to responsively engage with challenging behaviours, teachers need explicit training to do so, and constructive strategies such as restorative processes need to be explicitly taught in schools and early childhood services. In Chapters 5 and 6, Matla and Jansen argue that relationships in education involve teachers using a set of professional skills that need to be developed and practised; for example, restorative conversations (Matla, 2009). In Jansen's (2008) research, a teacher stated, "The building of the relationship is the talking with them ... but it's actually the skill of the teacher in the restorative chat; that is the crucial part" (p. 29).

Professional interest in restorative practice is exemplified in the reports of the recent sabbaticals of New Zealand principals Gattung (2007) and Stedman (2008), and a Massey University master's project (Signal, 2009). These studies have motivated school leaders' thinking on responsive pedagogical approaches, including the importance of constructive engagement with behavioural issues, connection with wider communities, curriculum connectedness and accountability. However, the strong demand for the services of New Zealand restorative practice facilitators Greg Jansen and Richard Matla, as well as Australian authority Margaret Thorsborne, shows that there is a real need for training and support in restorative practices at the teaching coal face. A key purpose in publishing this book is to ensure that such material becomes more accessible. However, a book cannot replace the fervour and enthusiasm of a dynamic facilitator, nor bring to life the narratives such as those shared in this book. We contend that if a school or early childhood education service is truly committed to restorative practice, then opportunities for staff training must be realised. In Chapter 9, Daley argues for a range of professional teacher support, including collegial peer support and relevant reading.

The Ministry of Education's (2009a) *Positive Behaviour for Learning Action Plan* indicates that training for teaching in this programme will include skills in relationship building with students, classroom management, collaboration with parents, teaching social skills and problem solving and reducing misbehaviour. The plan indicates that teachers and school leaders will be trained to "define specific inappropriate behaviours, analyse the behaviour, (and) specify and support replacement behaviour" (Ministry of Education, 2009b, p. 2). The extent to which such skill training will be universally available to teachers is still unclear. Even less apparent is why the plan refers only to school teachers, ignoring early childhood education: misbehaviour does not only occur beyond five years of age. In fact, it could be argued that a prime opportunity is being missed to apply positive behaviour for learning in settings where the youngest children may attend for 10 or more hours per day. Establishing a social sense of responsibility and accountability for actions early on is critical.

Just as we cannot expect teachers to implement restorative practice without training, there must also be time given to teaching core curriculum principles and values to other members of staff, the students, parents and key members of the community. Time spent teaching strategies for constructive relationships and social accountability is well served. In Chapter 4 Margrain and Dharan argue that culturally responsive, relationship-based practices are the legitimate task of all teachers, whatever the age of children and the curricula—*inside* the curriculum rather than external to teachers' regular work.

Aims

We learned in Chapter 7 (by Berryman and S. Macfarlane) that the restorative community conference approach of hui whakatika incorporates Māori cultural principles and processes, contextualised within phases of engagement and established through the process of pōwhiri. The following four principles from traditional Māori (pre-European) discipline underpin hui whakatika:

1. *reaching consensus* through a process of collaborative decision making involving all parties
2. *reconciliation*—reaching a settlement that is acceptable to all parties rather than isolating and punishing any one of them
3. *examining* the wider reason for the wrong with an implicit assumption that there was often wrong on both sides—not apportioning blame
4. being less concerned with whether or not there has been a breach, and more concerned with the *restoration* of harmony (McElrea, 1994).

These principles affirm the importance of relationship-based and responsive approaches to education. Organisations that commit to working responsively embrace all of the above principles, and each of them should be evident in all restorative actions, from chats to conferences.

Responsive pedagogy works from an aspirational paradigm. Using restorative practices in schools and early childhood services, for example, provides a contribution to greater society as we support young people to develop skills in relationship building, negotiation and responsibility. In this way, responsive approaches such as restorative practice address the aims of both the "here and now" and also the aims of the wider and future world. Schools and early childhood services need to have relevance to and for society, and restorative practice is one way that relevance can be demonstrated. Through restorative practice, democracy, citizenship and social responsibility are strengthened (Macfarlane, 2004, 2007). Chapter 4 asserts that curriculum implementation is, therefore, more than an educational practice. It is a social mechanism for enculturating young people with the norms valued by our society. Just as our curricula espouse the importance of responsibility and accountability, so these values presumably reflect the desire for responsibility and accountability within wider society. Conversely, society should value the responsive and constructive actions of schools and early childhood services as they actualise social agenda.

The social nature of restorative practice is also captured in the aim of individuals who are empowered and become more responsible and self-reflective. As Wachtel and McCold (2004) state:

> The fundamental hypothesis of restorative practices is disarmingly simple: that human beings are happier, more productive and more likely to make positive changes in their behaviour when those in positions of authority do things *with* them, rather than *to* them or *for* them. (p.1)

The aims of empowered individuals, effective relationships and responsive societies are developed further in the following section, bringing people to the fore of restorative practices.

Partnership

As a bicultural nation we are guided by the three principles inherent in the Treaty of Waitangi (Te Tiriti o Waitangi), signed by two partners in 1840. The Treaty is premised (first and foremost) on the principle of *partnership*, which encompasses such constructs as shared decision making, appropriate ways of engaging, interacting and communicating, and working together towards a shared goal. As the discussion of aims has indicated, responsive pedagogical engagement with challenging behaviours is essentially about working in partnership with others, developing positive relationships and restoring social harmony. Teachers are inherently drawn to their profession because of an interest in working alongside and with people: students, families, colleagues and community.

Emotional safety applies to both perpetrators and victims. The former need to feel they have a chance to regain social acceptance and earn respect, and the latter need to have their voice heard. Restoration of harmony and balance is important for both. Brantlinger (2009) argues that students who have actively engaged in restorative negotiations view themselves as part of a school collective: "us" and "we" rather than "them". Crucially, Glynn et al., in Chapter 3, remind us that "all members of a safe and caring classroom can benefit from regular interchanges of teacher and learner roles. This is especially true for students who are minoritised or marginalised" (p. 54).

The model provided by Pranis (2005, and discussed in Chapter 6), illustrates that there are more and less effective approaches to building trust and partnerships between people. Pranis argues that the steps of meeting and building relationships, and of listening to and hearing stories, should be addressed prior to the steps of exploring issues or concerns, and making plans and affirming common ground. All four steps are important, but taking the time to attend to the first two steps builds greater trust and strengthens partnerships between people.

Drewery (2003) argues that "the single most important idea behind restorative practices is that respectful relationships between people are what really count" (p. 7). Restorative practice, as a people-centred philosophy and practice, is neither new nor novel, although the more recent development of models and scripts adds structure, and there is a developing evidence base to support the practice. Case studies that illustrate the respectful development of relationships, using culturally appropriate protocols, are provided in Chapters 7 and 8:

> He aha te mea nui o te ao? He tangata! He tangata! He tangata!

> What is the most important thing in the world? It is people! It is people! It is people!

Universality

Responsive pedagogical engagement with challenging behaviours is an inclusive philosophy and concept. It can be applied to any educational setting, regardless of age or gender, socioeconomic, ethnic or cultural context. Relationships are universal, and so too are problems and issues. The nature of human interaction means there will always be situations to resolve; mistakes or misdemeanours are not the prerogative of any particular social group or age group. Equally, no education service should be able to retort that responsive pedagogy or restorative practice has little or no worth in an educational setting.

The New Zealand curricula for schools and early childhood education services (Ministry of Education, 1996, 2007, 2008) are aspirational and affirmative. The documents position learners as competent and capable, and recognise that learning is a social activity. Consideration of relationships, respect and responsibility are thus a core part of ensuring the curriculum is enacted and delivered across early childhood education and school sectors. Restorative practice is not something that should be limited to secondary schools as a panacea for expulsions, stand-downs and suspensions. It can be a universally applied philosophy and practice to support students and children across the education system and in wider society. Case studies of constructive responses to challenging behaviour in this book have included children in early childhood (Chapter 4) and in adult workplace interactions (Chapter 10).

Te Whāriki, the early childhood curriculum (Ministry of Education, 1996), values partnership between home and early childhood education, and includes consideration of the transition to school. *The New Zealand Curriculum* (Ministry of Education, 2007) illustrates links to early childhood education as well as to tertiary education goals. It is a strength that our curriculum aspirations in New Zealand are aligned so that there is the potential for universal, seamless education. However, we can do much more to smooth and strengthen transitions between sectors, and even between individual educational settings. The more concrete our aspirations become, the easier it will be to realise cross-sector and cross-organisational connections. For example, under present funding it is likely that as a child moves from early childhood to school (as special education funding moves from "early intervention" to "schooling"), then the special education case worker will also change. If, however, the same principles, practices and discourse of restorative practice are used by the new case worker and new teachers, then there is a greater chance of continuity for the student. We ought also to be constantly reminded that curriculum includes *Te Marautanga o Aotearoa* (Ministry of Education, 2008), and universality demands that all three curricula be to the fore of education.

Restorative practices are universal in as much as they are proposed as behaviours for living and acting as global citizens, not merely within the hours of 9 AM to 3 PM inside the school gates. We want young people to develop care and responsibility for others across society. We should also expect that teachers and members of the education community model restorative practices themselves, including in staff-to-staff relationships. These ideas were elaborated by Thorsborne in Chapter 10 of this book.

In discussing the universality of responsive pedagogy, we intentionally refer to principles rather than to explicit practices. Those in a specific educational setting must, of course, manage their own particular environment and be responsive to their own cultural/community context. Although principles such as respect and victim voice are universal, in practice they are managed in different ways. In Chapter 11 of this book, Prochnow, Macfarlane, and Glynn consider warmth and assertiveness as appropriate responses to the most intense challenging behaviours.

Wisdom

Goodfellow (2001) highlights the importance of teachers moving from notions of *best practice* to developing ideas of *wise practice*. As Kauffman (1997) acknowledges, there is more than one way of knowing, and some ways can be more useful than others at certain times. Equally, some practices are more wisely selected at certain opportune moments than others. We can all no doubt think of times when looking the other way allowed a situation to de-escalate, or times when discussion was more profitable after rather than during an event. For many teachers, wisdom comes with experience; for others, it is a combination of mentoring, observation, experience, explicit training, reading and reflection. Wisdom is more difficult for some individuals to attain, which supports the rationale of having effective leadership (see Chapter 9), and having lead teachers who can contextually connect restorative philosophy and practice wisely.

New Zealand's indigenous Māori heritage allows us to draw on traditional wisdom to inform contemporary practice. Contemporary examples of culturally responsive, relationship-based pedagogies that have developed from firmly grounded Māori world views include the *Te Kotahitanga* professional development project (Bishop, Berryman, Cavanagh, & Teddy, 2007, 2009), *The Educultural Wheel* (Macfarlane, 2004) and *Te Pikinga ki Runga* (Macfarlane, 2009). As Chapters 2 and 7 remind us, processes that provide positive outcomes for Māori also provide positive outcomes for non-Māori. Traditional perspectives can also allow us to reframe leadership wisdom. Chapter 3 acknowledges the role of rangatira and teachers, commenting on the importance of these people in serving and caring for the wellbeing of others.

Perhaps the wisest actions we can take include ensuring that responsive pedagogical engagement with challenging behaviours is well articulated, well evaluated and well aligned with other initiatives. Presenting responsive pedagogy, including restorative practice, as both common sense and universally good for society validates the commitment from schools and early childhood education services in New Zealand, and enhances the likelihood of further support.

Accountability

In this section we discuss accountability in terms of three areas of responsibility:

- responsibilities that schools and early childhood education services have to students, society and their own staff
- responsibilities for upholding the intent of particular notions within the Treaty of Waitangi
- the specific responsibilities and accountabilities that wrong-doers have to their victims.

Elsewhere in this book it is repeatedly argued that schools and early childhood education services should be places where students are able to feel safe and happy. The management and teachers in these services need to resist the urge to blame wrongdoers alone: the educational environment plays a significant part in the behaviour choices of individuals. Further, the specific policies and processes that are operating within an educational setting are the key to ensuring there are consequences and follow through to restore balance, in order for the place of learning to be safe and secure. If schools and early childhood education services do not accept this accountability, then problems will only be dealt with at a surface level. For example, stand-down or suspension is a short-term response to an incident, but not a solution to underlying issues, and expulsion simply shifts the problem elsewhere. However, as discussed earlier, if staff are expected to accept accountability, they need support and resourcing, including budgeting for professional development.

It is also important to acknowledge that schools and early child-hood education services are not only social-emotional or relationship-based contexts. They are predominantly designed as places of learning. If, as has been argued, restorative practices enhance the ability of students to learn and achieve academic outcomes, then schools and early childhood education services have a responsibility to apply these practices. Conversely if, by not applying restorative practices, student achievement is negatively affected, then educational services could be accused of being neglectful in their duty to students and society.

We also continue to acknowledge the intent of two particular notions inherent in the Treaty of Waitangi (Te Tiriti o Waitangi), signed in 1840. This treaty promised power sharing and self-determination for both Māori and non-Māori, and although there is contention about the extent to which the Treaty has been historically honoured, we can commit to these two particular notions in the present and future. It is also important to acknowledge inequities in power and discourse between the Treaty partners (see Chapter 7). Schools and early childhood services have a responsibility to actively seek to redress this imbalance. Important strategies include ensuring that assumptions and discourse about minority groups are not negatively biased, maintaining respect for traditional practices and wisdoms and empowering both parties. Restorative practices by their very design, are clearly a mechanism for actively promoting and modelling the Treaty of Waitangi notions of power sharing and self-determination through the facilitation of negotiation and accountability. Hui whakatika, in particular, is presented as a constructive approach for achieving positive and enhanced outcomes for Māori.

The final, but perhaps most important, area of accountability is to acknowledge victims. Fundamental to restorative practice is the recognition that harm has been done to others. As noted earlier in this book, Zehr's (2002) simplified definition of restorative justice has the following three principles:

- misconduct is a violation of people and relationships
- violations create obligations and liabilities
- restorative justice seeks to heal and put things right.

The victims must have the opportunity to share their voice and feel safe to participate in a restorative process. Outcomes could be as simple as an apology, or repairing or replacing property, they may include ongoing relationship building and they may also take time to achieve. Critical to restorative practice is the point that the wrongdoer understands the impact of what he or she has done to others. It should be remembered that this process can occur with the very youngest of children: even toddlers are developing a conscience and an awareness of the impact their actions have on others.

Evidence-based practice

Although we have argued that responsive pedagogy aligns strongly with teachers' people-centred practice, and for the importance of positive social interactions in greater society, Chapter 2 asserts that most research focusing on managing student behaviour has been conducted within a positivist, or scientific, paradigm. There is an urgent need for further research and evaluation literature that documents the outcomes of restorative practice approaches in New Zealand across a range of educational settings and at all levels of education, in order to build a critical mass of evidence across contexts and over time.

In Chapter 1 we discussed Bourke, Holden, and Curzon's (2005) model for evidence-based practice. This model asserts that three circles or "lenses" of evidence need to be considered: research; practitioner views; and individual/community views. Sometimes research simply serves to validate what we instinctively know as practitioners and individuals, and to authenticate what teachers and communities consider to be effective engagement with challenging behaviour. The following examples of research-based evidence relating to restorative practice are not likely to surprise many teachers, but they do reinforce the value of work that culturally responsive, relationship-based teachers instinctively use when engaging with challenging behaviour:

- Positive perception ratings from students, teachers and other staff, whānau and community members were noted from the use of conferencing, as well as enhanced awareness of the effects of participants' own behaviour on others (Adair & Dixon, 2000; Drewery & Winslade, 2003).
- Teachers' and students' perceptions of various indicators of school climate indicated a clear improvement in a study by Moxon (2003). In this study, 73 percent of teachers reported spending less time managing classroom disruption as a result of the Restorative Thinking Programme (p. 75), and 83 percent of students said that they returned to their classroom with the intention of putting things right with their teacher (Moxon, 2003, as cited in Signal, 2009).
- A substantial decrease in disciplinary action, such as suspension, was reported as a result of the Minnesota Restorative Practice Project (Carp & Breslin, 2001); 83 percent of administrators and caregivers reported that after three months the offending behaviour had not recurred.
- Many researchers have documented a reduction in suspensions and expulsions of students for serious wrongdoing as a result of implementing restorative practices (Cameron & Thorsborne, 2001; Drewery, 2003; Lewis, 2009).

- Evaluation of the first two years of restorative practices in 18 primary and special schools in Scotland (Kane et al., 2007) indicated the development of positive relationships, both in and out of classroom settings.

These positive indications support the extension of restorative practice initiatives for both affective engagement and effective outcomes. It is important that research and evaluation consider both these dimensions in judging success. However, we caution against studies that look at quantitative measures, such as expulsion and suspension, alone. These are likely to be influenced by individual school policies and values. It is also important to give equal consideration to the lenses of evidence, practitioner and individual/ community views. It may be that, in the short term, research evidence is less substantive than over the medium to long term, as a critical body of expertise and expectation develops. Thus, we also caution against outcome measures that are used too quickly or are too bound by a particular context. Narratives and case studies, as we have shared in this book, can provide powerful evidence of qualitative outcomes.

Looking forward

In addition to the need for further research and evaluation, there are still some members of society who are yet to be convinced of the validity of any approach to challenging behaviours other than a punitive one, or any other approach to evidence than quantitative research. However, constructive strategies that have been endorsed by writers throughout this book give guidance to practitioners in the face of possible scepticism:

- Be secure in your philosophy and values—relationships, respect, nonpunitive models.
- Ensure that responsive pedagogy is pervasive throughout the organisation, including staff–student, staff–staff and student–student relationships, and with the wider community.
- Provide explicit and ongoing training.
- Ensure effective leadership.

- Use solutions that are *for* and *with*, rather than *to*.
- Acknowledge the victims.
- Harness the curriculum and other connections.

In Chapter 3 the four principles of routines, relationships, responsibilities and respect are affirmed. These principles should provide the cornerstone to responsive pedagogical engagement with challenging behaviours. We have aimed within the book to provide case studies and a range of evidence that connect responsive pedagogical principles with examples of practice and action. We argue that both are important for teachers, administrators, policy makers and advocates.

In terms of restorative practice, our vision is to achieve the following outcomes:

- Punitive solutions are the exception rather than the default.
- Victims feel acknowledged and included.
- Restorative practices are evident at early childhood and all levels of schooling, and connect to the broader society.
- The Ministries of Justice, Health, Social Development, and Education collaborate in supporting initiatives.
- There is a broader and more extensive research and evaluation base on restorative practice, including both qualitative and quantitative outcomes.
- Restorative practice training is included in preservice teacher education, and support is readily available as ongoing teacher professional development.

How will we know if we are making positive progress? Perhaps in the future the media may report restorative outcomes with as much glee as they currently cover punitive measures. We will certainly have more narratives from participants in restorative schools and early childhood education services and communities, and less resistance to restorative approaches (Blood & Thorsborne, 2006). We will also find quantitative ways to document responsive pedagogical engagement with challenging behaviours, including restorative outcomes. Most of all, we will see responsive pedagogy in action across settings, with empowered students taking responsibility and working through constructive processes, resolution and restoration. This cannot be anything other than constructive for young people and the wider society of Aotearoa New Zealand.

Conclusion

Throughout this learning journey we have explored the breadth and width of responsive pedagogical engagement with challenging behaviours, why we need to consider (and therefore use) restorative approaches, and effective impacts on both the educational practices of teachers and the educational outcomes achieved by students. We have been propelled into a sense of urgency given the tensions that currently exist for teachers and whānau when trying to respond expeditiously and compassionately to challenging behaviours that are occurring with greater frequency and intensity in our educational settings. We have also taken a glimpse into the future by projecting a strong rationale for educational settings to articulate responsive pedagogy, and to embrace restorative practice as their core business. As an approach, restorative practice is clearly effective—socially, educationally and culturally: socially, because it reflects the social norms promoted by a society that embraces and espouses inclusion and human rights; educationally, because it serves to prevent, diffuse or resolve issues that can have a negative impact on learning and achievement by restoring harmony and not apportioning blame; and culturally, because it is able to be implemented from a kaupapa Māori/te ao Māori perspective.

Intention and action, however, are two different things. History is peppered with examples of good ideas being left to languish because follow-up and commitment appeared to be too onerous to advance past mere tokenism. The authors of the preceding chapters in this book all agree with the need for urgency. If educational settings are committed to relationships, respect, social justice and evidence-based practice, then engagement with challenging behaviours must be responsive and restorative.

References

Adair, V. A., & Dixon, R. S. (2000). *Evaluation of the restorative conferencing pilot project: Report to the Ministry of Education.* Auckland: Auckland Uniservices Ltd.

Ashworth, J., Van Bockern, S., Ailts, J., Donnelly, J., Erickson, K., & Woltermann, J. (2008). The Restorative Justice Centre: An alternative to school detention. *Reclaiming Children and Youth, 17*(3), 22–26.

Bishop, R., Berryman, M., Cavanagh, T., & Teddy, L. (2007). *Te Kotahitanga phase 3: Whanaungatanga: Establishing a culturally responsive pedagogy of relations in mainstream secondary school classrooms.* Wellington: Ministry of Education.

Bishop, R., Berryman, M., Cavanagh, T., & Teddy, L. (2009). Te Kotahitanga: Addressing educational disparities facing Māori students in New Zealand. *Teaching and Teacher Education: An International Journal of Research and Studies, 25*(5), 734–742.

Blood, P., & Thorsborne, M. (2006). *Overcoming resistance to whole-school uptake of restorative practices.* Paper presented at the International Institute of Restorative Practices, The Next Step: Developing Restorative Communities, Bethlehem, PA.

Bolstad, R., & Gilbert, J. (2008). *Disciplining and drafting, or 21st century learning? Rethinking the New Zealand senior school curriculum for the future.* Wellington: NZCER Press.

Bourke, R., Holden, B., & Curzon, J. (2005). *Using evidence to challenge practice: A discussion paper.* Wellington: Ministry of Education.

Brantlinger, E. (2009). Impediments to social justice: Hierarchy, science, faith, and imposed identity (disability classification). In W. Ayers, T. Quinn, & D. Stovall (Eds.), *Handbook of social justice in education* (pp. 400–416). New York: Taylor & Francis.

Buckley, S., & Maxwell G. (2007). *Respectful schools: Restorative practices in education.* Wellington: Office of the Children's Commissioner and Institute of Policy Studies.

Cameron, L., & Thorsborne, M. (2001). Restorative justice and school discipline: Mutually exclusive? In H. Strang & J. Braithwaite (Eds.), *Restorative justice and school society* (pp. 180–194). Cambridge: Cambridge University Press.

Carp, D., & Breslin, B. (2001). Restorative justice in school communities. In K. G. Herr (Ed.), *Bringing restorative justice to adolescent substance abuse: Special issue of Youth and Society, 33*(December), 249–272.

Drewery, W. (2003) *Restorative practices for schools—a resource.* Hamilton: School of Education, Waikato University.

Drewery, W., & Winslade, J. (2003). *Developing restorative practices in schools: Flavour of the month or saviour of the system?* Paper presented to the AARE/NZARE conference, Auckland.

Gattung, A. (2007). *Restorative justice programmes for students.* Sabbatical report to educational leaders. Retrieved 17 August 2009, from http://www.educationalleaders.govt.nz

Goodfellow, J. (2001). Wise practice: The need to move beyond "best" practices. *Australian Journal of Early Childhood, 26*(3), 1–6.

Jansen, G. M. (2008). *Restorative: Is it worth the time and effort?* Assigned project 2008. Christchurch: School of Educational Studies and Human Development, University of Canterbury.

Kane, J., Lloyd, G., McCluskey, G., Riddell, S., Stead, J., & Weedon, E. (2007). *Restorative practices in three Scottish councils: Final report of the evaluation of pilot projects 2004–2006.* Scottish Executive. Retrieved 8 August 2009, from http://www.scotland.gov.uk/Publications/2007/08/24093135/20

Kauffman, J. (1997). *Characteristics of emotional and behavioural disorders of children and youth* (6th ed.). Upper Saddle River, NJ: Prentice-Hall.

Lewis, S. (2009). *Improving school climate: Findings from schools implementing restorative practices.* A report from the International Institute for Restorative Practices Graduate School. Retrieved 21 August 2009, from http://www.iirp.org

Macfarlane, A. (2004). *Kia hiwa ra! Listen to culture: Māori students' plea to educators.* Wellington: NZCER Press.

Macfarlane, A. (2007). *Discipline, democracy, and diversity: Working with students with behaviour difficulties.* Wellington: NZCER Press.

Macfarlane, S. (2009). Te Pikinga ki Runga: Raising possibilities. *set: Research Information for Teachers, 2,* 42–50.

Matla, R. E. (2009). *What is required to make restorative conversations work?* Christchurch: University of Canterbury.

McElrea, F. W. M. (1994, February). *The intent of the Children, Young Persons, and Their Families Act 1989—restorative justice?* A paper presented to the Youth Justice conference of the New Zealand Youth Court Association (Auckland) Inc, Auckland.

Ministry of Education. (1996). *Te whāriki: He whāriki matauranga mō ngā mokopuna o Aotearoa: Early childhood curriculum.* Wellington: Learning Media.

Ministry of Education. (2007). *The New Zealand curriculum.* Wellington: Learning Media.

Ministry of Education. (2008). *Te marautanga o Aotearoa.* Wellington: Learning Media.

Ministry of Education. (2009a). *Positive behaviour for learning: Action plan, 2010–2012.* Wellington: Author.

Ministry of Education. (2009b). *Positive behaviour for learning: Summary of initiatives.* Retrieved 7 January 2010, from http://www.minedu.govt.nz/theMinistry/EducationInitiatives/PositiveBehaviourForLearning/SummaryOfInitiatives.aspx

Ministry of Youth Development. (2008). *UNCROC*. Retrieved 26 July 2010, from http://www.myd.govt.nz/working-with-young-people/uncroc/

Pranis, K. (2005). *The little book of circle processes: A new/old approach to peacemaking.* Intercourse, PA: Good Books.

Signal, K. R. (2009). *Restorative justice: An idea whose time has come: A critical literature review of restorative practices in schools in Aotearoa/New Zealand.* Master's research project, Massey University.

Stedman, G. (2008). *Investigating restorative justice models and their application for use in primary schools.* Sabbatical report to educational leaders. Retrieved 8 August 2009, from http://www.educationalleaders.govt.nz

Wachtel, T., & McCold, P. (2004). From restorative justice to restorative practices: Expanding the paradigm. Paper presented at the International Institute for Restorative Practices conference, Bethlehem, PA.

Zehr, H. (2002). *The little book of restorative justice.* Intercourse, PA: Good Books.

About the Authors

Mere Berryman

Dr Mere Berryman is of Tuhoe descent. She is a Senior Research Fellow, working with the Te Kotahitanga project at the Faculty of Education in Hamilton. This work, supporting culturally responsive practices for Maori learners in mainstream settings is internationally recognised and is widely published. Mere completed her PhD at the University of Waikato; her thesis is entitled, *Repositioning within indigenous discourses of transformation and self-determination*. This work covers 18 years of research undertaken by the Poutama Pounamu research-whānau of which she was a part.

Tom Cavanagh

Dr Cavanagh is on the faculty of the Richarrd W. Riley College of Education and Leadership at Walden University. He has two graduate degrees—one in organisational leadership from Regis University and another in educational leadership from Colorado State University. Following the award of his doctorate in 2004, he spent a year in New Zealand on a Fulbright Fellowship, and another 4 years there developing the theory of a culture of care in schools. As a result of this work, he is recognised internationally as an expert on applying restorative justice theory as restorative practices in schools to create a culture of care.

Jan Daley

Jan Daley is a Senior Lecturer at the University of Canterbury and coordinator of educational leadership programmes. Jan's professional background includes having been a lecturer in educational leadership, a teacher in-service educator, and a secondary principals advisor. She has held a variety of roles in secondary schools, including associate principal, deputy principal, guidance counselor, and transition educator. Jan's interests include brain-based learning, leadership and management, school improvement, teaching/learning, pastoral care, Māori achievement, student voice, special education, appraisal, managing student behaviour and restorative practices. She is co-author of *Learning to Learn*.

Vijaya Dharan

Dr Vijaya Dharan is a lecturer in the School of Psychology and Pedagogy, Faculty of Education, Victoria University of Wellington. She is a registered psychologist with a practising certificate and has worked for nearly 15 years with teachers, schools and early childhood services to make learning accessible for students who have significant behavioural and learning challenges. The experiences gained in working with children and families has reinforced to her that understanding lived experiences and restoring and re-storying lives of some children is pivotal for their long term wellbeing and thereby reducing their exclusion from learning opportunities. She has managed national projects providing professional development for teachers in early childhood and schools. As a passionate advocate for social justice, she is deeply interested in the area of "learning for all" and in particular the various beliefs, perceptions and attitudes of educators that can enhance or hinder this process. Her doctoral thesis examined the perceptions of beginning teachers about student diversity and the contextual impact on their perceptions. Vijaya is currently part of a team developing a programme to train educational psychologists.

Ted Glynn

Professor Ted Glynn is Foundation Professor for Teacher Education at the University of Waikato and a Fellow of the Royal Society of New Zealand. He researches and teaches in Māori and bicultural education, applied behaviour analysis and special education and for many years was a member of the special education research centre Poutama Pounamu, which is committed to improving learning and behavioural outcomes for Maori students. Professor Glynn has published prolifically in his field.

Greg Jansen

Greg Jansen is currently working with Richard Matla providing training, development and consultation for the educational sector and wider community organisations throughout New Zealand and abroad. Restorativeschools.org.nz, the consultancy they co-founded, focuses on developing strong teaching and learning relationships through the use of restorative approaches. Greg is highly motivated about working with people of all ages, and passionate about supporting them to reach their potential. His teaching background includes outdoor and physical education teaching, and he has spent many years working as a pastoral dean. Greg has a vast wealth of experience beyond mainstream education, ranging from working with marginalised and dysfunctional youth and leading alternative education programmes, to outdoor instructing and facilitating both in New Zealand and overseas. In his recent time at Kaiapoi High School, Greg, together with Richard Matla, led the whole school through the implementation of restorative approaches. He completed postgraduate research in 2009, asking the question "Restorative Practice: Is it worth the time and effort?"

Angus Macfarlane

Professor Angus Hikairo Macfarlane is of the Te Arawa waka and its confederate tribes in the central North Island. The thrust of his research activities focuses on the exploration of cultural concepts and strategies that influence educational practice. In 2003 he was awarded the inaugural Research Fellowship by the New Zealand Council for Educational Research. In 2004 his landmark book, *Kia hiwa rā! Listen to culture—Māori students' plea to educators*, was published, and he was a recipient of a Tohu Kairangi award, a citation for academic achievement in Māori education. Another book, *Discipline, Democracy and Diversity*, was published in August 2007, and this was followed in 2010 by *Above the Clouds*, an edited collection of readings on the cultural constructs of giftedness. In December 2010 Dr Macfarlane was presented with the Tohu Pae Tawhiti Award, acknowledging his significant contribution to Māori research over an extensive period. In 2011 he received a Good Practice Publication Grant from Ako Aotearoa, the National Centre for Tertiary Teaching Excellence. Dr Macfarlane is Professor of Māori Research at the University of Canterbury.

Sonja Macfarlane

Sonja Macfarlane affiliates to the South Island iwi of Ngāi Tahu; her hapū, Ngāti Waewae, is from the Arahura district. Sonja's conviction for improving outcomes for students at risk of educational failure has seen her move from classroom teacher, to Resource Teacher of Learning and Behaviour, to Special Education Advisor, to National Practice Leader of Services to Māori in the Ministry of Education. In 2011, she assumed a position at the University of Canterbury in the Health Sciences Centre. Sonja's research focuses on strengthening professional practice and service delivery to tamariki and whānau. This focus includes drawing from the best evidence available, so that practitioners are able to develop their own cultural competence so as to help realise the potential of Māori learners.

Valerie Margrain

Dr Valerie Margrain is a lecturer in Early Years education at Massey University in Palmerston North and formerly worked as editor of the *Kairaranga* journal. She has experience as teacher in classrooms, reading recovery and special education settings, and in early childhood, primary, tertiary and teacher education. Valerie's research interests focus on strength-based assessment in the early years, including gifted and inclusive education, parenting, children's voice, narrative assessment and early literacy. She has published widely from her 2005 PhD research on precocious readers. Valerie's current projects include involvement with a teaching-research nexus international collaboration with the University of Gothenburg, Sweden, and also the giftEDnz Early Years resource development project.

Richard Matla

Richard Matla currently provides training and development workshops and consultancy for schools and organizations throughout New Zealand and abroad as part of Restorativeschools.org.nz which he co-founded with Greg Jansen. Richard was born and raised in Christchurch and since 1990 has mixed a teaching career with extensive work abroad including establishing art cooperatives in Zimbabwe, youth development work in British Columbia and winter resort management in Europe. He began his career teaching art and spent a number of years leading a vibrant and diverse arts faculty. Through his work as a pastoral dean, Richard, along with Greg Jansen, led the restorative practice team at Kaiapoi High School. Richard recently completed postgraduate research at the University of Canterbury, with a particular focus on the effectiveness of restorative dialogue and conversations. Richard is passionate and committed to the needs of children and young people and their development and also to the professional growth of teachers and educators and the quality of teaching and learning relationships.

Jane Prochnow

Dr Jane Prochnow is a Senior Lecturer in the School of Educational Studies, College of Education, Massey University. Her background is in Educational Psychology and Applied Behaviour Analysis. Her particular interests are in theories and strategies for working with children with difficult behaviour. Her research has been in the areas of suspension, teachers' classroom needs for inclusion, and attitudinal, literacy and motivational variables related to disordered behaviour. One method of excluding students is through bullying, which she has recently examined in relation to text bullying in New Zealand schools. She has also examined the resistance and barriers to inclusion in the classroom experienced by students exhibiting difficult behaviour despite New Zealand's policy of inclusive educational practices. She is currently involved with research exploring the label of deficit theory and the damage that argument can do to supporting children experiencing specific learning or behavioural problems in the classroom.

Margaret Thorsborne

Margaret Thorsborne has a long history in education, guidance and counseling. Her passion has always been to find better ways to build and rebuild relationships between teachers, students, and other members of the school community, to enhance teaching and learning outcomes. In the early 1990s, she and like-minded colleagues were keen to discover more effective interventions to deal with those sorts of incidents in schools, such as serious bullying, abuse, conflict, and violence, that did not respond positively to traditional punitive sanctions. She was inspired by stories of restorative conferencing, at that time being used in justice agencies to divert young people away from the courts. Margaret convened the first ever school-based conference with a little telephone coaching from a police officer, and shortly afterwards, managed a ground-breaking pilot of restorative conferencing in her region. Now a private consultant, she continues to work with education departments in a number of countries, in schools and private and public sector workplaces, convening conferences for high level conflict and inappropriate behaviour and providing training in restorative facilitation for middle and senior management. As the use of restorative approaches continues to evolve as a preferred way to solve relationship and discipline issues in schools, Margaret's focus is increasingly on addressing the challenges of culture change and the development of restorative leadership.

Glossary

āhua demeanour; appearance

Aotearoa New Zealand

hāngi earth oven used to cook food

hapū subtribe or clan

hauora a name used by Māori health providers to reflect the provision of health care

hinengaro psychological characteristics

hōhā annoyed

hongi pressing of noses to signal unity

hononga relational characteristics

hui meeting held with Māori protocols

hui whakatika traditional meeting to resolve issues

iwi tribe

kaitakawaenga cultural adviser

kapa haka cultural performing arts groups

karakia traditional chant or prayer

kaumātua tribal elder

kaupapa agenda or issue

kaupapa Māori an understanding from within a Māori world view; ways that are Māori

kawa rules

koro male elder or grandfather

kotahitanga unity, bonding, working together

mana ascribed power, prestige and authority

mana motuhake personal self-concept; characteristics

manaaki support

manaakitanga commitment and care

manu kōrero language and oratory competition

māpuna treasure

marae traditional meeting place

mātua whāngai a name adopted by Māori agencies set up to help families with issues around parenting and caregiving; fostering; adoption

mihi whakatau a ritual of engagement, less formal than a pōwhiri

mihimihi greeting and introduction

Pākehā non-indigenous European coloniser

papakāinga original home; one's personal tūrangawaewae (walking place) pātai question

pōwhiri a very formal ritual of engagement

rangatira chief; leader

reo language

takiwā district

tamariki children

tapuwae footsteps

Tawhaingia te Pā Harakeke whānau/parenting support programme

te the

te ao Māori the Māori world

Te Kotahitanga the name given to a research and professional development programme implemented in schools, aimed at raising Māori student achievement

te reo Māori the Māori language

tikanga cultural beliefs and practices

tinana physical characteristics; the body

tuakana–teina peer tutoring role where there is a specific cultural expectation that the older or more skilled student assists younger or less skilled students

tūrangawaewae walking place

waiata song

whakanoa to make something safe again

whakataukī metaphorical saying

whakatika to correct or put right

whānau family and/or extended family

whānau whānui wider family

whanaungatanga exercising collective responsibility through engaging in family-like relationships

whāriki woven mat

whenua land

Index